KENTUCKY LIONS BREAKFAST
42ND ANNUAL CONVENTION
LIONS INTERNATIONAL
NEW YORK, NEW YORK
JUNE 30, JULY 1, 2, 3, 1959

# OHIO COUNTY, KENTUCKY

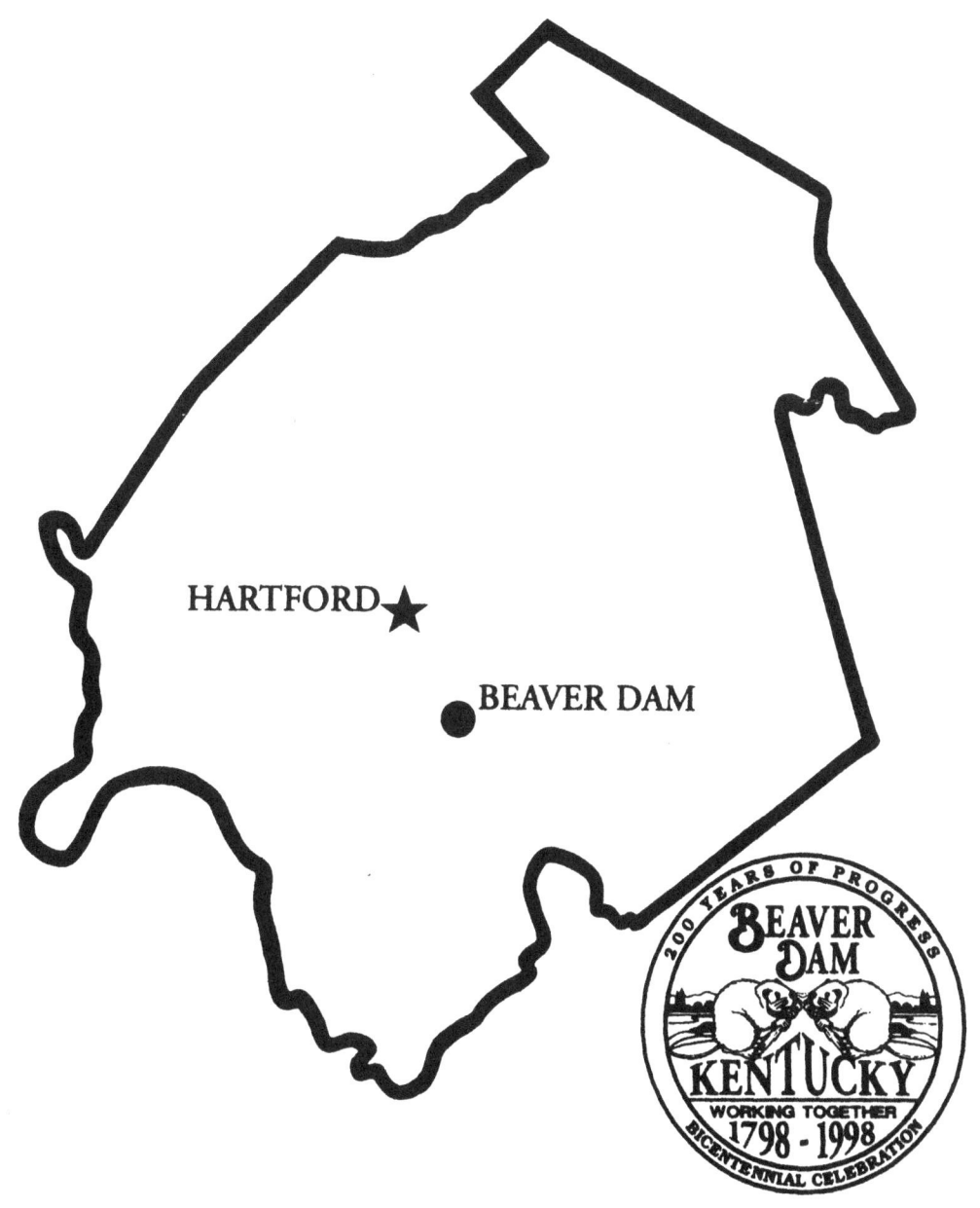

*Pictorial History*

TURNER PUBLISHING COMPANY

## TURNER PUBLISHING COMPANY
Publishers of America's History

Publishing Consultant: Keith R. Steele
Project Coordinator: John Mark Jackson
Designer: David Hurst

Copyright©1998 Turner Publishing Company
All rights reserved
Publishing Rights: Turner Publishing Company

This book or any part thereof may not be reproduced without
the express written consent of the publisher.

This publication was produced using available and submitted
materials. The author and publisher regret they cannot assume
liability for errors or omissions.

Library of Congress Catalog No. 98-87643

LIMITED EDITION
ISBN: 978-1-68162-574-4

## Contents

Publisher's Message .................................... 4
Preface ........................................................ 5
Book Committee ........................................ 5
Family Gatherings ...................................... 6
People & Families ..................................... 14
Towns & Communities ............................ 35
Fairs & Celebrations ................................ 42
Social Events ............................................ 47
Officials .................................................... 50
Fire Departments ..................................... 54
Professionals ............................................ 55
Transportation ......................................... 57
Trains & Depots ....................................... 59
Businesses ................................................ 63
Theatres & Memorabilia .......................... 80
Farming, etc. ............................................ 82
Coal Industry ........................................... 88
Veterans ................................................... 93
Schools ................................................... 106
Churches ................................................ 132
Clubs ...................................................... 145
Sports ..................................................... 148
Map ........................................................ 157
Post Offices ............................................ 158
Memorials & Tributes ............................ 163
Businesses & Organizations ................... 181
Index ...................................................... 200

# PREFACE

This book, by diligent trust and fervor, memories of the past, will be set forth far into the future of Ohio County, Kentucky. Thanks, to all of the contributors to the Ohio County Bicentennial Pictorial History 1798-1998. Thanks to the committee who has served faithfully the past year:

# BOOK COMMITTEE

Betty and Tommy Jackson
Brenda Dockery
Claude Taylor
Les and Jolene Johnson
Mayor David C. Taylor
Cheryl Morris
Noah Phelps Jr.,
Phillis Farmer
Dick Reid
Shirley Smith
Billy and Shirley Goodall
William and Virginia Hill
Winston Abbott
Ralph Warren

# FAMILY GATHERINGS

*J.A.C. Park homeplace, ca. 1920s. Farm is now part of Twin Hills Subdivision. Five members of this family were teachers. J.A.C. Park is the grandfather of Beaver Dam, also a teacher.*

Willie E. and Minnie Bell (Basham) Leach family reunion, Fordsville, Ky., 1988. Front, Robert Ralph, Julie Ralph, Brandon Thurman, Andrew Ralph, Kinsey Richards. 2nd: Mary Ann Rosencrans, Thelma Matthews, Helen Basham, Myrtle Mayer, Lorene Wright, Anna Mary Leach, Sheila Thurman. 3rd: Kenny Rosencrans, Kristy Richards, Norman Matthews, Lawrence Matthews, Teresa Miller (Cheek), Kathryn Miller, Joyce Leach, Jamie Leach (Johnston), Dennis Ralph, Judith Ralph, Debra Richards, Pat Richards. 4th: Jerl Dean Adkins, Russ Hobbs, Emogene Moseley, Clarence Miller, Lexter Leach. 5th: Charles Moseley, Barry Mosely.

Boswell Family. Charles Henry Ferree Boswell and Sarah Ellen (Bean) Boswell, children Alec Pigman "A.P.", Verna Loyal, Iva Galloway, Henry Wayne, Anna Woolsley, Utha Ellen Adams, Mary Jane Powers, ca. 1920.

*Grover and Cliffie Bennett families, ca. 1905, near Hartford, KY.*

*45th wedding celebration of Ray and Myrtle Hoskins, m. Dec. 23, 1927. Front: Melissa Hoskins, Myrtle and Ray Hoskins, Jed and Leah Stewart. Back: Donna, Michael, Connie, Gerald, Dennis, and Rhonda Hoskins, Coleen and Glen Stweart, John A., Keith, and Cheri Westerfield.*

*Wedding of Marlene Hoskins, Rockport, Ky., and John Westerfield, Beaver Dam, Ky., March 24, 1956. Attendants, Coleen and Glen Stewart. Flower girl, Teresa Shrull. Ring bearer, Randy Render.*

*J.E. Morris family. Back, Lula Warren, Oddist and Dona Morris. 2nd: J.E. Morris and wife, Warren and Ollie (Morris) James with Emmett (in lap). Middle child Roxie Morris (Craddock).*

*Ashley family reunion, Beda, KY.*

*Mystery picture. Those known: Edgar Barnard, row 2, 2nd. from left. Cecil Barnard, row 2, 9th from left.*

*Richard and Katie Baker Family, Taylor Mines.*

*Fisher Family Reunion, Sugar Grove Hill, 1920, McHenry, KY. Fannie Carnes Fisher, Mary Ellen Fisher Render, LoDema Fulkerson Fisher, Elizabeth Fisher Addison, Anna Espey Fisher, Martha Barclay Shoulders, Fannie Fisher Shoulders, Martha Frank Frank Fisher Hawes, Grace Clark Fisher, Rachel Fisher James.*

*Minton family reuinon, July 1928. Front, Alma Minton, Opal Minton, Beatrice Schroader, Lorine Day, Corine Minton, Christine Day. 2nd, Edith Minton, Bertie Schroader, Nannie Rudy Day, Etter Minton, Tarzina Minton, Beauty Burke, Celia E. Minton. Back, Billy Schroader, Henry K., Minton., Desie Minton, Ollie Minton, Ina P. Day.*

*50th reunion of 1926 BDHS. Front, Inez and Wm. Raley, Karl Brown, Helen Knight, Rhea Lender, Mildred Greer, Dr. Malcolm Barnes, V.M. Robertson. Back, Benmer Cohron and wife, Mrs. Hamilton Render, Ben Rummage, Lucille Chick, Audra Martin, Sterling Maddox, Lucille Couch, Hayward Stevens, Virgil Couch.*

LEFT: Knoics, Walhins, Rogers, Hughes, Ruth Oldham on an outing.

BELOW: Birthday party, 1900, Rockport.

Homecoming at M.F. Faught Williams Mines, KY., formerly known as Milton Parks Springs. From left, back rows, #1 Fanny Shoulders, #5 Anth (Maples) Tatum Hacker, #6, Ollie Hammond, #10 Cora Shoulders. Ora Bishop, middle front.

Fordsville excursion to the east bank of Rough Creek at Falls of Rough, May 31, 1891.

T.C. Trogden family, Washington community, Hartford. Back, Elsworth, Ulysses, Chesley, and Edward Trogden. Middle, Cora Trogden Tinsley, Gala Trogden York, Carson Trogden. Front, Mamie, Mr. and Mrs. T.C. (Lelah) Trogden, Katie Trogden Clark.

Homecoming at Wesley Chapel community, ca. 1912. Richard T, Nora Baize, and Clarence Gentry (F), Gilbert, Sara, Nancy, Reet Kirk and two daughters (F), Pastor Bro. Tichenor, wife and daughter, unk., unk., Arlavie, and Gabe Kirk, Clifton Shows. (F) indicates in front.

*John Barham Blankenship family at farm south of Beaver Dam, 1907. Front, John, J.L. Martha Joanna Rogers, Theadocia P. Bridges Blankenship. Back, Cecil, Jesse, Roy, Charles Elvis, and Okley Blankenship.*

*Schroader family, 1946. Top: Edward Lee, Mitchell Schroader, Willard Schroader. 2nd: Mary belle Schroader, Clara Benadinto, Mary E., Lillian L., Lon, Shelly, and Robert Schroader. 3rd. Venton McBride, ___ Benadinto, Isaac, Eva Jane, Connie, Alma, Mary L. and June Schroader. 4th: Donald and Shirley A. McBride, Emma J., Wanda D., Hugh E. Jenny Ray, Sonny, and Sherman Schroader.*

*Stonewall Cook, Maudie Stewart, Lethia C. James, Lucy Evans, Ray Cook, Nancy Elizabeth (Cook) Taylor. Nancy Elizabeth, Monroe, and MacClean Cook, Annie C. and Jimmie Albin.*

*Mr. and Mrs. Richard Baker with Minnie, Leonard, Lucille, Edgar.*

*LEFT: Vance family, ca. 1902-1903. Front, Raymond Alford Vance. 2nd: Delia Frances Murphy, Cephas Issac, John Wm. and Ethel Susan Vance (Thomasson). Back. Eva M. Vance (Arbuckle), Wilbur Vance, Iva A. Vance (Cox), Rena Vance. Concord.*

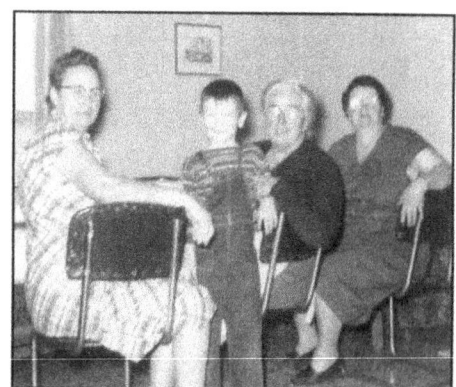

*ABOVE MIDDLE: 63rd anniversary, Ray and Myrtle Hoskins.*

*ABOVE: Quilting party, summer 1956. Eva Porter, Doug Cavender, Nannie Wallace, Mayme Stewart.*

*Crow family, April 9, 1877. Front: Evalena, Claborn Vinson, Vinson, Catherine Ann, Sallie. 2nd: Rosetta Ann, Susan Thursey, Marshall, Martha Ellen, Alonzo.*

*Park family. Joseph Cecil, Stella, Dr. Durwood, Everett, and Jesse Clint Park, Cecil Shown, Ellis Park. 2nd: Carrie Lowe Park Cooke, John Anderson, Jessie Thomas, and Roscoe Hubert Park, Mable Park Blanton, James Randall Shown, Antha Belle Park Shown.*

*Birthday celebration 1896, at Jobe M. Williams home, Rob Roy. Back: Joe R., Victoria, Mary, S.T., Rob and Roy, Mrs. S.T. holding Charles, Mrs. J.D. holding Edna, and Ora Williams. 2nd: J. Morton, Williams, Mrs. Jasper Leach, Mr. and Mrs. Jobe M., Essie, and J.D. Williams holding Altha, Jasper Leach holding Agnes Williams. Job Leach, Sofia Williams, Annie Leach, Eunice Williams.*

*McHenry group. Front: Mrs. Clarence Ashby, Clarence Ashby, Bertie Reedy, Will and May Duncan, Mary, Conrad, and Silas J. Tichenor. Girl with white and black hat Maude Render. Lady with white hat, Anne Leonine Duncan.*

*Top: Lockie (Butler) Morris, Owen Butler, Flossie Bina James. 2nd: Leona and Nan (Austin) Butler, Leona (Butler) and Clyde V. James. Front: John T. Jimbo, Catherine (Kitty Ann), and Aaron Butler, Martin James.*

*Phelps family. 1st: Weldon, Geneva, and Cecil Wakeland, Noel, Mabel, Lucy, T.J., Paul (behind), Vera (between), and Jeannie Phelps, Yandell, Chester, Marie, Virginia, and Eva Phelps McKenney, Ellis, Leon, and Arvil Phelps. 2nd: A.J. and Lola May Wakeland, William B. and Perna Chinn Phelps, Elmer McKenney, "Dude", and Myrtle Hunter Phelps. Back: Violet, Erpha, Noah Sr. and Ethel Phelps, Roy Baugh, Dessie Phelps Baugh.*

*Harber B. Taylor family, summer 1904. 1st: Ernest Taylor, Winona Stevens, Ione Taylor. 2nd: Lyman, Charles M., Sallie Rhoads, Hugh Edward, Harber Blackstone, Claude Liles, Octavia Chinn, and Lilburn Blackstone Taylor, Septimous T, Shelby, and Laura Ann Taylor Stevens. 3rd: Alva, Mary Blackstone, Willie Lewis, Shelby, Kittye Lee, Minnie Barnes, Robert Lee, Emma Elizabeth, Myron Hoy, Harber B. (Hob) Jr., and Margaret Stevens (Maggie) Taylor, Chester and Cecil Stevens.*

*Richard Baker family. Front: Wilson Randolph and Richard Baker, Augustus Baker Chick, Linda Sue Baker Kalnai, Catharine Baker holding Catharine Paulina (Kittye) Chick Brown, Kay Baker Fink, Danny Baker, Peggy Baker Nichols, Ava Baker Miller, Anna Baker Andes. 2nd: Minnie Lillian Baker Case Lee, Verna Lucille Baker Chick, Betty Ann Baker Jackson, Marshall Thomas, Richard Leonard, and Chester Maurice Baker, Jr. 3rd: Anna Lelia Baker Magas, Wallace Coakley Chick, Chester Maurice Baker holding Janet Baker Scalf, Kathleen Maine Baker holding Sylvia Baker Burchett, Edgar Clovis, Grace Westerfield, Leonard Augustus, and Ruby Taylor Baker.*

*William Volney Warren family. Front: William Volney, Cloman, Marvin, Yettie Goodall Warren, Lillian Ollie D., Anna, Myrl. Back: John Huston, Burrilla, William Orville, Minerva, Jospehine, Earcel, Loarn Cicero.*

*Clifton and Sara Jane Shown family, ca. 1912. Back: Lige and Essie Wells, Othmer, Lee (Bud), Bertha, and baby Hazel Shown, Geroge, Laura, and baby Basil Keown, Emel, Ethel, and baby Coakley Eskridge, Manford and Katie Brown. Front: Flora Wells, Calara Mae Shown, Stanley and Clarence Brown, Clifton and Sara Jane Shown, Letha Brown, Wilbert Wells, Golan and Gilbert Keown.*

*James R. Burgess and Thomas Southard family at home place below Prentis, KY., ca. 1900. Front: Robert Clifton, James Richard, and Mildred Servilla Rogeir Burgess, Corbett (chair), Thomas, Hubert (lap), and Mildred Ona Burgess Southard. Back: Tina Elizabeth, Lou Erna, Mattie Ethel, Richard Oda, James Grover and Jesse Lee Burgess.*

ca. 1917. Front: Myrtle Daugherty (Romans), Edith Daugherty (Smith), Myra Cochran (White). 2nd: Mary Dona Mollie Austin (Daugherty), W.J. (Will) Daugherty, John Shannon, and Sara Belle Burden Daugherty, Ina Daugherty (Cook), Rosa Daugherty (Baize, Cochran), John Thomas Cochran. 3rd: Ada Belle Daugherty, Ava Thomas Daugherty (Snodgrass), Gracie Havens (Evans, Gregory), Zora Romans (Simpson, Embry), Minnie Cochran, Jessie Ray Daugherty, Willie Quay Haven. Back, Ronnie Forest and Catharine Daugherty, Jewell Ferris, Verge Cook, Lonnie Daugherty, Versie, Herman, Minnie, John Cecil, Mack, Annie, Jane, and Morgan Daugherty.

Kinchen A. Martin and family, 1913. Front: Kinchen with Audra, Dianah Leach Martin with Grethchel. Back: Bertha Swarm and Eugene T. Martin, Carrie Roeder Martin holding Edward Tuel Martin, Birch B., Dona Rock, and Thomas Crittenden Martin.

W.S. Taylor family reunion. Back. Nellie Gray Schultz, R.B. Peters, Annie Tichenor Schultz, Rose Jackson, Ruth Taylor (Berryman), Edith Taylor (Reid). Mattie and Robert Jackson, Clead and Carl Austin, Nancy, J. Sam, and Anna Mae Gentry, Anna Elizabeth Shultz (Horton Luce), Irene, Bryant, and Ivan Shultz, Joe S. Roy, and Archie Taylor.

1917. Lizzie Taylor, Mrs. Willis, Robert and Geneva Taylor, Mamie Williams, Effie Mulhall, Martin Taylor. Bottom: Dr. Willis, Kitty Lee and Lymon Taylor, Hazel Hacker, I. Taylor, Kitty Rhoads.

1894. Top: Attye Austin Griffith, Cliffie Gray Brown, Virgil Hacker, Robert Coats Taylor, Lizzie Barren Taylor, Ella Snowden. Front, Beulah Coats, Mable ---, Annie McKenney Austin, Florence Tichenor, Sadie Austin Williams, Daisy Stevens Wright.

# PEOPLE & FAMILIES

Robert E., Susan M. Williams, and John Aubrey Barrett (baby) in buggy, Inez (Ina) Berrett Mauzy, Belle Taylor (by fence), Iva Taylor Hammons, Sally Mary and Joseph Matthew Barrett, in front of Joseph M. Barrett home, ca. 1909-1910.

C.C. Watts, Jr., Mrs. Maggart, W.P. Watts, McHenry, KY.

John and Jane Bennett, near Hartford, Ky., 1920.

Carlisle, John, and Latna Oldham.

Myrtle and Coleen Hoskins, 1929.

J. Frank Casebier.

Eva Garland Butler Barnard and Mae Whillinghill wearing their mothers' wedding dresses, ca. 1914.

Gronela Jessie and Glendon Brown.

*Martin and Delbert Daugherty, Centertown, Ky., ca. 1940s.*

*Robert Louis Bennett, Hartford, Ky., 1905.*

*Mr. and Mrs. E.W. Jackson.*

*Children of the Chester Bakers, Feb. 1938. Tommy, Chester, Jr., Betty Anne.*

*Will Lee, Charles and Jack Fisher.*

*Homer and Ethel Taylor Pean, wedding photo, Dec. 30, 1917.*

*Zora R. Embry, 1931.*

*Judge Mack Cook, county judge of Ohio Co., 1918-1923.*

*Lee and Ethel Bivins, m. April 25, 1927.*

*John Hamilton and Mary Elizabeth (Payton) Wilson, Sunnydale, KY.*

*Charles Henry Ferree and Sarah Ellen (Bean) Boswell.*

*Haven brothers. Top, Ira, Luther. Bottom, Jasper N., Henry, Arthur.*

*Oldham brothers. Carlisle, Austin, Latna, John, Jack.*

*Carson Trogden, on cow, Glendean and Chapman.*

*Rudy, Wilma, and Emma Haven, 1938.*

*Coleen, Marlen, Gerald, and Donna Hoskins, Rockport, KY, washing "Peanuts."*

William Mitchel and Mary Bell Hunter Overhuls.

Claude Park house, McHenry, KY.

Wallace Coakley and Verna Lucille Baker Chick.

James and Allie Ralph, 50th wedding anniversary, 1962, Whitesville, KY.

Myron, Claude, and Lilbern Taylor with father, Robert Lee Taylor.

Dee Maddox, Lodema Fulkerson Fisher, Hosea Fulkerson, Walter Scott, others unk., 1898, McHenry, Ky.

William "Will" Midkiff, Harriett Midkiff Ralph, Nelson Baugh.

RIGHT: Corinne Taylor Gregory, 1989, author and teacher.

BELOW RIGHT: Nick Hazelrig, Eunice (Loney) Brown, John Carter, Mae (Hazelrig) Lee, Geneva (Brown) Ross, Aaron Ross.

FAR RIGHT: The Cook brothers, 1908. Robert, Wm. A., Stephen, Mack.

Early Ford settlers of Ohio County. Edward Willett Ford, Louisa Jane Ford Wright, John William Ford, ca. 1900.

Ruby, Sheila, Allison, and Elizabeth Reid.

Willie and Martine Taylor, 1908.

Pearl Patton and Ethel Trogden.

Robert Lee and Emma Liles Taylor.

Claude, Myron, and Lilbern Taylor, sons of Robert Lee and Emma Liles Taylor.

Q.B. Brown Family Home built 1899 on Midway Road near McHenry. Picture taken ca. 1920. The first addition was made ca. 1912.

Quintis Blueford "Q.B." and Anna Elizabeth "Lizzie" (Chinn) Brown Family. Front: Quintis Blueford "Q.B." Brown, Bernice E. Brown m. Noble Rowe Everly, Artie V. Brown m. Herbert M. Porter, Walter C. Brown m. Geraldine Tomblinson, Anna Elizabeth "Lizzie" (Chinn) Brown. Back: Cecil W. Brown m. Marie VanBecelaere, E. Clay Brown m. Margaret L. VanBecelaere--Marie's sister, Percil A. Brown 1m. Marian E. "Birdie" (Hayes) Taylor and 2m. Mildred (Paye) Holdman, Oma L. Brown m. H. Cleveland "Clea" Adcock, Nola E. Brown.

Lee, Norwood, Grandpa Brown, Carl, Randal, Glendon, R.P., 1934-1935.

Samuel and Wm. Reynolds, Jr., 1927.

Barbara and son Jay Daugherty, late 1930s.

Layton and Jessie Brown and Children, R.P. Raymond, Carl, Louise.

RIGHT: J.L. and Myrtle Rowe Brown.

FAR RIGHT: Thomas and Mary (Mollie) Bennett.

*Early Ohio County musicians.*

*John and Susan Chapman of McHenry, KY, in Hot Springs, AR, April 1919.*

*Charlie Stewart, Bob Boyd, John Dehart, unk., Epp Geary, Beaver Dam, ca. 1919.*

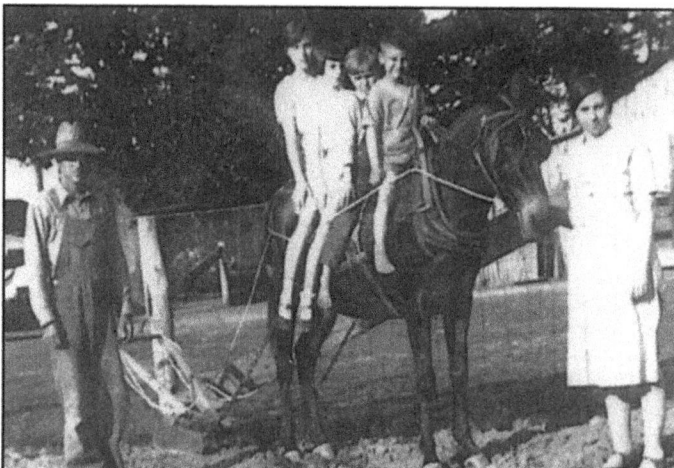
*Rupert and Lilpha Davis and children, Lee, Noel, Kathleen, Maggie Dean.*

*George Robinson and Nancy Cassandra McKinley Midkiff, m. Feb. 24, 1867.*

*Greta Whitehead, Centertown.*

*Cola James and Alfred Wing James. They had a delivery service in Centertown.*

*Family reunion, 1920. Top: Mary Catherine, Ethel, Archie, Robert, R.H. Taylor, Floye, Effie, Royd, Pete, Mittie. Middle: Ruby Taylor, Wiffie Swain holding Theda, P.A. Swain, "Sip" holding Temolian, Roy Morton Swain, Wendell Moore Swain, Maud. Front, Willie Lee, Natoma Swain, Wilma Taylor, Willie Pearl Swain.*

*Four generations. "Sip" Swain, Effie Swain Taylor, Wilma Taylor and Joe Harlan James.*

*Hunters in Ohio Co., Cromwell area, late 1800s.*

*James E. Trogden and Wm. "Curts" Trogden on 1934 Ford.*

*Alledore and Effie Render Brown.*

*Marietta Crief Easterday and Pearl Easterday.*

*A.L., Ollie, and Hazel Maddox holding Virginia Brown.*

Vonnie, Charlie, Carmen, and Myrtra Duvall.

Pearl A. Neal, Effie Renfrow, Mollie Ross, Vernie Johnson, unk.

Robert Lee Ambrose and Cletus Jacob, Bells Run.

Coleen and Jeanne Reneer, Centertown. Wanda Jacob, Bells Run.

Blacklocks, 1984. Larry, Avery, Sr., Hazel, Avery, Jr., Cromwell.

J.W. O'Dell house. First brick home in Fordsville, 1937. Fred Hevlin, contractor.

William Horton Luce and Annie Elizabeth (Schultz) Luce, returning from church, ca. 1932.

Horatio J. O'Dell, Elizabeth Melvin Clark, John W., Katie, and Eliza Jane O'Dell, 1881.

Wedding of Bobbie Joe James and Mary Jane Wilson, 1952. Charles R. Berryman, Mary Black, Wilson, James, Kenneth James, Noah Phelps, Jr.

Violet Harris and Mabel Hoover.

James and Curtis Trogden, 1940-1941

Lucy Chick Paxton.

Bess and Emma Barnes.

Emel and Effie Eskridge wedding photo, m. Dec. 15, 1909 near Fordsville.

Mrs. Earl Reid is baby.

Anna Mary Leach ringing dinner bell, 1939.

Willie Edgar and Minnie Bell (Basham) Leach, 1927.

Bobby Lee Baize, Henry Lee Baize, Carroll Moseley.

Myrtle Leach, Velma Leach Miller, Lexter and Anna Mary Leach, Lorene Leach Wright, March 1943.

Amy, Kerry, and Sherry Ratcliff, Beaver Dam, 1964.

Ira and Carrie Burden, Loucille Phelps and daughter Betty L. Burden, Iran Neil and Christopher Neil Burden, Corida Blair, Christmas 1972.

Jesse Lee James ran first radio station in Beaver Dam.

Four generations of Martins—Matt, Cecil, George, Bobby, Bells Run.

50th wedding anniversary, John and Susan Chapman, McHenry, KY.

Five oldest daughter of Richard and Minnie Barnard. Back: Ruth B. Mabrey, Esther B. Brown. Front: Martha B. James, Adah B. Raymond, Electra B. Chinn.

Jesse Franklin and Lucinda (Thomas) Berkeley, Henry Lewis and Sarah Matilda (Dockery) Thomas, Will and Nancy Margaret (Sorrels) Crowder. Back: Jesse Edgar Berkeley.

RIGHT: E.W. Jackson.

FAR RIGHT: Joe Henry Burgess and family. Pearl, Doris, Lonnie, Archie, Elizabeth, Willie, Kenneth, Henry Ellis.

Claude and Mille Burden, Echols, KY, on wedding day, Nov. 30, 1916.

Wedding photo of Henry Daniels and Nannie E. Bozarth, Cromwell, KY, Dec. 25, 1885.

William Townsley, born 1896.

Sallie Amelia (Minnie) Brown and Byron Lee Foster and children, Douglas Lee and Mildred Ruth Foster. Late November 1930.

Four generations. Dennie Allen, Kitrola Allen England, Jeanne England Baize, Bobbi Baize, 1864.

Broadway Pond, 1957.

Back: Grace Maddox, Lena Chinn, Ruby Nell White, Ada James, Marie Berryman, Lelane James, Nina Mae Williams, Claudine Warren. Front: Hilda Whitler, unk., Margaret Owens Westerfield, Geneva Warren, Jewel Parks.

*Sallie (Rowe) Barrett (chair), Susan Mariah (Williams), John Aubrey, Robert Wilson, and William Joseph Barrett, June 1939.*

*Hinton-Martin-Ambrose family, 1918. Back: Sagg and Maude Hinton, William Martin, Lillie King Ambrose, Robert Lee Ambrose, James J. Sharp (child), Les Taylor-Hinton, Charles McKinley. Front: Sally Hinton Martin, Hinton, Gus Sharp, Opal Sharp (child), Rosie Ambrose Sharp, Theresa Martin Huckleberry, Tootsie Hinton, Claude Ambrose, Susan Hinton Taylor.*

*1924 Sunday gathering. Lillian Buck, Zelma Lee Taylor, Glyndean Chinn, Jessie and A. Mercer, Lillian Lee, Frances Stevens, Boots Hazelrigg, Otis Johnson, Rick Chinn, Rhea Render.*

*Willie Edgar and Minnie Bell (Basham) Leach, Fordsville, 50th wedding anniversary, 1960. Children, Myrtle, Velma, Lorene, Lexter, Anna Mary.*

*Grandchildren of Spice Johnson, 1950-1951. Back: Glen, Tunney, Opel, Bill, Betty, Jewel, Liz, Junior, Clemmie, J.C., Anna Dean. 2nd: Dickie, Oscar, Dube, Alice, Pat, George. Front: Bonnie, Merle Lee and son, Pearl Stewart, Gladys.*

*James Walter and Ivy Mae Walton Blackburn. Children Ruby B. Martin (girl), Doris Gwen B. Williams (baby). Williams Mine, McHenry ca. 1907*

*Spice Johnson and children. Hernon, Cecil, Robert, James, Lillie, Spice Ann, Lizzie.*

*McKeown-Hale family, ca. 1900. John Carter and Martha Jane (Hale) Keown. Children, Floyd, Flora, Ida, Ada, Jess.*

*Ellen "Espy" Blackburn with Gwen Blackburn in front. Larrie, Gladys Watson, Lenas Watson, Ruby Blackburn, Nell Watson, Ivy Watson Blackburn holding Adrain Blackburn. McHenry, ca. 1909.*

*Hugh Eddie and Cynthia (Bishop) Duke and family.*

*Weymon Tucker, Alney Hayes, Larry and Ronald Tucker, 1957.*

*Willard Hess, McHenry, owner/operator of Hess Service Station.*

*Feeding the chicken on the Layton Brown farm. Lenwood, Lerese, and Glendon Brown.*

*Wayne and Catherine Hunter Tinsley, McHenry, 1948.*

*Sarah Belle (Burden) Dougherty.*

*Urbin Miller and Rae Miller Autry, 1918.*

*Quilt pieced by Matilda Stone, ca. 1915. Violin made with matches by Paul Moseley.*

*John Aubrey and David Williams Barrett, ca. 1912.*

*Sam James, Sr., Llanelly Wales, UK, ca. 1860.*

*Hosea and Lodema Fulkerson.*

*Joe Keown, druggist, Cromwell.*

*Duncan family reunion, 1942, Carlos, Autry, Leva Taylor, Irlis Duncan.*

*Louise and Helen Morris crossing Ohio River with pianist Orvix Burton, July 1935.*

*Guy and Bessie Chinn with son, Orville, 1912.*

*Mary Masterson Chinn, mother of John M. Chinn, 1860s.*

*John M. and Sarah Sublett Chinn, ca. 1890, parents of Guy Chinn.*

*Orville and Cleo Chinn, Dec. 7, 1945, parents of Sandra, Anita, and John.*

*Viola Williams Chinn standing in front of the Fielden Williams home, ca. 1900.*

*Going swimming at the new pond at McHenry, ca. 1947. Mary Jane Wilson James, Dodie Kendall Allen, Alta Jean, Annalee Johnson LeBlanc, Jenny Jo Refrow, Betty Lou McKerny Hull.*

*ABOVE: Ferguson family, ca. 1919. Lula Snodgrass Ferguson holding Lorene, Myrtle, Marvin, Arthur holding Ernest.*

*LEFT: Bruce Bishop and family.*

William Reynolds, owner of Reynolds Auto, Beaver Dam.

Leta T. Owens, McHenry, bookkeeper for W.S. Taylor and Son, Beaver Dam.

Lewis Easterday, father of Mabel Ross.

Henry S. and Harriett Garner Williams Duke, and daughter Lizzie Duke.

Margaret Porter, Clemmie Johnson, Sam Drake, Betty Read, Dorthy Crunk in front of Johnson's Cafe, Rockport, 1945.

Four generations. Archie L. and Hazel Brown, daughters Virginia and Lois Brown. Granddaughter Vicky Brown Cowell Goodman. G-granddaughter Meleney Cowell.

E.C. Heflin family. Gaynell Heflin Warren, Harold, Carrie, Fred, E.C., Myrtle Heflin Black, Helen Heflin Cook.

*Birthplace of P.A. Swain, Aug. 5, 1853.*

*Birthplace of P.A. Swain as it looked March 1998.*

*Oldest building in Hartford. Old Hartford Academy.*

*Myrtle Phelps and family, 1910. Ellis Leon, Arvil, Myrtle.*

*Relative of Mary C. Eskridge, late 1800s.*

*Hicks house, Old Echols, 1919-1921. Effie Hicks, Mrs. Mason Cup. Children unk.*

*Louise, Grace, Paulie Reynolds, McHenry, ca. 1930*

*Boxing in McHenry.*

*Robert Stone Sr. caught 38 lb. fish at Williams Mine pond, 1956.*

Mary Smith Bennett.

Eliza Jane McMillion Rains Dehart.

John Durall and Luther Geaves at Green River, Rockport.

Maurine Martin Wilson, Otto C. and Wade Franklin Martin.

Ray Miller Autry.

Thomas J. Phelps, McHenry, 1885.

Jess Bishop, McHenry, WWII.

Virginia Martin Flener, age 96, wife of Benjamin Franklin Flener.

Elbert Goodall, Centertown.

Lillian Beck Phelps, Charlie F. Beck, Irene Beck Hunter, Herbert Conway Beck, 1910.

Lilburn Taylor family. David and Peggy (Bozarth) Taylor, Bob and Betty (Turner) Taylor, Lilburn and Elizabeth (Cook) Taylor, L.B. and Tootsie (Burden) Taylor, Donald and Betty (Pierce) Taylor, Jerry and Betty (Coleman) Taylor, Charles and Defrosia (Richard) Taylor.

John and Ollie Render Maddox, Clifford and Mazie Maddox Growbarger, ca. 1900.

Wade Franklin Martin, ca. 1905-1906. South side of old court house.

Five generations. Baby Guy Nolan Ramney, Gwendolyn Martin Ramney, Otto C. Martin, Deliah A. Flener Martin, Virginia Martin Flener, early 1930s.

Harrison, Martin, and Columbus Flener.

*David and Peggy (Bozarth) Taylor.*

*Ruby and Wilma Havens, mid 1930s.*

*Phelps family, McHenry, spring 1923. Conrad, Lillian holding Natonie, Lucille.*

*Early 1900s. Back: Martin Flener holding Geneva, Stell Faught Flener, Isaac Cooper, Annie America Flener Cooper, Harrette Flener, Christopher Columbus Flener, Garin Flener Smith, Harrison Flener, Minnie Ramey Flener. 2nd: Leona Flener Stewart, Eliza Sandefur, Bejamin Franklin Flener, Virginia Martin Flener, Maurine Martin Wilson, Deliah A. Flener Martin, Raucem Basinel Martin. Minnie Cooper Wallace, "Spot" McKenney, Leatha Flener McKenney, Eura McKenney, Noka Flener Casebier, Wade Franklin Martin, Sigsby McKenney, Lucille Flener Scott. Virginia Sandefur Taylor, Floy Stewart Stevens, Gold Cooper West, Ruth Stewart Leach. Sitting: Otto C. Martin, Curtis Sandefur, Lillian Maurine McKenney, Rayburn McKenney, Fayburn McKenney.*

# Towns and Communities

*Main Street, Fordsville, before 1916 fire.*

*Street scene, Fordsville, early 1900s.*

*Main Street, Hartford.*

*Dundee, about 1900.*

*Beaver Dam, ca. 1950.*

*Community house, Old Echols, 1919-1921.*

*Sign on Hwy. 62 from Beaver Dam with new name.*

*Main Street, Fordsville, ca. 1900.*

*Hartford's famous town slogan.*

*Render, 1920.*

*"Hillside". Hartford house built by John Pendleton, 1861-1865.*

*General view of Echols, 1959.*

*Moving logs. Old Echols in background, 1919-1921.*

*Highway 71, near Beaver Dam, KY.*  *Hwy. 231 S.*

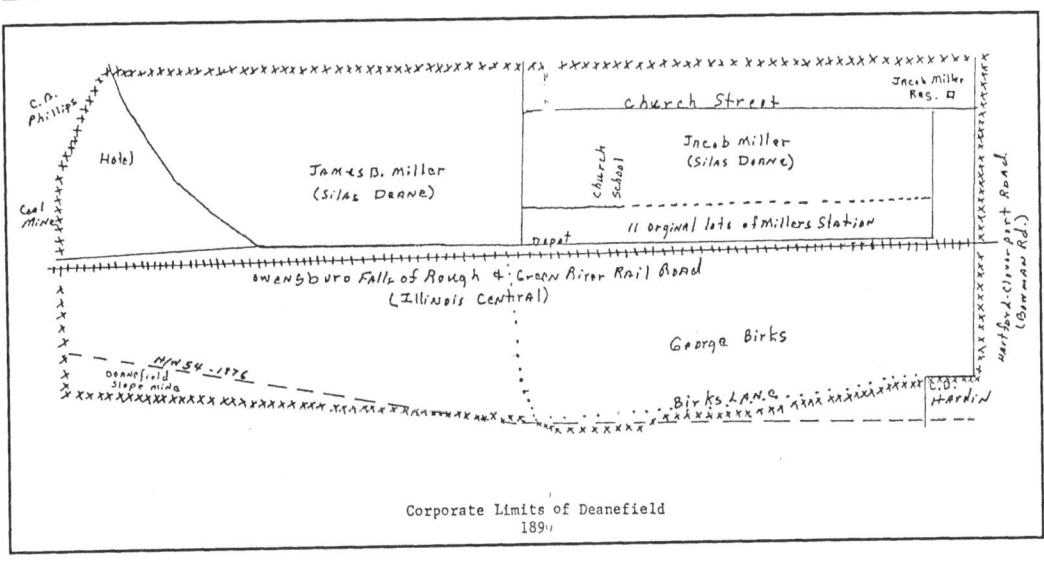

*Millers Station, 1889.*

*Corporate Limits of Deanefield, 1899.*

*Both sketches from "Deanfield, Kentucky, How It All Began", by Ellis and Bonnie Tierney.*

*Flood near depot, Rockport.*

*Willis Keys, streets of Rockport, KY.*

*Drawbridge, Rockport.*

*Ferry at Rockport, Jan. 1940. Woodrow on 14 inches of ice.*

*Tornado in Rockport, 1970.*

*Flood in 1937, Rockport.*

*Snow on Halloween, 1993. Home of Dennis and Judith Ralph of Reynolds Station.*

*Fort Hartford Stone Co. Owner, C. Hall.*

*Rochester Dam, 1921.*

*Railroad bridge, Rockport, 1937 flood.*

*Indian artifacts from Ohio County. Site along Green River are mostly "archaic," some "woodland" and "Mississippian". The most famous is "Indian Knoll" an archaic shell mound, excavated by W.S. Webb, a UK archeologist using CCC workers in the 1930s.*

Clemmie Johnson on the railroad bridge, Rockport.

Landmark at Rockport.

Old water tower, Horton, 1927.

Kenneth Hobdy pulling wagon, with Vernie Curtis riding. Result of an election bet.

Crew of wagon bet. Billy Allen, unk., Kenneth Hobdy, Vernie Curtis, unk. The 25 mile ride took more than ten hours. A huge crowd turned out for the finish of this election bet.

H.E. Allen and grandson, Douglas Allen, beside monument in honor of Granville Allen, the first Union soldier killed in West Kentucky.

First driver's license issued in Kentucky.

*McHenry, in the early days, looking southeast from mines.*

*Sewer construction on East Washington St., Hartford, February, 1911.*

### SQUARE DEAL TICKET

For MAYOR

C. B. Embry, Jr.   ( )

For COUNCILMEN

Douglas Ashby   ( )
John Render   ( )
David G. Givens   ( )
C. Webster Harris   ( )
James G. Sandefur   ( )
Robert "Bob" Shown   ( )

For JUDGE

Ellis G. Patton   ( )

# Fairs and Celebrations

*"The Spirit of No Creek," Ohio School Fair, 1929.*

*No Creek float, 1928, Ohio School Fair.*

*Hartford float, Ohio County School fair, 1923. Ellis Smith, driver, Lorena Bozarth making flag.*

*Echols Pink Hall School float, 1938, Mr. and Mrs. C.O. Brown, teachers.*

*Ohio County Fair, Sept. 11, 1900. Used by Mary Jo White for a well known painting.*

*Stretch car of Ohio Co. Shriners, built by Floyd Spriggs, early 1950s.*

*Ed Whitehead, Welburn Lee Ashby Post, Centertown horse show.*

*Ohio County Fair, 1957.*

*Ohio County Fair, 1957.*

*Fred and Ruth Heflin, 1958*

*Edwina Chinn, 1973.*

*Virgil Stewart, town marshal, clearing the street for school parade in Beaver Dam, 1966.*

*Octoberfest parade, Hartford, 1990.*

*Eula Rhea Wilson Barrett, with grandchildren, Joseph, Thad, Dawn, Scarlett, and Elizabeth Barrett.*

*Robert Stone and car, parade, Oct. 1992.*

*Drum majorette, Beaver Dam High, Shirley Barnes. Mascot Olive Hill.*

*First school fair in Ohio Co., held in Fordsville. Photo by J.W. Hale, early photographer in Fordsville area.*

*Karen McClain and Sandy Johnson, Beaver Dam Celebration Days, 1970.*

*Rockport school fair float, 1923.*

*"Masquerade Day," Beaver Dam, 1970. Tommy Jackson, Donnetta Crawford, Audra Hoxworth.*

*Drum and Bugle Corps, American Legion, Daviess Co., Post 9 at the unveiling of the Fort Hartford marker by Elna Hawkins (Moore).*

*Parade, Fordsville, ca. 1900.*

*Ohio County Fair, 1929.*

*Ohio County High School Marching Eagles at Rosine Centennial, Sept. 1973.*

*Rosine, 1996. Annual "Great Rosine Terrapin Race."*

*Ray Black and Son, Ohio Co. Fair, 1962.*

*Noah Phelps, Jr., receiving plaque at McHenry Centennial, 1980.*

*Christmas Parade, Beaver Dam.*

*Christmas Parade, Beaver Dam.*

*Winning float, 1935, Ohio County Fair.*

*South Beaver Dam school float, 1924.*

Mr. and Mrs. Ted Vincent, daughter Sheila Vincent Reid, Hartford Sesquicentennial.

Central Coal and Iron Co., Inc., McHenry, brass band.

Jackson family, picnic in the park.

1932 Beaver Dame Strawberry Festival. Back: Mary D. (Hocker) Parks, Rachel Shultz, Virginia (McKenny) Hill, unk., Katherine Chinn, unk, Ruby Bell, Lula Mae Fulkerson, Anna Frances Taylor, Naomi (Reid) Eskridge, Willie Pearl Swain, Grace Margaret (Williams) Albright, Jane Tichenor Hicks, Wilma Taylor. Front: Dora Belle Taylor, unk., Evaline Harreld.

1978 Alumni Banquet, McHenry.

# Social Events

*McHenry Centennial, 1980. Ruth Burris, Annabel Johnston, Mary F. Watts, Juanita Hughes, unk.*

*Carpet rug tacking at Mrs. Fred Miller's. Harriett Miller, Emma Miller, Vera Caldwell, Gladys Miller, Eva Burriss, Nell Blair, May Miller, Sue Blair, Annie Caldwell.*

*McHenry Centennial, 1980. McLean Co. Senior Citizens band entertains.*

*Parade, McHenry Centennial, 1980. Dr. and Mrs. Billy R. Allen.*

*Bill Monroe at KFC.*

Paul Keith Phelps, Art Linkletter, Gregory Dale Phelps at soft drink convention, 1962.

Wendell Patton and Vicky Brown, Beaver Dam, 1970.

Front: Pen Vandiver, Clarence Wilson. Back: unk., Flossie Wilson Hines, Versie Monroe.

Tom Thumb wedding, 1938. Front: Uneeda Smith, Martina Ross, Patsy Ruth Tilford, Robbie Nell Hert. 2nd: Don Smith, Wanda Jean Heltsley, Jimmy Barnard, Elizabeth Ann Crunk, Perry O'Neil Williams, Joyce Ann Campfield, Deward Glen Ross, Betty Jean Maddox, H. D. Bailey Jr., Martine Wilson. 3rd: Nancy Turley, Johnny Render, unk., Clemmie Everly, Noble D. Brown, Betty Tooley, Margaret Brown Wilson, Hazel Tooley, Jeannette Boswell, George Herbert Akins, Gracie Mildred Mabrey. Back: Ann Barnard, Billy Gene Welborn, Carolyn Smith, Hilda Robinson, Norman Cawthorn, Betty Reid, Deloris Dodge, Patsy Ann Render, Wanda lee Mabrey, Mary Brown.

Jim and Jessie, Rosine Bluegrass Fesitival, Rosine.

Beaver Dam's May Pole dance, 1951-1952.

Tom Thumb wedding. Gaynell Heflin, Willis Rowe, Lois Brown, Lawrence Pearl Bell, Jo Mitchell, Patsy Patton, Carol Evans.

Cecil Chinn estate auction, 1985, McHenry.

Wedding of George Hunter and Irene Beck, 1917, McHenry.

Bill Monroe, father of Bluegrass music, and James Hines, book and magazine publisher and songwriter. 1955.

Lee Bivins, front row, right, later a road contractor.

1st: Jessie Vernon, Lura Grobarger, Grace Elmore, Ann Grant. 2nd, Bee Blades, Jessie Hicks, Ida Kennedy, Tink Durham, Pearl Raines. 3rd: Will Vernon, Helen Bennett, G.G. Reid, Bee Cawthorn, Katie Chinn, Edith Wilson, Elsie Crunk.

The Rosine Barn Jamboree.

Wedding of Johnnie Culbertson and Gertie Goodman, Rosine, 1916. 1st: Rev. Ward Taylor, groom and bride. 2nd: Mrs. Ira Goodman, Arter Goodman, Ranzey Goodman (baby?), Levi Goodman, Lula Kessinger, Roberta Havens, Christy Ann Kessinger, Liza Hamilton, Eliza Goodman, Fannie Crowder. 3rd: Prudie Kessinger, Luke Griffith, Myrtel Culbertson, Estil Kessinger, John K. Goodman, Ira Goodman, John A. Goodman, Bob Rains, Martha Rains, Virge Kessinger, Cindrella Crowder, Tom Crowder. 4th: Edith Wallace, Betty Taylor, Loretta Crowder, Ann Haven, Ray Miller, Rosie Kessinger, Mae House, Hallie. 5th: Frank Kessinger, Van House, Mamie Leach., unk., Willie Goodman, Sarah Kessinger, Ollie Goodman, Custer Haven, Norman Hessinger.

Bill Monroe performs, Oct. 28, 1985.

# OFFICIALS

*James Franklin Carson.*

*Julian Ratcliff, 1958, Kentucky State Trooper.*

*Tom Butler, proprietor of Crescent Mills, sheriff.*

*Finley Nimmo, city policeman.*

*Joe S. Taylor, Beaver Dam Mayor, 1966-1968, city council, 1946-1957.*

*Fred Tatum, Ohio County Highway Department.*

*Ohio County Officials, 1897. Tom Black, top far right. R.B Martin, middle round far left.*

*Richard P. Beck, McHenry, Ohio Co. Tax Commissioner, 1928-1931.*

*Thomas H. and Lola (Stevens) Black. Thomas was sheriff of Ohio Co. from 1810-1813.*

*R.B. Martin, sheriff of Ohio Co., 1905.*

*Dora Beck Albin, 1928, Ohio Co Tax Commissioner early 1930s. Deputy jailer 1960s-1970s.*

*Mr. and Mrs. Richard P. Beck, McHenry, Ohio Co. Tax Commissioner, 1928-1931.*

*Carlisle and Latna Oldham, Mayor of Beaver Dam.*

*Latna Oldham, third mayor of Beaver Dam. Served for 28 years.*

*David C. Taylor, mayor of Beaver Dam. Served as commissioner and mayor for 24 years, ending in 1998.*

*Gayle and Steve Givens, 1952. Former City Commissioner.*

*Swearing in Rockport town board. Judge C.B. Embry Jr. W.L. Decker, Vernie Curtis, Shirley Smith, Darrell Curtis.*

*Wayland Render, 1964, State representative for Ohio and Hancock Counties.*

*Wm. Mitchel Overhults, chairman of Ohio County Soil Conservation, purchased a year's supply of the 1959 special issue soil conservation stamp from postmaster Forrest P. Bell, Hartford.*

*William Natcher speaking, businessman Charles "Dixie" Vinson far right.*

*Magistrate Earl Mattingly takes a drink of fresh water from one of the lines installed in the Narrows, Magan, and Fordsville Areas. James McGrew, right.*

*Lonnie Hawes, Eric Lee Chinn, Randall Sheffield, Burl Morris, Earl Mattingly.*

*Officials, 1900s. Top: L. Wilbur S. Tinsley, R.B. Martin.*

*Charlotte, Gwen, Otto Martin (judge), and Rance Ranney,*

*Ohio Co. Fiscal Court, ca. 1915. Warren Taylor back row, left.*

# FIRE DEPARTMENTS

*Firefighter Nancy Baker and Chris Shepard teaching children from Beaver Dam Elementary about fire safety, 1998.*

*Firefighter Jonathon James and Chris Shepard showing students from Beaver Dam Elementary about the fire hose and pressure, 1998.*

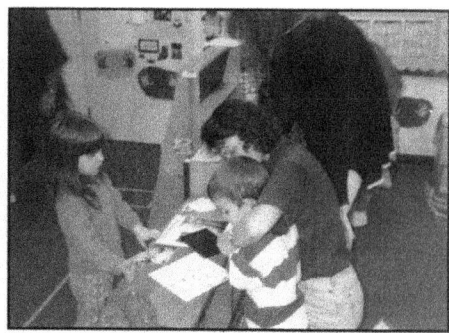
*Nancy Baker, volunteer firefighter fingerprints a student, 1998.*

*Ray Daugherty, Cecil Brooks, Fire Chief Gene King. Front: Roger Daugherty, unk., unk., ca. 1978.*

*City Commissioner Rex James, Mayor Hunter with firefighters.*

*Rosine Volunteer Fire Department. Back: Stoy Geary, Sonny Brown, Steve Geary, R.C. Davis, Sonny Whitely, Lea Taylor. Front: Bruce Leach, R. Swift, Tom Fitzgerald, Jerry Crumes, 1981.*

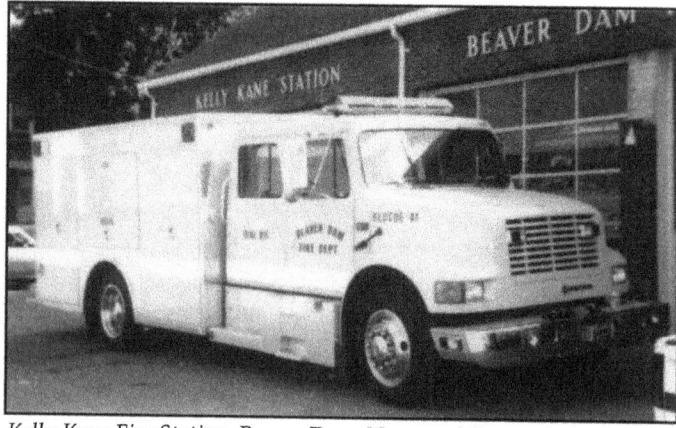
*Kelly Kane Fire Station, Beaver Dam. New rural fire truck purchased 1998.*

*Beaver Dam Fire Department.*

# PROFESSIONALS

Dr. Keith Martin, McHenry, retired from practice 1994.

Dr. Charlie Fisher.

Dr. William P. Watts, McHenry.

Monument of Rosine grocer, W. H. Pierce.

Bill Monroe Monument, Rosine Cemetery.

Bro. Richard Casey with Gospel Radio and TV Guide. Featured host on many radio and TV shows and pastor of Beaver Dam Community Church.

Dr. James A. Duff, Dundee.

Pendleton Vandiver monument.

*Introduction to the microscope, Sept. 13, 1944. Darlene Gripentrog, Dorothy Strandell, Betty Flickenger, Anne Fisher, Mary Seyffer, Pauline Griffith.*

*Dr. George Everly and family, 1937. Front: Homer and Gladys Boyd, Dr. Everly, George Anderson, Clemmie Park Hurst, George and Hazel Hurst (on either side of Dr. Everly.) Back: Jesse and Blanche Everly, George Boyd, Mr. and Mrs. Attison Park Everly. Clemmie Frances Everly, front.*

# Transportation

*Lofton Stewart, Echols, and 1928 Model T.*

*Coleen Hoskins Stewart and 1931 Model A Coupe.*

*First horse drawn hearse in Fordsville, purchased by Fuqua and Walker for $550.*

*J.P. Casebier with 1941 Packard.*

*Lee and Ethel Bivins out for a Sunday drive.*

*Mr. Morris drove the taxi service between Hartford and Beaver Dam. Fred Cooper, George Trought, Maurice Morris, John Bozarth, ca. 1912.*

*Car on frozen Green River, Jan. 1940. Driver Fred Heflin.*

*Richard Harlon Taylor, rural mail carrier, Beaver Dam.*

*Clarence Bernard Ross, 1924 Ford, Kronas.*

*J.F. Casebier store and hearse, Beaver Dam, early 1900s.*

*Nell Johnson, 1927 Overland Redbird.*

*Herman Johnson inside new car with Herman Jr., in lap. Brother Archie on fender.*

*Grandmaw Cardwell.*

*Lillie N. Cardwell.*

*Cecil Hacker, bookkeeper, Silas Tichenor Store, McHenry, ca. 1910.*

*Joe T. Fuqua, 1982.*

*Beaver Dam Bus Depot, 1949. Then Hwy 71, later known as Hwy. 231 S.*

*Fuqua Bus Lines, top of Lookout Mountain, 1934-1935.*

*1923-1924 model bus for Fuqua Bus Lines.*

# TRAINS AND DEPOTS

I.C. Railroad Depot, Fordsville, as it looked in the early 20s. At that time, Fordsville had two railroad companies with routes into and through it.

Fordsville Depot Museum, downtown Fordsville.

L&N Depot, Fordsville during its heyday. Three ladies around the freight and baggage truck.

ICG Depot, Horse Branch, KY.

Nov. 27, 1957. Last train between Louisville and Central City. Roberts, F. Durbin, H. Zirkel, C.S. Robinson, L.A. Wilmoth, E.G. Potts, C. Miller.

*Group that went to Mammoth Cave, 1914.*

*Beaver Dam Depot, 1913.*

*Depot, Deanefield, sometime in the early 1900s.*

*Horton Depot 1911. Children of Cary and Effie Crowder. Marion O'Connell, Grace Crowder (Potts), and Maude Crowder (Stevens.)*

*Railroad Depot and Creamery, Rockport.*

*Group at Beaver Dam Depot, ca. 1910.*

*Fordsville, 1890. Note large tobacco warehouse and train.*

*IC Railroad Depot, early 1920s.*

*L&N Train Station, Fordsville, early 1900s.*

*Clarence O'Brien, Ray Smith, Jr., Roy Smith, Okley Bratcher. Back: Russell Smith, Bill Jones. Standing: Mancie Jones, Sam Farris, early 1950s.*

*Rockport Bridge over Green River.*

*Gus Struder, Charlie McElroy, Nelie Evans, Charlie Duvall, Dof Tomes, Ben Davenport at Horse Branch.*

*Meeting the #22 train, McHenry, 1927.*

*Segregated restrooms at old Beaver Dam Depot.*

*McHenry Depot, 1927.*

*Train wreck in McHenry, May 15, 1903.*

*Head on collision, June 20, 1901, Beaver Dam.*

*Crew that built the MH&E Depot, Hartford.*

*Beaver Dam Depot, 1930s.*

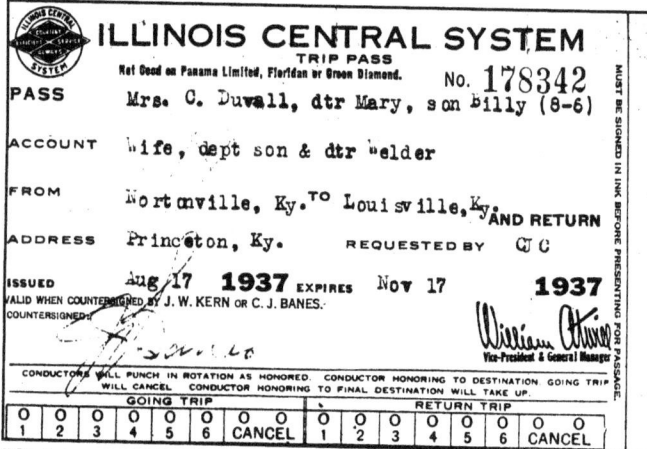
*ICS trip pass, 1937.*

*ICS Safety Club card of Charles Duvall.*

# BUSINESSES

Reid & Reid Store, Moseley J. Reid, right.

George Keown and Carl Westerfield, early 30s.

Inside Wilson's Restaurant. Unk., Carl Wilson, Hayden Curtis, Wm. Wilson.

Beaver Dam Planing Mill, 1909.

Carl Wilson, Wilson Bakery Wagon, Rockport.

Wilson Restauramt, Rockport.

First Band Mill at Rockport.

Building highway bridge over Green River, ca. 1939. Replaced ferry.

*Beaver Dam Milling Co.*

*Bevil & Johnson Truck Line. Earl Bevil, Bill Johnson, Elbert Slack.*

*Old Hartford Mill, constructed ca. 1830.*

*The Hartford House.*

*Gillespie Blacksmith Shop, started 1880. Photo early 1900s.*

*Cafe owned and operated by Mr. and Mrs. Joe Tate, Hartford. Foreground, Joe Tate and Conrad Gilstrap.*

*H.B. Stanley, Beaver Dam, 1962.*

*T.C. Martin, McCormick Deering Implement Co, Beaver Dam, 1930s.*

*Central Coal & Iron, McHenry.*

*Jail on bottom level, Rockport.*

*Dundee Store, Dundee.*

*Virginia Lee Brown, Young Office.*

*Clive Iler's store, Hartford.*

*Rockport Deposit Bank. Incorporated Oct. 1903; dissolved June 1926.*

*Rex James.*

*Ray James.*

*Norval P. Brown, McHenry Mfg. & Machine Co., 1910.*

*Ads, 1930s.*

*Leach's Grocery ad.*

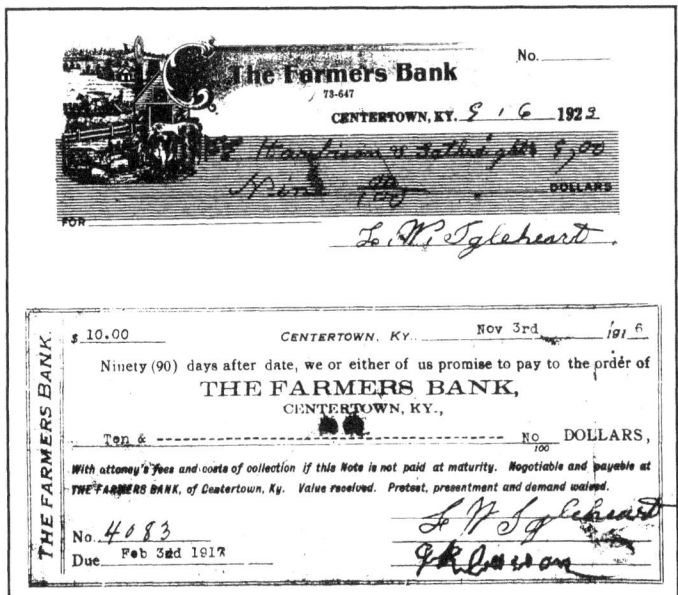

*Farmers Bank, Centertown documents. Check, 1923; Note 1916.*

*Cook's General Store, off Bethel Church Road. James Lewis Cook and wife, Martha Kuykendall.*

*Community group at Cook's Store, ca. 1914. Bottom: Densie Minton, Dillard Minton, Dillard Schroader, Bennie Long, Ben Peach, Dave Kuykendall, Harrison Schroader, Mode Schroader, Charlie Schroader, Pone Burton. Top: Lou Kuykendall, Albert Long, Mary Minton Long (sitting) holding Stella Long, Nannie Minton, Martha Cook, Lewis Cook, Pearl Bennington, Rene Schroader, unk., unk., unk., Provie Nelson, Rene Minton, Lincoln Schroader.*

*E.P. Barnes Store, Beaver Dam, early 1900s. Site of current Beaver Dam Deposit Bank.*

*Ozie Taylor Grocery, Cromwell. Mr. and Mrs. Taylor, unk.*

*Bishop's Sundries, Centertown. Owners Mr. and Mrs. Guy Bishop. Cynthia Bishop outside.*

*Logan C. "Bud" Shown has repaired shoes in Beaver Dam since 1944. Now semi retired, Shown is one of the few small town cobblers still around.*

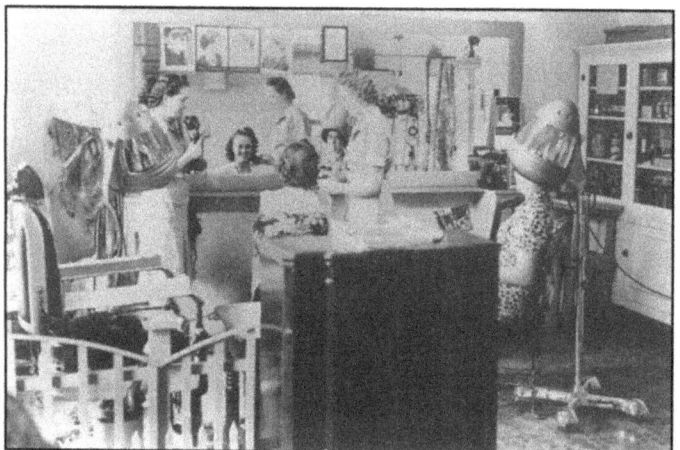

*Beaver Dam Beauty Salon, 1930s.*

*Royal Crown Cola Bottling Co, Main St., Beaver Dam. Early 1960s.*

*Hocker & Company Store, late 1800s.*

*Barnes Automotive, Beaver Dam, 1930s.*

*Casebier's Garage, First Street, Beaver Dam.*

Lacefield Grocery, 1950s. Standing: Lewis Southard, Walter Lacefield, Alva Southard. Sitting, Ernest McConnell, Sharon Lacefield Barrett, Oscar Allen.

Sharon Lacefield Barrett grew up listening to folklore at Lacefield Grocery.

Moseley's Grocery, Taffy. Joe and Arlayne Moseley, owners.

Bennett Apple House, ca. 1940. Back: Edna Earl Wilson, Clara Bennett. Front: Robert Wilson Barrett, Charles Bennett, Alva Bennett.

Overhuls & Bullock Cash Store, built ca. 1910, Equality. Photo, 1912.

C.T. Leach & Son Grocery, Beaver Dam. Ora Maddos, William Taylor and Chester Taylor Leach.

Johnson Brothers saw mill, early 1900s.

Carlos B. Embry Sr., and Zora R. Embry and staff of Ohio County Messenger, 1940.

*Veller Drug Co., Beaver Dam. Paxton Veller, unk., John Veller.*

*Standard Oil Co., R.B. Blankenship, Distributor. Filbert Eskridge, Murray Davis, Kenneth Alford.*

*Inside Espey's Grocery, Render. Bill and William Espey.*

*Beaver Dam Cafe. Betty Dale, E.J. Knight, Ida M. (Tootsie) Givens. Located on Main Street. Still in operation.*

*Ira Haven Grocery, Hwy. 231S, Cromwell, ca. 1930. (Both photos.)*

*Wilson Restaurant, Rockport.*

*Barrel parts makers, mid 1800s. On Green River, where bridge is now.*

*Home where Beaver Dam Health Care Manor is now located. Hwy 231 S. toward Cromwell.*

Wallace and Louise English, built and operated 231 Grill, Pleasant Ridge.

231 Grill, Pleasant Ridge. July 13, 1959- March 28, 1995.

Hotel Vinson, Beaver Dam. Ada Vinson and maids.

Mr. and Mrs. Argle W. Leach's Grocery Store, Hwy. 231 S.

Making molasses. Herman and Lola Render farm near Centertown.

Cross Road Grocery, South Beaver Dam, 1944. Owner Gene Coleman. In front: James Dennis, Frank Stevens.

Last Cross Road Grocery, South Beaver Dam. Owner Gene Coleman.

Oller's General Store, Olaton. Owned by Alvey Oller, March 1, 1935-Nov. 8, 1971.

Hess Service Station, McHenry, 1930.

W.E. Taylor and his store, early 1940s.

*Daugherty's Grocery, Thanksgiving 1975. Fred (d. 9/28/76) and Barbara Daugherty, Ken and Adam Daugherty, Daniel Dockery.*

*Wendell Maddox, 1920.*

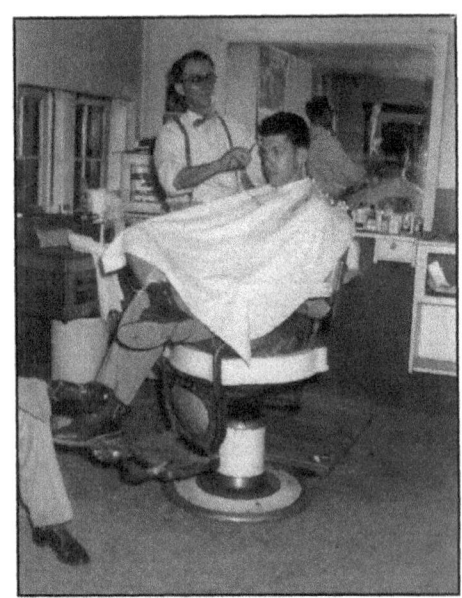
*Raymond (Dick) Render Barber Shop, Centertown. Ed Whitehead in chair, 1950.*

*Merlin and Freeman Shultz opened the first Western Auto Store, Beaver Dam, Nov. 1948.*

*C.E. Ford & Co., corner of Hwy. 54 and 69 S. Present Wemhoener Building.*

*Old Wilson Store, Fordsville, late 1800s.*

*McHenry Mfg. & Machine Co. First owner Ed Nelson; then Frank Lawrence. Currently owned by Bill Wallace.*

*Rex and Ray James. McHenry Mfg. & Machine Co.*

Black's Superette, opened in 1953. First supermarket in Beaver Dam.

Ferry at Livermore, Ky.

Main Street, Fordsville, ca. 1900, showing second location of Fordsville Bank.

Early 1900s, Junius Litsey Blacksmith Shop, Fordsville.

W.S. Taylor & Sons, Roy and Joe S. Garage founded Dec. 7, 1927.

Fordsville.

F.K. Casebier Co, Beaver Dam.

Ira Neil Burden and Avery Blacklock Sr. Molasses Mill, Cromwell.

*Store in Olaton, burned Nov. 8, 1971.*

*Beaver Dam Drug Co, Kentucky Utilities, Main Street, Beaver Dam.*

*Cecil and Madge Pirtle Leisure.*

*Leisure's Modern Court.*

*Main Street, downtown Beaver Dam. Old Tilford Hotel, Hub's Cafe, Jewelry Store, Old Livery Stable behind hotel.*

*Downtown Hartford, north of Union Street.*

*Young's Lumber Co., S. Main across railroad tracks, Beaver Dam.*

*Grocery Store of J. Dyer White, Hartford, early 20th century. James Lyons, left behind counter. J.D. White (child), J. Dyer White, right rear, Mrs. J. Dyer White, right behind counter. Others unknown.*

*R.A. Rowan Sawmill, Rough River, ca. 1906*

# OLD HOTELS

*Commercial Hotel, 1910, Beaver Dam.*

*Williams Mines Hotel, McHenry.*

*Old Commercial Hotel, Rockport, owned by Katherine O'Bannon and Betty Brown.*

*Taylor Mines Hotel before 1900, sold and dismantled 1937.*

*Daniels Mototel, Beaver Dam.*

*Cromwell Hotel. Warren Shields, Pernecy Lane Jackson, Verna Porter Jackson, baby James Benjamin Jackson, unk.*

# Theatres and Memorabilia

*March 1939, Beaver Dam.*

*Opera House entrance, McHenry, 1908.*

*Pantomine, early 1960s. Martha Heflin Barrass, Don Barrass.*

*Hartford Opera House, 1933, Tom Thumb Wedding.*

### PROGRAM
CENTERTOWN, KENTUCKY.
### Thursday, March 9, 1922.
## ALAMO THEATER
DOORS OPEN AT 7 P. M. PERFORMANCE BEGINS AT 8 P. M.

### SPECIAL NOTICE!

We carry a full line of Star Brand Shoes (none better) with prices reduced to almost normal.

Big line of horse collars and harness such as you need every day.

Most any kind of field and poultry fence at reasonable prices.

Nice line of the celebrated O. K. Stoves and Ranges; every one fully guaranteed.

All kinds of Staple and Fancy Groceries, Seed Potatoes, Field Seeds, Chicken Feed, Tea, Tar, Turpentine, Tacks, in fact most anything you want (except white mule.)

We also buy all kinds of produce at the highest price.

DEXTER & VINCENT.

---

**The Farmers Bank**

CAPITAL - - $15,000.00
SURPLUS - - $10,000.00
Motto: "Security"
Come to see us.

DO YOU KNOW WHAT THE P. T. A. IS DOING?

Come to the school March 17th and find out.

☞ Good program.

*Alamo Theater Program, March 9, 1922*

*Olive Brown Walton McHenry Opera House, 1910.*

*The Kentucky Theatre is listed on the National Register of Historic sites. Built in 1936 by WPA.*

*Cast of "An Arizona Cowboy." Standing, Glenn Cook, Claude Taylor, John Barrett, Horace Taylor, Asberry Hocker, Joe Barrett. 2nd: Belle Taylor, Dora Belle Boswell, Mattie Taylor, Minnie Lou Boswell, Elizabeth Boswell. Sitting: Lilburn Taylor, Ovid Barrett, Durwood Black.*

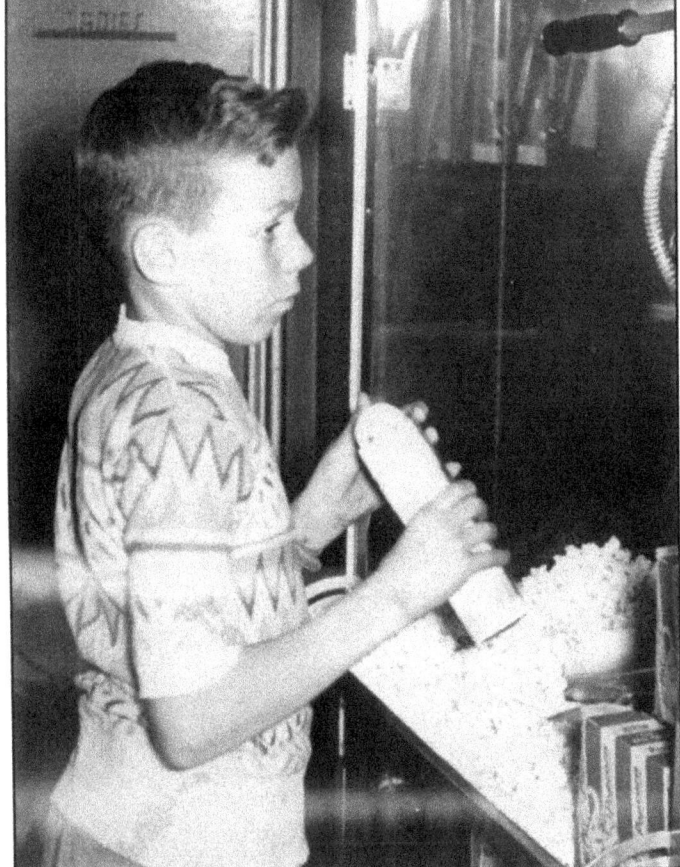
*Bobby Shown, Majestic Theatre, Beaver Dam, 1947-1948. Andy Anderson, owner; Virgil Stewart, manager.*

# Farming and Miscellaneous

Ira S. Burden and his black mule at Blacklock's Sorghum Mill, Cromwell.

Alva Blacklock Sr., Cromwell Sorghum Mill, first in Ohio County.

The thrashing outfit of P.M. and Norval P. Brown, ca. 1912, McHenry.

*Refinished horse drawn road grader Lee Bivins used to build highways.*

*L.A. Stevens, Beaver Dam.*

*Christopher Neil Burden, 12, Cromwell.*

*Robert (Bob) Goodall, sons Roma, Foster, Oakley and John, Wysox community. Farmers with horse-Jack, Bell, Dock and Julie.*

*Timber from Centertown area.*

*Ray Black Sr., Ray Black Jr, Barabara Black, ca. 1946.*

*Robert (Bob) Goodall, sons Roma, Foster, Oakley and John, Wysox community.*

*Chesley Trogden working at Westerfield Dairy.*

*Jewell Martin, 1939.*

*Ira S. Burden, 1967.*

*One of the first wheat thrashers in Ohio County, early 1900s.*

*Layton Brown, 1948-1949.*

*Bailing hay, ca. 1900.*

*James Wade (Hess) Martin, 1940.*

*Jeremiah Williams, obtained original land grant for Knob Hill farm, 1806.*

*James Clellon Renfrow, 1944.*

*Processing sorghum, 1972. Mule belongs to Ira S. Burden.*

*John Aubrey Barrett, Barrett Orchard, Liberty Road, Beaver Dam, ca. 1925.*

*Robert Elijah Barrett spraying apple trees, Barrett Orchard, ca. 1925.*

RIGHT: *Wyman Tucker, 1950.*

FAR RIGHT: *Nell Johnson, logging at Goshen, 1950.*

*Sep Williams farm, Rob Roy community. Mary Barnard, Elizabeth Taylor holding Bob Taylor, Pauline Williams, Rachel Williams front, Anna Williams back, Rob Williams, Emma Taylor, Lilburn Taylor, Annie Williams, Sep Williams, Claude Taylor, Clarcy Williams, Cecil Barnard, Thomson Taylor, Agnes Taylor, Annie Taylor, Cecil Barnard, Mary Elizabeth Barnard, L.B. Taylor, Louise Taylor, Charlie Williams.*

*Edgar, John, Irlis, Autry, and Carlos Duncan, 1926, working in wheat field, Rockport.*

*Mary Barnard, Clarcy Williams, Mary Elizabeth Barnard on bumper, Agnes Taylor. Trip to Hopkinsville, ca. 1934.*

*Susan Mariah (Williams) and Robert Elijah Barrett, owners of Barrett Orchard, ca. 1925*

*Fred Latney Oldham with bees, 1940s.*

*FFA judging team, Louisville, 1951. Bill Hines, John Ragland, Bill Johnson, Alva Barnard.*

*Ed, Tony, and J.R. Whitehead beside hay stacks.*

*Bedford Gasaway Snodgrass, Centertown, operated this wheat thrasher.*

# Coal Industry

*Shovel No. 2, steam powered, boom 120 ft. Standing on shovel, Bob Snodgrass, Jasper Whitehead, Lawrence Snodgrass, 1 unk.*

*Old Echols.*

*Rockport Mines.*

*Beaver Dam Coal Co., Taylor Mines, 1905. Herman Stewart, Beety Stum, Dit Martin.*

*Echols Mine sign.*

Cherry Hill Miners from Ohio County. Front: John Render, Claud Maple, Lou Francis, Cecil McCoy, Dennie Saling, James "Fat" Givens, Sam Durham. Back: Bookkeeper, Mitchel Curtis, Earl Porter, Herman King, C.L. Marlow, Roy Hoskins, Hulet Curtis, Jeff Curtis, Dellie Singleton, Russell Blades, unk., Martin Durham.

Norval P. Brown, fifth from left, on tipple at McHenry Mines before 1916.

The store at Williams mines, McHenry. Guy Stateler, Roscoe Beward, unk., Dr. Deard, Anna L. Williams, Georgie Larkins, 1 unk.

Old Render tipple.

Entrance to Holt Mines, McHenry. Guide Rupert Davis, Zilpha Davis, Hayden and Polly Moorman.

McHenry.

Front: Homer Crume, Barney Baugh, Arvin Leisure, Jess Dudley Smith, Jim McDowell, Ernest Baldwin, Joe Mo McKenney, Arlis Parks, Glendon Stevens Jr., Dub Williams, Dan Lamb, Joe Shep Taylor, Maurice Burden. Back: Bryan Barnes, Dr. W.H. Washburn, Carl Hobdy, Kelly Kane, Bill Casebier, unk. Everett Hill. Volunteer firemen, ca. 1946, standing in front of first rural truck, built by Peabody Coal Co.

Kirk Leach, McHenry, paper carrier, Courier Journal.

Charles C. Watts, McHenry, superintendent of Beaver Dam Coal Co.

Ella Johnson Hocker, bookkeeper, Duncan Coal Co, McHenry, ca. 1910.

Render Mine, 1890.

CWA workers, 1939. Elbert Himes is in group.

*Old Render, 1906, Robert Simpson on front row.*

*Tokens from Beaver Dam Coal Co.*

*McHenry tipple, 1895.*

*"Script" used in Coal Co. stores, McHenry, Taylor Mines.*

Camp No. 1 mine, "West" Team. Morganfield. Front: Trainer Junior Chandler, Tommy Gipson, Jeff Gatten, Jack Willingham, David Acker. Standing: Mine Superintendent Terry Hurd, Gerald Mills, Philip Day, Jim McGill, Brent Roberts, Gary Birchwell.

*Taylor Mines, 1915.*

*Mines, 1905. Note Mules that pulled coal, carbide lamps, and dinner buckets.*

*Simon Janes, superintendent of Render Coal Mines, owned by DuPont family.*

*Miners from Kentucky Coke Co, Echols, Sept. 26, 1919. Those identified: seated front, Floyd Hoskins, third in front Della Singleton, fourth Roy Shaw. Standing second row, Dave Sneeden, seated behind him, Sam Shaver and John Myers, behind Shaver is Oval Cooper. First one on right in second row is D.A. Woodburn, third from right Midge Maples. Also in third row Shirley Geary.*

*Kentucky Coke Co. Echols, Company Store, Sept. 26, 1919.*

# Veterans

*Co. G, 13th Kentucky, V.R. Hartford Camp #202, Woodmen of the World, 1902.*

*WWII scrap metal drive at Beaver Dam High School, 1942*

*Kentucky State Militia, Co. H, 3rd Regt., Hartford, Capt. James Deweese in command. Top: 2nd from right, Sgt. Allison Barnett. 2nd: 3. Charlie Hawkins, 4. A.D. Kirk, 12. ___ Morris. 3rd: 1. Lt. Shown, 2. Capt. Deweese, 4. Marvin Hoover, 6. Arthur Minton.*

*American Legion Post, Hartford. Sixth person from right on back row is Clyde H. Wallace.*

# OHIO COUNTY CIVIL WAR TIMES
## Volume 1, Number 1            18 April 1865

We must gratefully acknowledge the labors of two Ohio County Civil War students who have contributed so much to the compilation of the following roster of Ohio County Civil War veterans who were natives of, resided in, or were buried in Ohio County. Many of the following names were first assembled by John Blackburn of Fordsville for the New Years Eve edition of the Ohio County Times in 1969. Secondly, we must extend our thanks to Bill Phelps of Beaver Dam who personally visited the Ohio County cemeteries and combed Civil War records for hours on end to add to Mr.. Blackburn's list and to locate the final resting places for the great American heroes of the following list. It is with deepest respect to the generation of our great-grandfathers that we include this roster of those who contributed so much to our American heritage. If any errors have occurred in the following roster by including some non-Ohio County veterans, the compiler felt that it would be better to include a few who lived barely into an adjacent county than to omit a deserving veteran.

| NAME | US/CS | GRADE | COMPANY | ORGANIZATION | CEMETERY | COMMUNITY |
|---|---|---|---|---|---|---|
| ABBOTT, William C | US | PVT | H | 18 Kentucky Inf | Rochester Cemetery | Rochester |
| ACTON, William H | | | | | Mt Vernon | Hwy 1164 |
| ADDISON, John | US | | M | 100 Pennsylvania Inf | Render | McHenry |
| ALLEN, Arthur | US | PVT | G | 12 Kentucky Cav | Lone Star Church | Falls of Rough |
| ALLEN, David | US | PVT | H | 12 Kentucky Cav | Rosine Cem | Rosine |
| ALLEN, Eli B | US | SGT | B | 17 Kentucky Inf | | |
| ALLEN, Granville | US | PVT | D | 17 Kentucky Inf | Leach | Horse Branch |
| ALLEN, Joseph | US | PVT | D | 17 Kentucky Inf | Union Temple Cem | Ohio County |
| ALTMIER, David | US | PVT | E | 3 Kentucky Cav | Prentiss | Beaver Dam |
| AMBROSE, William C | US | CPL | E | 12 Kentucky Cav | Buelah Cemetery | Beda |
| AMBROSE, William L | US | PVT | G | 17 Kentucky Inf | Private Cemetery | Sunnydale |
| ANDERSON, John W | US | PVT | I | 17 Kentucky Inf | Fairview | Baizetown |
| ARNOLD, Job | US | PVT | I | 17 Kentucky Inf | Private Cemetery | Arnold Ridge |
| ARNOLD, John | US | PVT | C | Mid Green River Bn | Old Salem | Horse Branch |
| ARNOLD, Stephen Z | US | PVT | I | 17 Kentucky Inf | Private Cemetery | Arnold Ridge |
| ASHBY, William Jr | US | CPT | G | 17 Kentucky Inf | Walton's Creek | Centertown |
| ASHLEY, Woodford | US | PVT | A | 17 Kentucky Inf | Barnett's Creek Church | Ohio County |
| ASKINS, J. J. | US | PVT | A | 17 Kentucky Inf | Evans' Farm | Askins, KY |
| AULL, A. S. | CS | PVT | K | 4 Kentucky Inf | | |
| AUSTIN, J. Rolla | CS | PVT | C | 9 Kentucky Inf | prob Stones River NB | Murfreesboro, TN |
| AUSTIN, John | US | PVT | B | 26 Kentucky Inf | Liberty Methodist Ch. | Beaver Dam |
| AXTON, Isaac | US | | | | KIA in Ohio County, by guerrillas | |
| AXTON, Levi M | US | PVT | A | 26 Kentucky Inf | | |
| BABBITT, Hiram | US | PVT | D | 12 Kentucky Cav | Pleasant Hill Cemetery | Magan |
| BABBITT, Sylvester | US | | | United States Navy | Hopewell Church | Askins, KY |
| BAIRD, J. A. | US | | | | Alexander Cemetery | Hartford |
| BAKER, Augustus | US | PVT | F | 11 Kentucky Inf | Rochester Cemetery | Rochester |
| BALES, L. R. | US | PVT | K | 3 Tenessee Inf (US) | Taffy Cemetery | Taffy |
| BARNARD, Ignatius P. | CS | PVT | C | 9 Kentucky Inf | Cave Hill | Louisville |

| NAME | US/CS | GRADE | COMPANY | ORGANIZATION | CEMETERY | COMMUNITY |
|---|---|---|---|---|---|---|
| BARRY, Samuel L | CS | | | 9 Kentucky Inf | | |
| BASHAN, C. D. | US | PVT | D | 26 Kentucky Inf | Willis Gilliam Farm | nr Fordsville |
| BEAN, Cortez X | US | PVT | F | 17 Kentucky Inf | Mt Vernon Cem | Hwy 1164 |
| BEAN, William Riley | US | PVT | F | 17 Kentucky Inf | Fitzhugh Cemetery | Dundee |
| BEGGARLY, Jessie N | US | PVT | F | 13 Indiana Cav | Cool Springs | Cool Springs |
| BENNETT, Jacob T | US | PVT | C & I | 17 Kentucky Inf | Walton's Creek | Centertown |
| BENNETT, Lindsey | US | PVT | F | 17 Kentucky Inf | Buelah Cemetery | Beda |
| BENNETT, Stephen A | US | PVT | A | 17 Kentucky Inf | Mt Herman Church | Beda |
| BENNETT, William G | US | 2LT | E | 12 Kentucky Cav | Oakwood Cemeery | Harford |
| BENTON, Joshua | US | PVT | A | 26 Kentucky Inf | Buelah Cemetery | Beda |
| BISHOP, John M | US | PVT | H | 17 Kentucky Inf | Central Grove Church | Centertown |
| BLANKENSHIP, William | US | PVT | D | 12 Kentucky Cav | Beaver Dam Baptist Church | Beaver Dam |
| BLACK, David | US | 2LT | A | 12 Kentucky Cav | | |
| BOWLES, Thomas | US | | B | 26 Kentucky Inf | | |
| BOYD, John W | US | 1SG | K | 17 Kentucky Cav | Bethel Church | McLean County |
| BRANDON, Robert J | US | PVT | B | 3 Kentucky Cav | Friendship Church | nr Fordsville |
| BRATCHER, F. K. | US | SGT | F | 5 Kentucky Inf | Ceralvo Cemetery | Ceralvo |
| BRATCHER, William E | US | PVT | B | 17 Kentucky Inf | Gary Cemetery | Horse Branch |
| BRIGGS, William W | US | CPT | B | 17 Kentucky Inf | | |
| BROOKS, Samuel | CS | PVT | C | 9 Kentucky Inf | KIA, 5 Aug 62 | Baton Rouge, LA |
| BROWN, Christopher | US | PVT | I | 17 Kentucky Inf | Fordsville Cemetery | Fordsville |
| BROWN, F. D. | | | | | Sugar Grove Church | Magan |
| BROWN, John G. | US | CPT | | 11 Kentucky Inf | | |
| BROWN, G Washington | US | PVT | H | 12 Kentucky Inf | | |
| BROWN, John F | US | RCT | A | 26 Kentucky Inf | | |
| BROWN, Samuel T | US | PVT | A | 17 Kentucky Inf | West Providence Church | Centertown |
| BRYANT, John W | US | PVT | D | 26 Kentucky Inf | Patterson Cemetery | Silver Beech Road |
| BULLOCK, James | US | CPL | I | 17 Kentucky Inf | Equality Cemetery | Ohio County |
| BUNGER, George | US | SGT | F | 17 Kentucky Inf | Oakwood Cemetery | Hartford |
| BYERS, Avery | US | CPT | H | 35 KY Mtd Inf | Spurrier Cemetery | Horse Branch |
| BYERS, Daniel | US | PVT | B | 17 Kentucky Inf | Spurrier Cemetery | Horse Branch |
| BYERS, James D | US | PVT | B | 17 Kentucky Inf | | |
| BYERS, John H | US | CPL | A | 17 Kentucky Inf | | |
| BYERS, William S. | US | SMG | Regt | 35 KY Mtd Inf | | |
| CAIRNES, Peter | US | MUS | A | 17 Kentucky Inf | Rockport Cemetery | Rockport |
| CALLOWAY, Calvin | US | PVT | A | 17 Kentucky Inf | Walton's Creek Cemetery | Centertown |
| CALLOWAY, John M | US | PVT | H | 17 Kentucky Inf | Mt Pleasant Church | Magan |
| CANNNON, James | US | PVT | F | 17 Kentucky Inf | | |
| CANNON, John W | US | PVT | F | 17 Kentucky Inf | | |
| CARTER, Amaziah | US | PVT | A | 17 Kentucky Inf | Walton's Creek Cemetery | Centertown |
| CARTER, James A | US | PVT | A | 17 Kentucky Inf | Providence Church | Centertown |
| CARTER, Prince W | US | PVT | B | 26 Kentucky Inf | Walton's Creek Cemetery | Centertown |
| CARTER, Thomas E | US | PVT | A | 17 Kentucky Inf | Providence Church | Centertown |
| CARTER, William H | US | PVT | A | 17 Kentucky Inf | Providence Church | Centertown |
| CHANCELLOR, William | US | | H | 35 KY Mtd Inf | Lone Star Church | Ceralvo |
| CHAPMAN, Joseph | US | PVT | D | 26 Kentucky Inf | Patterson Cemetery | Hartford |
| CHAPMAN, Samuel | US | | F | 10 US Infantry | Deanfield cemetery | Deanafield |
| CHAPMAN, William R | CS | PVT | C | 9 Kentucky Inf | Beaver Dam Baptist Church | Beaver Dam |
| CHINN, Charles T | CS | PVT | C | 9 Kentucky Inf | | |

| NAME | US/CS | GRADE | COMPANY | ORGANIZATION | CEMETERY | COMMUNITY |
|---|---|---|---|---|---|---|
| CHINN, James S | CS | PVT | C | 9 Kentucky Inf | Sunnyside | Beaver Dam |
| CHINN, John | CS | PVT | C | 9 Kentucky Inf | Sunnyside | Beaver Dam |
| CHRISTIAN, Charles V | US | PVT | K | 17 Kentucky Inf | | |
| CLARK, Fleming J | US | PVT | K | 12 Kentucky Cav | Warren's Mill Cemetery | Gilstrap |
| COBB, James W | US | PVT | H | 17 Kentucky Inf | | |
| COLE, William S | US | PVT | B | 17 Kentucky Inf | Midkiff Cemetery | Hwy 1164 |
| COLEMAN, James W | US | SGT | D & H | 17 Kentucky Inf | West Providence Church | Centertown |
| COLEMAN, William D | CS | PVT | G | 11 Kentucky Cav | | |
| COLLINS, Luther | CS | PVT | C | 9 Kentucky Inf | Oakwood Cemetery | Hartford (CS Roll of Honor) |
| CONDOR, Leroy | US | PVT | I | 17 Kentucky Inf | Petty Cemetery | Narrows |
| CONDIT, Cincinnatus | US | 2LT | A | 12 Kentucky Cav | | resided Hartford |
| CONDIT, Isaac | US | 2LT | G | 17 Kentucky Inf | | |
| CONDIT, Willie F | US | PVT | H | 17 Kentucky Inf | | |
| COX, John W | US | PVT | C | 17 Kentucky Inf | | |
| COX, Lemand T | US | PVT | H | 17 Kentucky Inf | Elmwood Cemetery | Owensboro |
| COX, Samuel K | US | CPT | A | 17 Kentucky Inf | Oakwood Cemetery | Hartford |
| CROWDER, Francis M | US | PVT | H | 12 Kentucky Cav | Mt Pleasant Cemetery | nr Rosine |
| CRAIG, Joel | CS | PVT | C | 9 Kentucky Inf | | resided nr Hartford |
| CURTIS, James A | US | PVT | I | 17 Kentucky Inf | | b nr Centertown |
| DANIEL, Nicholas C | US | SGT | F | 17 Kentucky Inf | Green River Cemetery | Cromwell |
| DANIEL, U C | US | PVT | F | 17 Kentucky Inf | | |
| DAVIDSON, James | CS | SGT | G | 9 Kentucky Inf | Fordsville Cemetery | Fordsville |
| DAVIS, Eli | US | CPL | A | 17 Kentucky Inf | Patterson Cemetery | Hartford |
| DAVIS, J C | US | PVT | D | 17 Kentucky Inf | Prentiss Cemetery | Slater Creek |
| DAVIS, John T | US | PVT | I | 17 Kentucky Inf | Brick Church Cemetery | Beaver Dam |
| DAVIS, Robert M | US | CPT | H | 17 Kentucky Inf | Mt Pleasant Church | Centertown |
| DAVIS, Thomas D | US | 2LT | Regt | 17 Kentucky Inf | Oakwood Cemetery | Hartford |
| DAVIS, Thomas L | US | PVT | A | 17 Kentucky Inf | Sunnydale | Sunnydale |
| DEAN, Noah C | US | 2LT | K | 20 Kentucky Inf | Elmwood | Hartford |
| DeBRULER, James W | US | PVT | I | 20 Kentucky Inf | Pleasant Grove Cemetery | Shreve |
| DOCKERY, John E | US | PVT | B | 17 Kentucky Inf | | |
| DODD, William | US | CPL | F | 26 Indiana Inf | John Haynes Cemetery | Fordsville |
| DOHERTY, John | US | CIV | | US Army Ordnance Forces | | |
| DOUGLAS, George F | US | SGT | D | 12 Kentucky Cav | Shields Cemetery | Cromwell |
| DUFF, Robert J | US | PVT | F | 17 Kentucky Inf | Midkiff Cemetery | Hwy 1164 |
| DUVALL, Benjamin | US | CPT | H | 12 Kentucky Cav | | |
| DUVALL, John W | US | PVT | H | 17 Kentucky Inf | Gary cemetery | Horse Branch |
| ELMORE, A. N. | US | PVT | G | 17 Kentucky Inf | Sunnydale | Sunnydale |
| EZELL, Burrell | US | PVT | H | 17 Kentucky Inf | | |
| EZELL, George W | US | PVT | H | 17 Kentucky Inf | Ealton's creek cemetery | Centertown |
| FARMER, John H | US | PVT | B | 26 Kentucky Inf | Sugar Grove Church | Magan |
| FAUGHT, Bagges M | US | PVT | B | 17 Kentucky Inf | Central Grove Church | Centertown |
| FERGUSON, John G | US | 2LT | G | 17 Kentucky Inf | | |
| FERGUSON, Samuel | US | PVT | I | 20 Kentucky Inf | White's Run Cemetery | Horse Branch |
| FORBES, Edwin | US | SGT | A | 17 Kentucky Inf | Hayne's Cemetery | Fordsville |
| FORD, Burrell | US | | | KIA? | | |
| FORD, David | US | | | | | |
| FORD, Isaac | US | PVT | F | 1 Kentucky Cav | | |
| FORD, James W | CS | 2SGT | C | 9 Kentucky Inf | Oakwood Cemetery | Hartford |

| NAME | US/CS | GRADE | COMPANY | ORGANIZATION | CEMETERY | COMMUNITY |
|---|---|---|---|---|---|---|
| FORD, John W | US | CPL | A | 12 Kentucky Cav | | |
| FORD, Joseph | CS | CPL | I | 2 Kentucky Cav | | |
| FORD, Newton J | US | PVT | A | 17 Kentucky Inf | | |
| FORD, Samuel Burrell | US | PVT | C | 17 Kentucky Inf | | |
| FORD, William | US | PVT | C | 2 Kentucky Cav | | |
| FOX, Joseph | US | CPT | I | 17 Kentucky Inf | | |
| FRAZIER, Absalom D | US | TMSTR | D | 17 Kentucky Inf | died PW Camp | Richmond, VA |
| FRAZIER, Allen L | US | PVT | D | 17 Kentucky Inf | | |
| GAINES, William W | US | PVT | G | 21 Kentucky Inf | Rochester Cemetery | Rochester |
| GAITHER, Halbert H W | US | PVT | F | 12 Kentucky Cav | Render Cemetery | McHenry |
| GARRETT, Smith A | US | PVT | K | 35 KY Mtd Inf | Centertown Cemetery | Centertown |
| GENTRY, James H | US | PVT | H | 17 Kentucky Inf | Pleasant Grove Cemetery | Fordsville |
| GILLMORE, James P | US | PVT | B | 17 Kentucky Inf | Fordsville Cemetery | Fordsville |
| GILLMORE, W. H. | US | PVT | K | 17 Kentucky Inf | Wells Cemetery | Fordsville |
| GILLSTRAP, FRANCIS | US | CPT | B | 26 KY Vet Inf | | resided Cromwell |
| GIVENS, Richard W | US | SGT | H | | nr Hopewell | Horse Branch |
| GODSEY, Samuel A | US | PVT | A | nr Falls of Rough | Falls of Rough | |
| GORMAN, John F | US | PVT | C | 2 Kentucky Cav | Westerfield Cemetery | Bell's Run |
| GREEN Joseph A | US | PVT | H | 17 Kentucky Inf | Elmwood Cemetery | Owensboro |
| GREER, Benjamin T | US | PVT | F | 26 Kentucky Inf | Mt Herman Church | Beda |
| GREER, Bluford C | US | PVT | F | 26 Kentucky Inf | | |
| GREER, Capp | US | | | | Antioch Church | Ralph Community |
| GREER, Thomas | US | PVT | B | 26 Kentucky Inf | Antioch Church | Ralph Community |
| GUNTHER, Louis A | US | | | 2 Kentucky Cav | Oakwood Cemetery | Hartford |
| HALL, James C | US | PVT | G | 17 Kentucky Inf | | b. nr Olaton |
| HAM, John C | US | 2LT | H | 11 Kentucky Inf | b Ceralvo | |
| HARDEN, James Ray | US | PVT | D | 26 Kentucky Inf | resided nr Fordsville | |
| HARDER, Joseph | US | | | | Providence Baptist Ch. | Dundee |
| HARRISON, Asbury | US | PVT | F | 17 Kentucky Inf | Asbury Cemetery | nr Dundee |
| HARRISON, James B | US | 2LT | A | 17 Kentucky Inf | | |
| HATLER, Francis M | US | PVT | H | 35 KY Mtd Inf | | |
| HAYNES, John | US | CPT | | Adams Fork Home Guard | | |
| HEDRICK, Mason | US | CPT | D | 12 Kentucky Cav | | |
| HICKS, Brice J | US | PVT | G | 12 Kentucky Cav | Patterson Cemetery | Silver Beech Road |
| HICKS, , Daniel | US | PVT | D | 12 Kentucky Cav | Patterson Cemetery | Silver Beech Road |
| HILL, Charles | US | PVT | K | 5 Tennessee Cav (US) | Lone Star Church | Ceralvo |
| HILL, Samuel E | US | CPT | G | 12 Kentucky Cav | | |
| HIMES, William H | US | SGT | A | 17 Kentucky Inf | | buried in Utah |
| HINES, Alexander | CS | 1SGT | C | 9 Kentucky Inf | Mt Pleasant Cemetery | Beda |
| HOAGLAND, John | US | | | | Prentiss Cemetery | Slater Creek |
| HOCKER, J. B. | US | PVT | D | 17 Kentucky Inf | Beaver Dam Baptist CH | Beaver Dam |
| HODGES, Asa | US | SGT | B | 12 Kentucky Cav | | b. nr Olaton |
| HOOVER, Massa | US | PVT | B | 17 Kentucky Inf | | |
| HOSKINS, James A | US | PVT | B | 12 Kentucky Cav | Providence Baptist Ch | Duyndee |
| HOWARD, George P | US | PVT | E | 17 Kentucky Inf | | |
| HUBBARD, Edward C | US | SMG | Regt | 33 Illinois Inf | | |
| HUDSON, A. P. | US | 2LT | D | 12 Kentucky Cav | Westerfield Cemetery | Bell's Run |
| HUDSON, James | US | CPT | D | 17 Kentucky Inf | | prob buried TN |
| HUDSON, James E | CS | | | | | resided Cromwell |

| NAME | US/CS | GRADE | COMPANY | ORGANIZATION | CEMETERY | COMMUNITY |
|---|---|---|---|---|---|---|
| HUDSON, Porter | US | 2LT | D | 12 Kentucky Cav | | resided Hartford |
| HUFF, William J | US | PVT | D | 26 Kentucky Inf | Wesley Chapel Meth Ch | Fordsville |
| HULL, Charles | US | | | 5 Tennessee Cav (US) | | |
| HUMPHREY, Rollie | CS | PVT | | 1 Kentucky Cav | | |
| HURT, Berry | US | PVT | F | 17 Kentucky Inf | Bethel Church | Horton (OH County) |
| HURT, Henry | US | PVT | F | 17 Kentucky Inf | Midkiff Cemetery | Hwy 1164 |
| IGLEHART, James B | US | PVT | G | 17 Kentucky Inf | | |
| IGELHART, John D | US | PVT | I | 17 Kentucky Inf | USA Cemetery | Nashville, TN |
| JAMES, Eugene P | US | CPL | I | 11 Kentucky Inf | Riverview Cemetery | Morgantown |
| JAMES, John A | CS | PVT | I | 4 Kentucky Inf | Green River Bapt Church | Cromwell |
| JAMES, Samuel M | US | SGT | H | 17 Kentucky Inf | | b. Centertown |
| JENKINS, Benjamin F | US | PVT | H | 17 Kentucky Inf | Elmwood Cemetery | Owensboro |
| JERNIGAN, James A | US | PVT | A | 17 Kentucky Inf | | |
| JOHNSON, John F | US | PVT | D | 17 Kentucky Inf | Petty Cemetery | Narrows |
| JOHNSON, Martin | US | PVT | G | 35 KY Mtd Inf | Echols Gen Bapt Ch | Echols |
| JONES, J. H. | CS | PVT | C | 1 Kentucky Cav | Brick Church Cem | Beaver Dam |
| JONES, James H | US | PVT | H | 17 Kentucky Inf | Brick Church Cem | Beaver Dam |
| JONES, S. W. | US | PVT | I | 37 Kentucky Inf | | Centertown |
| JONES, Samuel | US | CH MUS | Regt | 17 Kentucky Inf | | |
| KEOWN, Samuel #1 | US | PVT | B | 17 Kentucky Inf | | |
| KEOWN, Samuel #2 | US | PVT | B | 17 Kentucky Inf | Wells Cemetery | Fordsville |
| KEOWN, Thomas M. | US | PVT | H | 17 Kentucky Inf | Keown Cemetery | Select |
| KESSINGER, Daniel C | US | PVT | F | 12 Kentucky Cav | Rosine Cemetery | Rosine |
| KESSINGER, Nicholas C | US | PVT | C | Middle Green River Bn (Home Guard) | | |
| KING, Daniel J | US | QM | Regt | 12 Kentucky Cav | | resided Hartford |
| KING, William T | US | 1LT | H | 17 Kentucky Inf | | |
| KING, Zachariah A | US | PVT | B | 3 Kentucky Cav | Bell's Run | Hwy 1414 |
| KING, J. T. | US | PVT | E | 12 Kentucky Cav | Bell's Run | Hwy 1414 |
| KIRBY, Thomas J. | US | CPT | G | 17 Kentucky Inf | | |
| KUYKENDALL, Abraham | US | PVT | G | 17 Kentucky Inf | Salem Church Cemetery | Rosine |
| LAKE, J. B. | US | PVT | B | 10 Kentucky Inf | Bell's Run | Hwy 1414 |
| LANDRUM, William J. | US | CPT | E | 17 Kentucky Inf | KIA, Atlanta Campaign | Georgia? |
| LEACH, Henry C. | US | PVT | D | 21 Kentucky Inf | | |
| LEACH, James H | US | PVT | H | 17 Kentucky Inf | | |
| LEE, James S | US | PVT | G | 11 Kentucky Inf | Sunnydale Cemetery | Sunnydale |
| LeGRANDE, Joel | US | PVT | I | 52 KY Mtd Inf | Fordsville | Fordsville |
| LEWIS, Hunt | US | PVT | I | 52 KY Mtd Inf | Sunnydale Cemetery | Sunnydale |
| LLOYD, Solomon | US | PVT | A | 17 Kentucky Inf | | Falls of Rough |
| McCLEARY, Robert | US | | | | resided Ohio County; born state of Ohio | |
| McCOY, John R | US | PVT | H | 17 Kentucky Inf | Sunnyside Cemetery | Beaver Dam |
| McDOWELL, James | US | CMSY | REGT | 26 Kentucky Inf | | resided Ceralvo |
| McGill, James | US | PVT | B | 17 Kentucky Inf | Rowe Cemetery | Centertown |
| McHENRY, John | US | COL | REGT | 17 Kentucky Inf | Elmwood Cemetery | Owensboro |
| McINTIRE, William | US | PVT | A | 17 Kentucky Inf | | b. Ceralvo |
| MADDOX, JOHN | CS | PVT | A | 4 Kentucky Inf | Mt Pleasant Church | Beda |
| MAGAN, Jessie W | US | | | | Midkiff Cemetery | Hwy 1164 |
| MANNER, I. F. | US | PVT | E | 84 Ohio V Inf | Mt Pleasant Church | Beda |
| MARLOW, Josiah M | US | PVT | B | 17 Kentucky Inf | Miles Cemetery | Fordsville |
| MARLOW, William H | US | PVT | A | 12 Kentucky Cav | Miles Cemetery | Fordsville |

| NAME | CS/US | GRADE | COMPANY | ORGANIZATION | CEMETERY | COMMUNITY |
|---|---|---|---|---|---|---|
| MARTIN, Robert K | US | PVT | C | 11 Kentucky Inf | Echols Gen Baptist Ch | Echols |
| MATTHEWS, C. M. | US | PVT | D & K | 12 Kentucky Cav | Rosine Cemetery | Rosine |
| (listed as Cornelius in KY AG Report) | | | | | | |
| METCALF, Henrty S. | US | PVT | A | 7 Kentucky Cav | | |
| MIDKIFF, George R | US | PVT | B | 20 Kentucky Inf | Pleasant Hill | Magan |
| MIDKIFF, Samuel L | US | PVT | I | 17 Kentucky Inf | | |
| MIDKIFF, William P | US | PVT | I | 17 Kentucky Inf | | |
| MILES, Elisha H | US | PVT | H | 17 Kentucky Inf | pvt cem, Miles Farm | nr Fordsville |
| MILLER, Ben T | CS | PVT | H | 1 Kentucky Cav | Fisher Cemetery | McHenry |
| MILLER, C. Waller | CS | PVT | C | 9 Kentucky Inf | | |
| MILLS, Ashford | US | PVT | F | 12 Kentucky Cav | Alexander Cemetery | Hartford |
| MITCHELL, Elijah | US | PVT | F | 17 Kentucky Inf | US Army Cemetery | Chattanooga, TN |
| MITCHELL, James B | US | PVT | C | 9 Kentucky Infantry | KIA, Shiloh, TN | buried Pittsburg Landing |
| MITCHELL, William | CS | COL | REGT | 9 Kentucky Inf | KIA,m Shiloh, TN | buried in unmarked grave |
| MOORE, John W | US | PVT | C | 11 Kentucky Inf | Private Cemetery | Wysox |
| MOORE, William Jr | US | CPL | K | 17 Kentucky Inf | | |
| MOORE, William Sr | US | PVT | K | 17 Kentucky Inf | | |
| MORGAN, Van Buren | US | CPL | B | 3 Kentucky Cav | Adaburg Cemetery | Adaburg |
| MORRIS, Holland* | US | PVT | H | 17 Kentucky Inf | DOW, Kingston, GA | USA Cemetery, Marietta, GA |
| MORRIS, Wm Holland* | US | PVT | B | 17 Kentucky Inf | Ceralvo | Ceralvo |
| MORTON, David | CS | PVT | A | 1 Kentucky Cav | | |
| MORTON, James S | CS | PVT | C | 9 Kentucky Cav | Oakwood Cemetery | Hartford |
| MORTON, John P | US | PVT | B | 17 Kentucky Inf | Oakwood Cemetery | Hartford |
| MORTON, Preston | US | CPT | A | 17 Kentucky Inf | KIA, Shiloh, TN, buried nr Pittsburg Landing | |
| MORTON, Timolen | CS | 1LT | A | 15 Kentucky Cav | | |
| MORTON, William C | US | PVT | G | 26 Kentucky Inf | Elmwood | Owensboro |
| MOSELEY, David | US | PVT | B | 3 Kentucky Cav | Bell's Run | Hwy 1414 |
| MOSELEY, Dillis | CS | PVT | A | 1 Kentucky Cav | Ralph Cemetery | Ralph Section |
| MOSELEY, J. W. | CS | PVT | A | 1 Kentucky Cav | | |
| MOXLEY, Samuel | US | PVT | A | 17 Kentucky Inf | b. Falls of Rough | |
| MURPHY, James A | US | PVT | A | 17 Kentucky Inf | Fordsville Cemetery | Fordsville |
| MURPHY, John | US | PVT | B | 17 Kentucky Inf | Wesley Chapel Church | Fordsville |
| MURPHY, William T | US | PVT | K | 17 Kentucky Inf | b. nr Fordsville | |
| NEIGHBORS, William | US | PVT | A | 17 Kentucky Inf | Axton Cemetery | Dundee |
| NELSON, V. A. | US | SGT | A | 12 Kentucky Cav | Bell's Run | Hwy 1414 |
| NELSON, William | CS | CHAP | REGT | 1 Kentucky Cav | | |
| NETTER, Gabriel | US | LTC | REGT | 15 Kentucky Cav | KIA- Panther Creek | resided Cromwell |
| NEWTON, Benjamin | CS | 1SGT | Bell's Battery | | | |
| NICHOLSON, James W. | US | PVT | D | 6 Kentucky Inf | Barnett's Creek Cemetery | Hwy 1414 |
| O BANNON, George L | US | SGT | H | 17 Kentucky Inf | | b. Select |
| OWENS, William R | US | | E | 3 Wisconsin Inf | Render Cemetery | McHenry |
| PARK, James A | US | PVT | D | 26 Kentucky Inf | Buelah Cemetery | Beda |
| PATTON, J. J. | US | | | | Resided Hartford | |
| PEARSON, Jordan | US | PVT | H | 12 Kentucky Cav | Sugar Grove Church | Magan |
| PELL, John | US | CHAP | REGT | 12 Kentucky Cav | resided Hartford | |
| PENDLETON, John Ed | CS | SURG | REGT | 9 Kentucky Inf | Oakwood Cemetery | Hartford |
| PETTY, Benjamin P | US | CPL | F | 17 Kentucky Inf | | resided Narrows |
| PIERCE, Edward | US | PVT | B | 17 Kentucky Inf | Rosine Cemetery | Rosine |
| PIERCE, James W | US | PVT | B | 17 Kentucky Inf | Bratcher Family Cemetery | Horse Branch |

| NAME | US/CS | GRADE | COMPANY | ORGANIZATION | CEMETERY | COMMUNITY |
|---|---|---|---|---|---|---|
| PIERCE, Martin V | US | PVT | B | 17 Kentucky Inf | McCord Cemetery | Rosine |
| POLLARD, James H | US | PVT | A | 17 Kentucky Inf | Pleaaant Grove Church | Fordsville |
| POLLARD, William T | US | PVT | H | 17 Kentucky Inf | family cemetery | nr Fordsville |
| RAFFERTY, Benjamin P | US | PVT | H | 17 Kentucky Inf | Keown Cemetery | Select |
| RAGLAND, Moses S | US | CPL | H | 17 Kentucky Inf | Rosine Cemetery | Rosine |
| RAINES, George W | US | COMSGT | REGT | 17 Kentucky Inf | Shi8elds Cemetery | Cromwell |
| RAINES, Van Buren | US | PVT | I | 17 Kentucky Inf | Mt Pleasant Cemetery | Rosine |
| RALEY, Benjamin | US | PVT | H | 17 Kentucky Inf | | |
| RALEY, Henry J | US | PVT | H | 17 Kentucky Inf | | |
| RALEY, JonathinS | US | PVT | G | 17 Kentucky Inf | | |
| RALPH, Andrew J | US | PVT | I | 17 Kentucky Inf | Ralph Cemeery | Ralph Section |
| RALPH, William | US | PVT | F | 17 Kentucky Inf | Ralph Cemetery | Ralph Section |
| RAYMER, Curren P | US | CPL | I | 17 Kentucky Inf | | |
| ROACH, Joel H | US | CPL | B | 3 Kentucky Cav | Sugar Grove Church | Magan |
| ROARK, Warren T | US | PVT | D | 17 Kentucky Cav | Walton's Creek Cemetery | Centertown |
| ROBERTS, George A | US | PVT | K | 17 Kentucky Inf | | |
| ROTHROCK, Charles W | CS | PVT | C | 9 Kentucky Inf | | |
| ROWAN, Stephen W | CS | 4SGT | C | 9 Kentucky Inf | Pleasaant Hill Methodist Church | McLean County |
| ROWE, John K | US | PVT | B | 26 Kentucky Inf | Lone Star Church | Ceralvo |
| SANDERS, Willford | US | PVT | K | 23 Indiana Inf | Cool Springs | Cool Springs |
| SIMPSON, Robert | US | PVT | D | 17 Kentucky Inf | Leach Cemetery | Horse Branch |
| SIMPSON, Sansfor | US | PVT | H | 17 Kentucky Inf | Leach cemetery | Horse Branch |
| SMITH, Thomas | US | PVT | D | 26 Kentucky Inf | Patterson Cemetery | Silver Beech Road |
| SHULTZ, Zeb W | | | | | Midkiff Cemetery | Hwy 1164 |
| SORRELLS, Richard P | US | CPL | H | 17 Kentucky Inf | Old Mill Cemetery | Hartford |
| SPENCER, John | US | PVT | A | 17 Kentucky Inf | Clark Cemetery | Fordsville |
| St CLAIR, Adam | US | PVT | D | 17 Kentucky Inf | | resided Cromwell |
| STEPHENS, Richard H | US | PVT | G | 19 Kentucky Inf | Brick Church Cemetery | Beaver Dam |
| STEVENS, William T. | US | PVT | | | Alexander Cemetery | Hartford |
| STEWART, John M | US | PVT | H | 17 Kentucky Inf | Leach Cemetery #2 | nr Rosine |
| STEWART, Willis | US | | | Enrolled Militia | small cemetery nr Rosine | |
| STOUT, Alexander | BvtBG | US | REGT | 17 Kentucky Inf | | d. Chicago, IL |
| SUTTON, James O | CS | PVT | B | 5 Kentucky Cav | | |
| SUTTON, John T | CS | PVT | E | 10 Kentucky Cav | | |
| TANNER, Samuel | US | PVT | C | 17 Kentucky Inf | Pleasant Hill Cemetery | Magan |
| TATE, William P | US | PVT | A | 17 Kentucky Inf | Pleasant Grove Church | Fordsville |
| TATUM, William F | CS | PVT | C | 9 Kentucky Inf | Old Liberty Church | Beaver Dam |
| TAYLOR, Hugh | US | PVT | H | 17 Kentucky Inf | | resided Cromwell |
| TAYLOR, Richard F | US | 1LT | I | 17 Kentucky Inf | | resided Cromwell |
| TAYLOR, William | CS | PVT | M | 2 Kentucky Cav | | |
| TAYLOR, William H | US | 1LT | | 17 Kentucky Inf | Brick Church Cemetery | Beaver Dam |
| THOMAS, James A | US | QM | REGT | 12 Kentucky Cav | | |
| TILFORD, W. G. | US | PVT | B | 17 Kentucky Inf | Green River Cemetery | Cromwell |
| TINSLEY, George M | US | PVT | D | 26 Kentucky Inf | US Army Cemetery | Nashville, TN |
| TINSLEY, James H | US | PVT | B | 26 Kentucky Inf | | resided Ceralvo |
| TINSLEY, Monroe | CS | PVT | C | 9 Kentucky Inf | | resided Hartford |
| TINSLEY, Woodbury | US | CPT | E | 125 USCT | Alexander Cemetery | Silver Beech Road |
| TRACY, Daniel | US | SMG | C | 17 Kentucky Inf | | |

| NAME | US/CS | GRADE | COMPANY | ORGANIZATION | CEMETERY | COMMUNITY |
|---|---|---|---|---|---|---|
| TROUT, Daniel B | CS | | | 4 Missouri Mtd Inf | | resided nr Cromwell |
| | | PVT | A | 4 Kentucky Cav | | |
| TRUMAN, Henry C | US | PVT | B | 17 Kentucky Inf | Fordsville Cemetery | Fordsville |
| TUTTLE, James F | US | PVT | A | 17 Kentucky Inf | US Army Cemetery | Nashville, TN |
| TUTTLE, William A | US | PVT | A | 17 Kentucky Inf | USA Cemetery | Lebanon, KY |
| VINCENT, Jonathon P | US | PVT | D | 5 Kentucky Cav | Central Grove Church | Centertown |
| WALL, William B | US | MAJ | REGT | 25 Kentucky Inf | | |
| WALLACE, Samuel | US | CIV | | 13 Grandsons and one son in US Army | | |
| WALLACE, William A | US | PVT | F | 17 Kentucky Inf | | d. Leitchfield |
| WARD, George W | US | PVT | B | 26 Kentucky Inf | Wesley Chapel Church | Fordsville |
| WARD, Hiram D | US | PVT | F | 17 Kentucky Inf | Private Cemetery | Beda |
| WARD, William E | US | CPT | B | 11 Kentucky Inf | Beda Cemetery | Beda |
| WEBB, Achilles | US | PVT | F | 17 Kentucky Inf | Buelah Cemetery | Beda |
| WEBSTER, W. G. | US | PVT | B | 3 Kentucky Cav | Bell's Run | Hwy 1414 |
| WESTERFIELD, Galen | US | PVT | H | 35 KY Mtd Inf | | |
| WESTERFIELD, Jacob | CS | SGT | A | 1 Kentucky Cav | Oakwood | Hartford |
| WESTERFIELD, James A | US | PVT | G | 17 Kentucky Inf | KIA Shiloh | resided Dundee |
| WESTERFIELD, Joseph | CS | PVT | A | 1 Kentucky Cav | Bell's Run | Hwy 1414 |
| WESTERFIELD, Stephen | | | | | Brick Church Cemetery | Beaver Dam |
| WESTERFIELD, William H | CS | | | 3 KY Mtd Inf | KIA in Alabama | |
| WHITE, James T | US | PVT | B | 17 Kentucky Inf | Whittinghill Cemetery | Fordsville |
| WHITE, Stephen B | US | PVT | E | 17 Kentucky Inf | Pleasant Grove Cemetery | Fordsville |
| WHITE, Sylvester | US | CPL | E | 17 Kentucky Inf | McCord Cemetery | Rosine |
| WHITE, William J | US | 1LT | A | 17 Kentucky Inf | | resided Hartford |
| WHITTEN, Jarvis H | US | | | | | resided Fordsville |
| WILLIAMS, G. N. | US | PVT | A | 17 Kentucky Inf | Walton's Creek Cemetery | Centertown |
| WILLIAMS, Larkin | US | PVT | A | 17 Kentucky Inf | Central Grove Church | Centertown |
| WILLIAMS, Thomas E | US | PVT | A | 17 Kentucky Inf | Walton's Creek Cemtry | Centertown |
| WILLIAMS, Warden | US | PVT | A | 17 Kentucky Inf | Walton's Creek Cemetery | Centertown |
| WILSON, Ancel | US | WGNR | G | 17 Kentucky Inf | Mt Vernon Cemetery | Hwy 1164 |
| WILSON, John C | US | PVT | A | 17 Kentucky Inf | Mt Zion Cemetery | Ohio County |
| WILSON, Nimrod | CS | | | | | |
| WILSON, Samuel H | US | PVT | H | 17 Kentucky Inf | McCord Cemetery | Rosine |
| WILSON, Thomas B | US | PVT | F | 17 Kentucky Inf | Boyd Cemetery | Horse Branch |
| WILSON, Valentine | US | PVT | G | 35 KY Mtd Inf | Rosine Cemetery | Rosine |
| WILSON, William | US | | F | 14 Illinois Inf | Whittinghill Cemetery | Fordsville |
| WHITAKER, Alexander | US | | H | 11 Kentucky Inf | Private Cemetery | nr Matanzas |
| WHITAKER, Acquila L | US | SGT | E | 12 Kentucky Cav | Walton's Creek Cemetery | Centertown |
| WHITTINGHILL, E. W. | US | CPT | D | 17 Kentucky Inf | Private Cemetery | nr Rosine |
| WRIGHT, B. F. | US | SGT | D | 27 Kentucky Inf | Mt Moriah Cemetery | Taffy |
| WOODFORD, Elijah | CS | PVT | C | 9 Kentucky Inf | | |
| WOODWARD, John | CS | PVT | | Schoolfield's Battery | | |
| WOODWARD, John L | US | CPT | D | 12 Kentucky Cav | | |
| WOODWARD, Stephen | US | 1LT | A | 26 Kentucky Inf | | |
| YOUNG, Pleasant M | US | PVT | H | 17 Kentucky Inf | resided Cromwell | |

\* Mr. William Morris, West Point, KY, great-grandson of Holland MORRIS resolved the evasive Holland MORRIS mystery for us. There were two Privates MORRIS, Holland and William Holland. As shown above, Holland died of wounds at Kingston, GA, and William Holland is buried in the Cemetery at Ceralvo.

*Col. John McHenry.*

## GENERAL HYLAN B. LYON RAVAGES OHIO COUNTY COURTHOUSE

WEATHER FORECAST. CENTRAL KENTUCKY, Early December, 1864. Snow, up to six inches. Temperature, freezing, down to -20 degrees at night. River conditions, flooded. Roads, hazardous, frozen, and slick. Provide shelter for all your stock.

Brigadier General Hylan B. Lyon (PACS) crossed into Kentucky from Paris, Tennessee, on 10 December 1864 with abut 1,400 cavalrymen to draw defenders away from Nashville as General John B. Hood (PACS) was preparing to invade Tennessee. Lyon (West Point, 1856) formerly commanded a brigade in the vaunted cavalry corps of Lieutenant General Nathan Bedford Forrest (PACS), but the regiments of Kentucky recruits he brought in his latest endeavor were mere shadows of the highly respected organizations he had commanded earlier in the war. The men were poorly equipped and even worse clothed for the rigors of winter campaigning in one of the worst early winters encountered in recent years in Kentucky. General Hood had ordered Lyon "to capture Clarksville and to tear up and to destroy all the railroad and telegraph lines leading to Nashville, and to put all mills running in the region to the use of the (Confederate) government." Lyon found Clarksville too strongly defended and settled for interrupting the rail and telegraph lines between Clarksville and Hopkinsville, Kentucky - thus threatening the environs of Hopkinsville.

At the same time, the information available to the Union command in Nashville indicated that Lyon's objective was Bowling Green, Kentucky, and the L & N Railroad, the main supply route for Major General George H. Thomas' Army of the Cumberland. As the fortunes of war had it, Brigadier General Edward M. McCook's (USV) Second Brigade, First Cavalry Division, Army of the Cumberland, was then at Horse Cave, Kentucky, returning to Nashville after having received remounts at Louisville. McCook formed up his columns at Franklin, Kentucky, with Brigadier General Louis Watkins (USV), formerly commanding the Sixth Kentucky Volunteer Cavalry, Colonel Oscar LaGrange's Second Brigade, and the Eighteenth Indiana Battery. Private John Rippetoe, 18th IN BTRY, reported that the roads were so slick when they left Franklin that his mare fell twice - the men had to dismount and lead their horses as the search for Lyon began. McCook proceeded through Russellville where Colonel Samuel Johnson's Seventeenth Kentucky Cavalry was picked up and attached to General Watkin's brigade. The command marched out of Russellville for Fairview, Kentucky. McCook's forward elements reached Fairview about 1700 hours on 15 December with Lyon operating two separated brigades. One brigade under Colonel J. O. Chenowith occupied Hopkinsville while Lyon accompanied Colonel J. J. Turner's (originally 30th TN Infantry) Brigade on an expedition toward Cadiz, Princeton, Eddyville, and Princeton. Finding the courthouses in those cities being occupied as barracks for US Colored Troops, Lyon torched the temples of justice in Cadiz and Princeton. The courthouse at Eddyville was spared because Lyon's daughter was seriously ill nearby and could not stand the excitement. For burning those courthouses, and later those at Madisonville, Hartford, Leitchfield, Elizabethtown, and Campbellsville, Lyon was given the sobriquet, 'Courthouse Burner.'

McCook attacked Chenowith's brigade on a prominent ridge just west of Hopkinsville near the site of the present day state hospital. Watkins was to have sealed off the Confederate escape routes and to have attacked from the north simultaneously in conjunction with the attack by LaGrange's Second Brigade. As the situation developed, Colonel John K. Faulkner (Seventh Kentucky Cavalry) mistakenly identified the troops to his immediate front as friendly units and did not conduct a timely attack, thereby allowing most of Chenowith's command to avoid battle and capture. Most of Chenowith's Confederate soldiers joined Lyon's other brigade at the Tradewater River west of Hopkinsville.

The action at Hopkinsville netted McCook an artillery piece, 57 men and four officers, and about 30 enemy soldiers killed or wounded. Included among the captured officers was one Lieutenant Colonel Reuben Ross (West Point, c 1860). The pursuit was mounted and continued to the Tradewater River where the bridge had been destroyed to interfere with McCook's pursuit operation. Overnight, a foot bridge was constructed while the horses were rested. The next morning the men crossed on the foot bridge while the horses swam across this obstacle. LaGrange's Second Brigade resumed the pursuit while Watkin's brigade and the 18th Indiana Battery were returned to Hopkinsville to prevent Lyon from doubling back into Tennessee. That night the Second Brigade bedded down in a cold camp about six miles southwest of Madisonville while Lyon was burning the courthouse in his precipitous flight through that city.

LaGrange's advance guard caught up with Lyon's rear guard about three miles south of Ashbyburg at 1600 hours on 19 December with darkness closing in rapidly. Flooded swamplands on both sides of the highway made the narrow road the only available avenue of approach for the pursuers who were delayed by Lyon's rear detachment while Lyon employed the available boats to escape with most of his command across the flooded Green River. After LaGrange closed into Ashbyburg a number of Lyon's Confederates who had not already been ferried across the river were

*Marker at site where Private Granville Allen fell.*

*GAR Marker at site where Granville Allen fell.*

either shot or drowned trying to complete their escapes. Captain Frank P. Gracey, formerly of Cobb's Battery, led a group of about 200 mounted Confederates who had not already escaped across the Green River. Captain Samuel Dickerson, Company M, Fourth Indiana Cavalry, commanded a squadron from his regiment in tracking down most of Gracey's renegades. LaGrange was delayed at Ashbyburg until he could round up boats to cross his command during the night of 20-21 December. Buildings near the river banks were burned in order to provide illumination for the river crossing operation.

Lyon led his dwindling division up the Green and Rough Rivers to Hartford where the Ohio County courthouse suffered the same fate as the others he had earlier encountered. About 40 home guard defenders at Hartford surrendered without resisting and were subsequently paroled. The courthouse at Hartford was built between 1813 and 1815 for $3036 by a citizen named Charles Wallace. Its basic construction was of brick laid on a stone foundation, with an adjacent two-room annex to house the office and records of the Clerk of the Ohio County Circuit Court. Dr. J. S. Waller, later of Hanson, Kentucky, who participated in the raid as a private soldier under Lyon, described the Hartford experience briefly as, " . . . on our way to Hartford. At the latter place we encountered a small force of the enemy, about 50 in all, but they surrendered without giving us a fight. From there we went to Elizabethtown…" One thing worth mentioning about the Hartford courthouse is the fact that Dr. Samuel O. Payton was able to dissuade Lyon from burning the annex building and all the Ohio County records by appealing to Lyon's sense off decency as a fellow-Kentuckian".

The pursuers approached the flooded Rough River near Hart ford to find it a raging torrent. A local Unionist guided La Grange to a ford, described in the OR's by that officer as, "a mile wide and half way up on our horses' sides." Before fording the Rough, LaGrange ordered his wagons and led animal s to report to Captain Dickerson at Bowling Green in order to speed up the pursuit.

The Confederates departed Hartford with stragglers and deserters increasing by the hour. Many were picked up by pursuing elements and the county home guards while some others escaped capture and returned to their homes in other western Kentucky counties. Lyon's flight continued through Caneyville and Leitchfield to Elizabethtown where an action occurred in which the pursuers captured two majors, two lieutenants, and 40 men. By this time, Lyon's command had almost totally disintegrated. General Lyon himself attested to the sorry plight of his command in his report in the OR's. "At this place, Elizabethtown, I learned of Hood's defeat and withdrawal from Tennessee which had a very demoralizing effect upon my command, and within two days, 500 of my men deserted." McCook turned over the pursuit at General Burbridge at Elizabethtown with Lyon and a few vaunted warriors bugging out to Tennessee through Hodgensville, Campbellsville, and Burksville. The courthouse at Campbellsville suffered the same fiery fate as the others he had passed on his courthouse burning spree. Upon returning to Tennessee, Lyon's entire division could boast no more than a company's strength. Again, thanks to the honesty of Dr. Waller, "Sypert's and Cunningham's regiments were depleted until there were scarcely enough to form a respectable company of soldiers fit for duty. Major Owsley's battalion was reduced to three men, one major, one captain, and one private.

## OHIO COUNTY NATIVE EARLY CIVIL WAR CASUALTY

Ohio County was the center for recruiting activities for both the union and Confederate armies in the early autumn of 1861. Sergeant J. H. Westerfield rode off to Bowling Green on 5 October to rank among the first Confederate volunteers from Ohio County. The next day, Dr. John Ed Pendleton led another contingent of future Johnny Rebs into Confederate military service with the Ninth Regiment of Kentucky Volunteers, a regiment destined to join the First Kentucky (ORPHAN) Brigade. At the same time, Union recruiting efforts were increasing in

*Grave of Pvt. Granville Allen, Leach Cemetery.*

*Grave of Pvt. Robert Simpson, Leach cemetery.*

and all around Ohio County . Camp Silas Miller in Owensboro became the temporary headquarters for the Third Kentucky Cavalry Regiment (COL James S. Jackson), the Seventeenth Kentucky Infantry (COL John H. McHenry), and the Twenty-sixth Kentucky Infantry (COL Stephen G. Burbridge). Colonel Pierce Hawkins and Colonel Charles D. Pennebaker were also forming the Eleventh Kentucky Infantry and the Twenty-fifth Kentucky Infantry at nearby Rochester on the Green River. Daviess County had too small a population to support the recruiting of three regiments simultaneously, so Colonel McHenry returned to his native Hartford to fill the ranks of his regiment. He established his base of operations at Camp Chesley Callaway, named for a Revolutionary War hero and arly settler in the No Creek area of Ohio County. Camp Callaway was located near the present site of the Ohio County Hospital in Hartford.

General Albert S. Johnston (CSA) commanded a Confederate defensive line from Cumberland Gap through Mill Springs to Bowling Green, then south westward to Forts Donelson and Henry just across the line in Tennessee, then northwestward to Columbus, Kentucky, and then westward through Missouri into Kansas. General Johnston had occupied Bowling Green with two divisions commanded by Major General William J. Hardie (PACS) and Brigadier General Simon B. Buckner (PACS). The Confederate command at Bowling Green was naturally interested in Union activities in Butler county immediately to the north. General Buckner dispatched a battalion of Colonel Wirt Adams' First Mississippi Cavalry Regiment to the vicinity of Morgantown to determine who, when, where, and in what strength the Unionists were engaged in that region. The calendar advanced to 27 October 1861 when friendly Unionists in Butler County informed Colonel McHenry that a Confederate force was prowling around Butler County. Such reports from civilians probably exaggerated the Confederate numbers.

The actual Confederate strength, as determined by reports in the OR's, amounted to a squadron (two companies) under a Major Hagan and a single company commanded by a Lieut. Bondurant. Colonel McHenry received reports with alarm and requested assistance from Colonel Burbridge in Owensboro. The latter joined forces with McHenry at Hartford, and the two commanders displaced their men to a forward assembly area near Cromwell. The strengths of the combined Union forces numbered no more than 400 officers and men: 125, 17th Kentucky; 100, 26th Kentucky; 100, 3d Kentucky Cavalry; maybe 50 Cromwell Home Guardsmen; and a section of 6-pounders served by no more than one lieutenant and 20 men. The commanders determined in a council of war at Cromwell on the evening of 28 October that McHenry would cross the Green at Borah's Ferry at daybreak the next morning while Burbridge and the artillery section would march southward at the same time. The latter would cross the Green at the Woodbury Ferry ; then both forces would converge upon the Confederates in a pincers movement.

The scouts dispatched from Cromwell earlier did not return by daybreak with the sought information, but the two senior commanders moved put according to plan. Friendly civilians informed McHenry, on the march, that an enemy force was ahead of him near Morgantown. He headed his column in that direction on an old gravel road that paralleled today's Logansport Road in Butler County. Approaching Big Hill, about a mile north of Morgantown, McHenry's pickets reported that a mounted enemy unit was approaching. McHenry deployed his company-sized regiment ion line of battle along the military crest of Big Hill with a small line of skirmishers forward. A brisk firefight soon erupted with Lieutenant Bondurant reporting the action as, ". . . encountering a superior force of nfantry under cover on both sides of the road. After a brisk exchange of shots, I withdrew in good order to make my report." The casualties that occurred included: Confederate, 3-WIA; and Union, 1-KIA and 3-WIA. The man killed was Private Granville Allen, Company D, Seventeenth Kentucky Infantry. He was one of the early Kentucky soldiers killed on Kentucky soil in the Civil War. The commonly accepted story of how Allen met his death is that he and other skirmishers were about 40 yards ahead of McHenry's line of battle. With such a small force present on such a narrow frontage, Colonel McHenry would naturally have employed only a minimum number of skirmishers forward. Such forward troops would have been instructed to have taken advantage of the available cover and to lie low to the ground. Allen's party of skirmishers were in a covered position near a large chestnut tree. Private Allen stepped out from behind his shelter to get a better shot at the enemy and was struck by the fatal musket ball. Lieutenant Bondurant retired his force in an orderly manner to prepare his report of theaction.

Later on that same day another skirmish occurred with part of the Confederate force just south of Morgantown, and a third one took place at Woodbury after Burbridge's command crossed the Green River at the Woodbury Ferry. The Union forces returned to the Cromwell assembly area where the regimental commanders decided that the enemy had returned to Bowling Green. They then marched their own commands back to their camps in Hartford and Owensboro.

Private Allen's body was escorted back to his home at nearby Horse Branch, Kentucky, by an old friend, Private Robert Simpson, also of Company D, Seventeenth Kentucky Infantry. Allen was buried in the Leach Cemetery near his native community. Today, long after the last guns were fired and "Taps" have ended the hostilities of the American Civil War, the Leach Cemetery is still the final resting place of two old wartime comrades and lifelong friends. The bodies of Privates Allen and Simpson lie near one another in the Leach Cemetery. In the years following the American Civil War, Granville Allen was honored by the Morgantown Camp of the Grand Army of The Republic which named its encampment after Private Granville Allen. Private Allen is still remembered as one of the earliest Kentucky soldiers killed on Kentucky soil in the American Civil War.

### *OHIO COUNTY CIVIL WAY HERO CITED POTHUMOUSLY*

Brigadier General Smythe Williams, Assistant Adjutant General (ARMY), State of Kentucky, presided over the awarding of the KENTUCKY DISTINGUISHED SERVICE MEDAL (posthumously) for heroism displayed on the field of battle at Shiloh, Tennessee, on the 6th of April, 1862, by First Sergeant (later Captain) Samuel K. Cox, Company A, Seventeenth Kentucky Volunteer Infantry (US). The reasons that the state's highest military decoration was awarded are stated in the following order:

PERMANENT ORDER 275-005
2 October 1997
Award: KENTUCKY DISTINGUISHED SERVICE MEDAL
Dates of Period of Service: Year, 1862
Authority: KYARNG 600-8-2 Reason For: First Sergeant Samuel K. Cox, Company A, Seventeenth Kentucky Volunteer Infantry (US) exhibited exceptional bravery and unselfish devotion above and beyond the call of duty on the field at Shiloh, Tennessee, on the 6th of April in 1862. The Seventeenth Kentucky, as a part of the Third Brigade, Fourth Division, Army of The Tennessee, was on line with the 25th Kentucky, the 31st Indiana, and the 44th Indiana and was receiving deadly small arms and cannon fires with the entire line's being threatened by an overwhelming enemy force advancing upon its position across an open field. The brigade was ordered to hold its fires as the enemy quickly closed the distance between the lines. The enemy advanced upon the entire brigade behind increasing artillery barrages and small arms fire with the friendly units taking increasing casualties accordingly. Cox' brigade was ordered to open fire upon the advancing enemy who then sustained heavy casualties. The friendly fires, in turn, attracted more enemy artillery fire which increased in tempo until the brigade was ordered to counterattack the enemy force in the open field to the front. The brigade had withstood a galling enemy attack for more than five hours during which time it had faced steadily increasing enemy fires and had suffered a heavy toll in casualties. By the time the Seventeenth Kentucky gained its assigned objective and began to return the enemy's fires in kind, it had exhausted its own supply of ammunition, and its casualties were mounting steadily. At this point in the action, Captain Preston Morton, commanding Company A, Seventeenth Kentucky Volunteers, fell beside First Sergeant Cox with a deadly serious wound. Under heavy enemy fire, and without regard to his own safety, First Sergeant Cox packed Captain Morton upon his back more than a mile, disregarding shot and shell falling all around him, to an aid station near Pittsburg Landing. Even though the wounds proved fatal to Captain Morton, First Sergeant Cox' conduct in attempting to save the life of his commanding officer at a great personal risk to his own ranks as a matter of the greatest personal bravery, honor, and unselfish devotion above and beyond the normal call of duty. First Sergeant Cox, with his dedication to his comrades and his devotion to his colors, to his state, and to his nation, epitomizes the highest military standard of courage on the field of battle that any one soldier may attain..
FORMAT: 320
BY ORDER OF THE
GOVERNOR: DONALD C. STORMS
LTC, INF, KYARNG
Military Personnel Officer
CAPTAIN SAMUEL K. COX
SEVENTEENTH KENTUCKY INFANTRY

*Capt. Sam K. Cox.*

*Slate Riffle Hill viewed from Rough River.*

## OHIO COUNTY'S OWN CIVIL WAR BATTLE

Point Pleasant, Kentucky, July 25, 1864. A few days ago, bullets were flying in anger on nearby Slate Riffle Hill as Daviess County Home Guards exchanged deadly fires with mounted partisan rangers from Union County. The raiders, under a Captain (probably Bill) Yates had been raiding the eastern portions of Daviess County and exchanging broken down horses for the best available mounts in Davis County. Needless to say, Captain Yates' party was well experienced in such one-sided bargaining. Years of ravaging their Unionist neighbors had taught them how to bargain with their neighbors at gun point to the best advantage.

When the partisan rangers first entered Davis County on this foray, A Captain Wilson, with prior military service in one of the Kentucky volunteer regiments, assembled the local home guard outfit near Boston. The home guards were drilled and taught the basics of loading and firing their muskets for a couple hours and permitted to return to their homes overnight with orders to reassemble on Old Boston Hill at 0800 hours the next morning. A note about their muskets may be in order at this point. Kentucky Home Guard units were usually armed with smoothbore muskets which were notoriously ineffective and cumbersome. It was estimated that the Belgian musket (the "punkin-shooter") was totally ineffective at a range greater than 25 yards - some authorities said, 25 feet. Some 30 members of the home guard unit arrived at the appointed place and hour under arms as the law directed, but a greater number was conspicuously absent with "sudden sickness" or "urgent business" elsewhere. The cows had to be milked on time, or a sudden attack of the gout certainly was more important than running off into an adjacent neighborhood chasing rebels who might shoot back. After all, the business of the home guard was to guard the home, not to go chasing off after a bunch of rebels into the next county which was far from home.

Captain Wilson received word that the raiders were visiting Whitesville about the time his troops assembled on Old Boston Hill. His latest information indicated that the rebels had departed Whitesville past St. Mary's of The Woods Church and had taken the road toward Point Pleasant in Ohio County. Captain Wilson's mounted column headed out to take up the same route with overtaking the enemy force as its main objective. Night overtook the opposing forces a few miles north of Slate Riffle Hill as the troops bedded down alongside the roadway with their campfires illuminating their immediate areas.

As the march was resumed the next morning, sympathizers in the area alerted Captain Yates that the Daveiss County home guardsmen were following. He was apprised of the local geography and of the fact that Slate riffle Hill offered an excellent ambush site. The raiders hurried to Slate Riffle Hill to set the trap and quickly deployed the main force on line with a few skirmishers (security guards) left behind to provide early warning of the approach of the pursuers.

But, the best laid plans of mice and men go astray. As Dame Fortune dealt the cards for that hand, a Mrs. Caroline Sutton was heading northward to her home after spending the previous evening assisting her daughter who had given birth to a baby boy. The new grandmother was in hurry to return home to care for another daughter who was sick and urgently required her presence. Crossing Rough River at a trot, Mrs. Sutton was challenged to halt by a sentry who suddenly appeared from his concealment alongside the road. Holding his rifle at the port, the sentry informed Mrs. Sutton that she could not proceed and that she must return from whence she had come. While explaining her plight to the sentry, she edged closer, but he still demanded that she turn around for points south of Rough River.

Nothing equals the fury and resolution of a determined woman! Mrs. Sutton feigned her misunderstanding while she sidled her spirited mount closer to the guard. At the proper instant she stung her horse sharply on the flank causing the horse to bolt suddenly forward and catching the guard who was prepared for such a sudden movement. The unprepared sentry was knocked to the ground with his rifle out of arm's reach by the horse as it bolted out at the speed of a thoroughbred. Mrs. Sutton raced through the flat bottom land alone without a pursuit's being mounted.

She raced up the roadway at top speed a mile or so until she encountered Captain Wilson's home guard column. Checking her flight, she informed Captain Wilson of the rebel trap on Slate Riffle Hill and cautioned him that death awaited, that he should turn back. Among those assembled around Captain Wilson and Mrs. Sutton was a local Unionist named Midkiff who had joined the column. Midkiff, who knew the local area like the palm of his hand, informed the captain of a route passing by the Leo Wimsatt farm that offered total concealment and that would allow them to get behind the ambuscade to give the rebels a taste of their own medicine. Midkiff led them back up the road a piece to turn off on another old gravel roadway. After awhile, he led them into the woods and along a path until they approached a big hill where he cautioned the party to dismount and to proceed quietly to the top of the hill. The home guards stealthily climbed to the top of the hill and saw the rebel line stretched out in plain view.

The inexperienced guardsmen were anxious to clean up the grisly task at hand and opened a premature fire with their notoriously ineffective muskets. The rebels turned around to answer the fire in kind as both lines suffered a number of casualties. The affair ended almost as abruptly as it had begun with a couple exchanges of fire. The home guards retired taking their five dead and one wounded with them while the raiders assessed their own casualties. The known Union dead included men named Cecil, Hinton, Wooten, and two others. Bill Shively was wounded in the action, but he recovered and lived to observe his hundredth birthday in Daviess County. Among the Confederate casualties were Captain Yates and an unidentified enlisted man. Another partisan ranger, seriously wounded, was left for treatment at the Virgil Renfrow home as the rangers packed up. Captain Yates and the dead private were buried on site until August of 1866 when their bodies were exhumed and returned to Union County for proper burials. The five home guardsmen killed in the action were taken back to Boston in a straw-filled wagon for burials. As soon as the Confederate force determined that the home guards had left the area of Slate Riffle Hill, they mounted up and rode away. Thus, the Battle of Slate Riffle Hill ended almost as abruptly as it had erupted.

*Abraham Bradley Stanley, Civil War tintype.*

*Ellizabeth Ann Hill and Abraham Bradley Stanley, ca. 1863.*

*These "Billy Yanks," all veterans of the Union Army during the Civil War gathered on May 30, 1910, at the Clark Cemetery about four miles south of Fordsville. C.C. Brown, S.C. Babbitt, H. Babbitt, Joseph Sapp, Robert Brannon, Crit Truman, Luke Hunt, Joseph Harder, G.H. Osborne, Cornelius LeGrand, Jim Cooper, W.R. James.*

*DAV Chapter 11 and DAV Auxiliary.*

*Albert Cummins, killed at Norman Beach, 1942-1943.*

*Rosine, Oct. 1, 1994, 50th anniversary memorial service in honor of Pfc. Wesley Phelps, USNC Medal of Honor.*

*A farm class of WWII veterans from Centertown. Standing: J.V. Coleman, James Smith, Durwood Porter, Woodrow England, Wallace Roe, Edwin Clark Brown, Ecklas Williams, Rodney Brown, Claud Shrull, Douglas James, Carl Hopper, Noel Cavender, Rollie Smith, Martin Williams. Seated: Purcel Hopper, James Brown, Burlie Shrull, Johnny Bilbro, Conway Addington, Hollis Whittaker, Alvey Ashby, Edwin Martin, Jack Abner, Tom Abner, Eldred Schacklett.*

*Draftees, Ohio Co., 1918.*

*Leonard Bishop, Centertown, WWI.*

*Gen. D.C. Buell, settled in Muhlenberg Co, but came to Rockport for mail.*

*Lois and Tip Cardwell, when first married. Tip was in WWII.*

*Card from Leonard Bishop to wife, Rena.*

*Clyde H. Wallace on motorcycle during WWI. He drove for his commander during the war.*

*Guy Bishop, WWII, owner of Bishop Sundries, Centertown.*

*Hemon Johnson Jr., WWII.*

*Margaret Mae Blackburn, McHenry. WWI nurse.*

Sidney Williams, owner of Williams Grocery Store, Hartford.

Ovid Willams Barrett, May 1944. Killed in Germany, WWII, Sept 1944.

Civil War veteran, John Blackburn. Buried Render Cemetery.

John Givens Jr., USAAF 1944-1946

Andrew Ralph, Hartford, WWII veteran. 1942.

Argle Leach and Roscoe Embry, Germany, ca. 1917-1918.

Thomas L. Jackson, 1943, WWII.

John Wesley Moseley Jr., Civil War veteran, celebrating 100th birthday, Oct. 17, 1936.

Edward Snyder, Pleasant Ridge.

Pfc Wesley Phelps USMC, MOH, April 12, 1923-Oct. 4, 1944—the only Ohio Countian to receive the Medal of Honor. Also, the first Kentuckian to receive the Medal posthumously for service in WWII. The medal was presented to his mother, Lida Phelps, at a ceremony in Rosine Cemtery, April 26, 1946. Right: his monument.

Charles Fisher, USMC, WWII.

Malcolm Fisher, USN, WWII.

Tec/5 Ted Vincent receives bronze star medal from Lt. Col. Harry Holman, July 1945.

Verdie, Theron, Eulema Kessinger, WWII.

Unveiling ceremonies at grave of Edward Williams, Revolutionary Soldier, Aug, 17, 1930. Decendants and members of the Hartford Chapter DAR.

# SCHOOLS

*Rockport Grade 1, 1950. 1: Paul Tarrance, Jerry Dozier, Jackie Holland, Gerald Hoskins, Roland Wilkerson, Billy Growbarger, Ray Geary, Wendell O'Brien. 2: Alma Geary, Martha Curtis, Bonnie Geary, Jerry Decker, Kermit Geary, Charlene Harris, Velma Scott, Nancy Brown, June Williams, H.T. Kennedy Jr., David McCoy. 3: Mary Baggarly, Helen Devine, Connie Coy, Roland Decker, Patsy Farris, Ronnie Harper, Phillip Chapman. 4: Judy Stewart, Phyllis Devine, Joyce Casteel, Carol Ingram, Marquetta Thomas, Mary Lou Brown, Freddie Welborn, Jerry Saling, Francis Byrd, Barbara Rippy, Eunice Shaw, Jo Ann Geary, Dale McKee, Lonnie Fulkerson. Teacher, Cliffie Austin.*

*McHenry 5th grade, 1928. Back: Mary Langley, Vernie Bishop, Thomas Davis, Martine Trail, Thelma Hibbs, Aeriel Porter, Wilma Hammond. 3: Claudine Maddox, Marguerite Warner, Mabel Pierce, Clara Shropshire, Leota Miller, Wanda Miller, Mary Brown. 2: Harold Leisure, Juanita Shaw, Irene Hawes, Martine Taylor, Elizabeth Watson, Lois Maddox, Ruth Maddox, Inez Peach, Paul Maddox. 1: Carter James, Joe Sondefur, Charles Allen, James Smith, Johnnie Maddox.*

*Class Night, 1931. 1: Beulah Warren, Vernon McConnell, Thelma Miller, Dickie Cairnes, Winnie R. (Pete) Tatum. 2: Thelma Parks, Eva Chapman, Marie Parks, Waconda Parrott, Zora Romans, Opal White. 3: Bessie Raymer, William Fuller, Joe Mathis, Ernest Fuller, Emma Ford, Frankie Wade.*

Senior Class, 1946-1947, Rockport High School. Back: Claude Snodgrass, Audrey Maddox, Nobel Brown, Glen Stewart, Bette Tooley, Corbett Farris teacher. Front Coleen Hoskins, Gladys Robinson, Marjorie Elder, Martha Rains, Anona Kimmel, Jane O'Brien.

McHenry, 1934-1935, 8th grade. Back: unk., Irwin Daniel, ___ Mitchell, Montye Bibb. 4: Dan James, Charles R. Fisher, Hugh Warner, Jim Culbertson, Beulah James, unk., Laura McIntyre, Irene Menton, Wilma, Lois Bishop, Claron Jones. 3: Alva C. Hert, Reva Moseley, Bud Hawes, Russell Crowe, J.C. Hoskins, Marion R. Chumley, Alvie Givens, James Dowell, Pattie Peach, Jouette Crowe, Elizabeth Matthews, Edith B. Wallace. 2: James Blackburn, Nina Mae James, Jewell Park, Geneva Warren, June Blackburn, Natomi Phelps, Zora Simpson, Mary Leisure, Margaret Hunter, Anna Vernon Myers, James Watt. 1: Jack Warren Rondal Raymond, Conrad Craddock, Willard Warren, John R. Owens, C.C. Watts Jr., Charles Maddox Jr., Charles McDaniel.

McHenry, 1938-1939, 6th grade. 1: Bonnie Moore, Margaret Stewart, Marchetta Williams, Donnie Carnes, Mabel Douglas, Beutonne McDaniel, Donnie Wakeland, Emogene Miller, Louise Phelps. 2: Joanne Miles, Geneva Alford behind, Bobby Smith, James Turner, Dorothy Minton, ___ Moore, Jack Cox, Bobby Borah, Wanda Moore, J.R. Vincent, James Barnes, Elmer Phelps, Noah Phelps, Jr. 3: Karl Brown teacher, Laburn Likens Jr., Ronnie Carnes, Olivia Craddock, James Phelps, Maxine Price, Vitula Baize, Billie Autry, Margaret Butler, Margie Davis, Naomi Bishop.

1951 Sophomore class, Rockport. Back: Dudley Tanner teacher, Billy Sharp, William C.D. "Doodie" Givens, Bobby Singleton, Ralph Fuller, Lake Saling, Harold Welborn, Billy O'Brien, Jimmy Sheffield. Front: Anna Lee Fulkerson, Norma Jean Lewis, Clemer Curtis, Shirley Blair, Lillian Key, Gleta Brown.

McHenry, Senior Class, 1934. 1: Stasha Wallace, Thelma Park, Mitchell Maddox, Mary Langley, Marguerite, Lois Maddox, Charles L. Allen, Martine Taylor. 2: Lena Scott teacher, Denver Maddox, James Logan Warren, Hannah James, Rose Catherine James, Mary Lee Kelley, R.W. Chapman, Willard Mosley, Wavy D. Royal. 3: Wanda Miller, Ronald Givens, Simon James, Noble Joe Sandefur, Eugene Ashby.

1948. 1: Anna Lee Nelson, Claron Berryman, Clemon C. Nance, Wanda Matthews, Bobby Joe James, Mary E. Albin. 2: Fostine Lacefield, Bobby Main, Billy Russell, Bobby Espey, Gene Warren, Laymon Hoskins. Teacher, D.B. Lutz.

*Tribe 73, Order of Redmen. 1: Azzie Adcock?, John Woodburn. 2: Harry Woodburn, Will Vernon, unk., Roy Deeter, Earl Maple. 3: Tom Tooley, Mack Hendricks, Tandy Porter, Cecil Dunn, unk., ___ Landrum. 4: Bert Reid, unk., Ben Woodburn.*

*Olaton School, grades 1-5, 1940-1941. Front: Wesley Lindsey, R.J. Keith, Chester Decker, James Lindsey, Blackman Patterson, Oneal Decker, James Mattingly, Earl Martin, Wendell Keith. Middle: Mary Lou Boswell, O'Dell Decker, Morris Decker, Jean Keith, Martha Lou Faught, Edna England, Joyce Patterson, Garnet Cooksey, Helen Sapp, Leona Patterson, Silva Sapp, Clifton Downey. Top: Hoover Patterson Louise Berkley, Earl Sapp, Robert Lindsey, Thelma Decker, Verblee Lindsey, Herman Payton, A.D. Martin, Carrie Payton, Mrs. Willie Pearl Oller teacher, Nora Patterson.*

*1930 Oakland School. Bottom: Neumare "Bill" Knight, Tommy Fulton, Foster "Steve" Knight, Billy Nall, Rayburn Taylor, Cecil Dortch, Paul R. Brown. 2: Leland Chinn, 4 unk., Loretta Boyd, Carrie Baggarly, Lewis Davenport, Wester Cook, Kenneth Taylor. 3: Richard McKee, Reed Taylor, Richard Nall, Evelyn Knight, Walter Dortch, Katherine Slack, Ettah Knight, Dora Mae Fulton, Edna Robinson teacher.*

*McHenry, 1927, 5th grade. Bottom: Carter James, Vernie Bishop, Paul Maddox, Charles Allen, James Smith, Noble Sandefur. 2: Juanita Shaw, Lois Maddox, Eva Pierce, Martine Taylor, Ruth Maddox, Mary Elizabeth Stevens, Verda Ruth Hanes, Thomas Mitchell. 3: Irene Hawes, Clara Shropshire, Mary Hibbs, ___ Herrel, ___ Trail, Anna R. Wakeland, Leota Miller, Wanda Miller, Carroll Leisure, Johnny Maddox, Joe Mitchell, sitting. 4: Wilma Hammon, Marguerite Warner, Velma Langley, Mary Langley, Aral Porter, Henry Maddox, Theo Davis, Maurice McDaniel.*

*Echols School 1936-1937. Mr. and Mrs. C.O. Brown teachers. Grades 1-8. 1: Johnie Hulse, Earl Ray Tinsley, Chas. Vinson, Wm. Earl Jones, Adrell Smith, Billy Gene Hicks, James Decker, ___ McCoy, Johnson Kincade, James Ed Curtis, ___ Ezell, Hildred Brown, Andrew Geary, Clyde Woodburn. 2: Neal Decker, Freeman L. Jones, Paul Ezell, Evelyn Woodcock, Christine Hill, Edith Mae Hulse, Edwina Phelps, Virginia McCoy, Dorsie Lee Bratcher, Nellie Janette Burden, Lottie B. Wilcox, Margaret Helen Porter, Opal Lee Johnson, Anita Minton, Flora Mae Johnson, Thema Baize, Lorene Johnson, Rena Woodcock, James Farris, Chas. Farris. 3: Estil Geary, David Woodburn, Richard Hill, Marie Woodcock, Chas. Ezell, Billy Bratcher, Frankie Hulse, Geneva Johnson, Nell Susan Curtis, Edna Mae Burden, Anna Rae Burden, Lizzie Woodcock, Hildred Porter, Mitchell Minton, Bert Neal Wilcox, Heamon Johnson Jr., Irene White, Dorothy Farris. Back: Mrs. Brown, Bonnie Mae Tinsley, Joyce Maddox, W.L. Phelps, Margie Bratcher, Judson Brown, Stoy Bratcher, Rexford Maddox, Violet Geary, Virginia Wilcox, Maline Johnson, Gladys Key, Kathleen Vinson, Harry Kincaid, Carl Ezell, Mr. Brown.*

*Rockport School. Burned Sept. 1, 1967*

*Jubilee School 1913. Front: Irvin Clark, Goebel Fulton, Almont Fulkerson, Darrell Cummins, Paul Russell, Wm. (Bill) Russell, Carroll Stom. 2: Mabel Chinn, Ada Lee Cummins, Sally Mae Kirtley, Evelyn Hunley, Gladys Fulkerson, Ollie Mae Stom, Maudie Kirtley, Edith Chinn, Maqdaline Shull. 3: Dayton Clark, Guy Russell, Bessie Russell, Justus Shull, Dimple Fulkerson, Nina Clark, Louise Russell, Goebel Chinn, Minnie Brown, Henry Douglas. 4: Euclid Shull, Neva Fulton, Carrie Brown, Elsie Russell, Hazel Cummins, Merle Miller, Dewey Williams, Ava Lou Kirtley. 5: Charlie Overton, Nova Williams, Weber Clark, Vera Miller, Roscoe Engler, Mabel Russell, Walter Overton. 6: Ethel Russell, Olga Hunley, Jim Coleman, Maud Miles, Aaron Ross teacher.*

*Number 19 School, 1914. Front: Clara White, Everett Chinn, Harry Wydic, Wango Ross, Luther Payton, Oscar Tomblin, Vivian Robertson, Alva Ross. 2: Lillie White, Raymond Shafer, Sam Ashby, Wallace Fulkerson, Orville Robinson, Earl Payton, Rosco Robinson, Ursel Chinn, Clarence Bowen, Lofton Stewart. 3: Agnes Ashby, Jessie Graham, Mary Jane Quinn, Madeline Crowder, Mary Jane Fulkerson, Gustie Stewart, Sofia Fulton, Martha Southard, unk., Mary Fulkerson, Frank Robinson, Leslie Bowen. 4: Geneva McConnell, Ethel Shafer, Pauline Wydic, Pecola Fulton, Mary Ashby, Anna Thelma Chinn, Clemmer Stewart, Marie Graham, Lorena Ross, unk., Walter Fulkerson, Earl McConnell, Aubry Dale Robertson. 5: Bea McConnell, Marvin Ross, Maud Geary, Marie Crowder, Edith Fulkerson, Bessie Graham, Dummie Turner, Acmey McConnell, Anna Bowen, Effie Fulkerson, Chester Fulton, Clyde Robinson, Clifton Robinson, Harvey Robinson. 6: Anna Shafer, Lizzie Chinn, Carrie Southard, Altha Robinson, Ruth Graham, Nolva Ross, Ethel Dowel Robertson, Ruth Hammond teacher, Clarice Chinn, Maggie Hunter, Maggie Tomblin, Mary Sue Johnson, Oval Cooper, Roy McConnell.*

*Cave Ridge School, 1928, near McHenry.*

*Liberty School, 1889.*

*LEFT: O.L. Shultz, Ohio Co. educator. Principal of Central Park School, 1933-1944.*

*FAR LEFT: McHenry School, 1909. Teachers Ozna Shultz, Lula Midkiff*

*Olaton School 1936-1937, grades 1-4. Front: J.B. McCoy, Glendal Daniel, Earl Sapp, Carl Calloway, Harry Grant Ford, James Lindsey, Blackman Peterson. 2: Anderson Dudley Martin, Stella Myers, Mable Keith, Billie Faught, Eloise Berkley, Thelma Decker, Willa Nena (Billie) Daniel, Maurita Daniel, Willie (Bill) Burden, Joyce Patterson. 3: Chester Decker, Curtis Payton Jr., Flossie Sapp, Anona Patterson, O'Dell Lynch, O'Dean Ford, Christine Whitley, Mary Lillian Keith, Hacker Patterson, James Louis (Sam) Ford. 4: Willie Pearl (Landrum) Oller teacher, Ray Cooksey, Agusta Embry, James Martin, Claudia Lindsey, James Louis Sapp, Pearl Burden, Ray Martin, Robert Lindsey.*

*Hartford, 1930, 1-2 grades, Miss Rhodes. Included: Chas. Oldham, John Oldham, Chris Ranney, Denver Chungler, Mack Wade.*

*Independence School, McHenry, 1905. Mabel Easterday Ross, teacher.*

*Independence School, McHenry, 1909. Mabel Easterday Ross, teacher. 1: Paul Phelps, ___ Hoops, Ellis Phelps, Leslie Carnes, Carl Givens. 2: Spencer man with two children, Katy Moseley, Ethel Phelps, Bessie Cates, P.D. Carnes, Wavy Givens. 3: Ethel Marie Phelps, ___ Spencer, Jim Moseley, Cecil Hoops, Robert Cates, Jim Rock, Noah Phelps, Elbert Phelps, Clarence Render, teacher. 4: Dewey Chapman, Owen Hudson, Fannie Carnes, Norma Wade, Pearl House, Erpha Phelps. Elsie Carnes. Effie Carnes between rows 3 and 4. 5: Dudley Carnes, Minnie Lee Wade, Stella Phelps, Cordie Hudson, Genevieve Render, Mae Suegeon, Mary Moseley, Ed Rock, John Moseley.*

*Junior class 1943-1944. Back: Noah Phelps Jr., Bobby Borah, Lyndon Raymond, Ann Ross Langford, Imogene Mill Hines. Front: Olivia Craddock Warren, Donnie Carnes David, Donnie Wakeland Valentine.*

*1928 Senior girls. 1: Grace Reynolds, Belle Chapman, Anna M. Fisher, Bertha Chinn, Myrl Bishop. 2: Artie Tatum, Mable Shoulders, Flossie Chapman, Edith Brizendine, Lois Chinn.*

*Independence School, McHenry.*

*Goshen, 1930. Bottom, 4 unk., Russel Cooper, James Gray, Shorty Chinn. 2: 2 unk., ___ Wade, Frances Moorman, Margaret Lillian Barnes, Hazel Chinn, Clara Mae Moorman, unk., Charles Gray. 3: Leonard Miller, Cesia Miller, ___ Ford, Wilma Gray, Ozna Shultz, unk., Earl Moorman, Walter Myres, teacher.*

*Liberty School, ca. 1888. Those identified from the top: Susan M. William Barrett, row 2 #3 from left; Lydia Williams, row 4 #3 from left; Inez (Ina) Barrett Mauzy, row 4 #4 from left; Robert Elijah Barrett, bottom, extreme right.*

*National Honor Society, 1953-1954. Jean Geary, David Pryor, Ann Byers, Rachael Render, Nila Jean Chinn, Janice Wallace, Sandy Pearl, Billy Lace, Martha Heflin, Anita Jo Buck, Shirley Barnes (back), Hilda Stearns (front), Emma Haven, Edwin Render, Perry Lewis, Nelda Barnes, Bonnie Robinson, Carl Leisure, Prof. Forsythe, Peggy Render.*

*Rockport PTA officers, ca. 1950. Grace Fulkerson, Juanita Ashton, Alma Durham, Charlene Hill, Carrie Devine.*

*Rockport School. Burned ca, 1933.*

*LEFT: Bartlett School, 1914, on Taffy-Bells Run road. 1: Elvena Chapman, Verona Chapman, Tincy Bartlett, Gus Chapman, Noel Massie, Schultz Chapman. 2: Mrs. Owen Wells holding Evelyn, Gola Bartlett, Wilma Chapman, Dee Bartlett, Miss Harriet Midkiff teacher. Back: Della Bartlett, Belle Bartlett, Mollie Smiley, Mrs. Bell Long Bartlett.*

Goshen, 1933-34. Back: Iva Render teacher, Francis Moorman, Dorotha Baize, Bryce Carter, Clara Mae Moorman, Gilbert Hoskins. 3: Glendon Chinn, Virginia Coleman, Ruth Raines, Eva Jean Westerfield, Margaret Barnes, Edwina Baize, William S. Stevens. 2: Margaret Johnson, Bobbie Chinn, Azilee Chinn, Wendell Raines, Jessie Lee Johnson, Margaret Hoskins, Ney Shepard Hazelrigg, Jenny Belle Barnes, Margaret L. Barnes. Front: ___ Coleman, Donald Hazelrigg, Jewel (Bud) Moorman, Hugh L. Ford, Jackie Raines.

Rockport, 5-6 grades, 1948. 1: Kelly Harris, Winferd Boyd, Gordon Geary, Lester Geary, Emma Geary, Betty Welborn, Mildred Geary. 2: Frances Chapman, Nola White, Marlene Hoskins, Jimmy Brown, Fay Fulkerson, Milton Brown, James Geary, William Givens, Russell Geary. 3: Evelyn Fulkerson, Peggy Render, Bonnie Robinson, Kaye Smith, Betty Maddox, Pearl Chapman, Lake Holland, James Fuller, R.L. Goff.

Echols School, 1933, grades 4-8. Front: David Woodburn, W.L. (Bill) Phelps, W.J. Porter, Wm. Powell Wilcox, Hildred Porter, Arthur C. Ingram, Charles W. Vinson, Jessie L. Hoskins, Valdie Elmore. 2: Margie Bratcher, Joyce Maddox, Nellie Bell Garrett, Vacova Garrett, Goldie Burgess, Kathleen Vinson, Ruth (Dean) Curtis, Essie Mae Burgess, Reba Elmore, Violet Geary, Bertha Ellen Burgess, Virginia Mae Wilcox. 3: Rodney Bratcher, Dorothy Belle Brown, Stoy Bratcher, Marjorie Burton, Nell Susan Curtis, Rexford Maddox, Naomi Burden, Bonnie Mae Tinsley, Archie Crabtree, Aila Burton, Cecil Curtis. Back: C.O. Brown teacher, Ernest L. (Jack) Vinson, Ruth Hicks, James R. Ingram, Clara Mae Hoskins, Orville Elmore, Naomi Hoskins, Edward (Ted) Key.

Horton, Nov. 1909. Miss Ethel Raines teacher. Ethel Raines Tilford Bivins, right side of photo, fourth row. She also helped establish the Beaver Dam Hotel and Cafe, one of the oldest businesses in Beaver Dam.

Ricketts School, 1940-1941.

Bennett's School, Hartford, 1922, Rhoda Whitehouse teacher.

Rockport School.

*Midway School, 1938-1939. Front: Russell Ball, Glen Chapman, Allen Ezell, Jimmy Chapman, Randall Blanchard, Maurice Ball, Nelson Blanchard Jr., Bobby Heflin, Willis Blanchard, Roy Francis, Ercie Ball. 2: Charles Bishop, Kenneth Ezell, Marvin Rowe, Ruby Blanchard, Maridean Yonts, unk., Anna Murl Blanchard, Reba Joyce Rowe, Kathryn Belle Brown, Mary Bishop, Louis Ezell, Hayward Ball, Charles Ezell. 3: Christine Blanchard, Letty Belle McIntyre, Willard Blanchard, Amos Blanchard, Bob Jennings, Cyril Ross, Ada Blanchard, Flossie Heflin, Hazel Blanchard, Hazel Heflin, Vonell Chapman, Hattie Ward, Wilda Ezell. Teacher Wayne White.*

*Walton's Creek School, 1916. Seated: Anna Carter, Lois Bishop, Idola Render, Cassie Kincheloe, Viola Hoskins, Fred Williams, Alfred Ashby, Rethel Hoskins, Ralph Bishop, Rayburn Render, Robert Hoskins. 2: John Bishop, Myrtle Render, Jessie Carter, Irene Rhodes, Emma Tichenor, Anna Tichenor, Emma Carter, Bessie Hoskins, Pauline Render, Ida Marie Bennett, Emma Boyd, Robert Render, Leslie Williams. Back: Bessie Carter, Ada Carter, Martha Ashby, Tom Bennett, Mattie Jane Bennett, Evert Boyd, A.B. Rowe, Loga Williams, Byron Tichenor, Alney Ashby, Raymond Render.*

*The Bend, 1930. 1: unk., Edward Lee Thomasson, William Barnard, J.C. Burgess, ___ Patton, Ray Smith Bradshaw, Chester Geary, J.T. Barnard. 2: 3 unk., Virginia Ferguson, Mildred Geary, Fonda Gail Bradshaw, Naomi Bratcher, Evenell Geary, Ruby Bratcher, 2 unk. 3: unk., Daniel Bratcher, J.B. Thomasson, Charlotte Bratcher, Elizabeth Patton?, ___ Oliver, unk., Goerge Bradshaw, Albert Bratcher, Elmer Geary. 4: Mayburn Stewart, Imogene Barnard, Dena Mae Bradshaw, Daisy Ferguson, Helen Bullock, Edna Geary, Jim Ferguson, Eva Thomasson.*

*Fordsville Academy, Nov. 20, 1908, O.L. Shultz, principal.*

*Front: Estella Ralph, Anne Barnes teacher, Mildred Hocker, Grace Margaret Williams, Katheryn Boswell, Claribel Daniels. 2: Wilma Taylor, Dorothy Dexter, Louise Bennett, unk., Mildred Taylor, Doris Likens, Mary Belle Smith. Back, unk.*

*West No Creek, 1907, one room school.*

*McGrady School, 1894. Front (begins near center) Alva Peach, Everett Peach, Rena Vance, Cecil Murphy, Henry Lamb, Cora Lamb, Murdie Dever, Alice Plumer teacher, Mittie Ballard. 2: Robert Lamb, Ida Fieldon, Remus Fieldon, Hattie Davis, Mary Peach, Willie Gidcombs, Irgile Murphy, Grover Murphy, Frank Dever, Burt Cox, Tom Cox, Tom Sutton, Zeb Davis, George Cox, Wayne Dever, Claudie Gidcombs, Aldolphus Murphy. 3: Dona Gidcombs, Miles Dever, Ida Ballard, Delia Ballard, Mary Morris, Charolette Mitchel, Martha Morris, Willye Ballard, Belle Dever, Cora Cox, Ed Gidcombs, Lara Gidcombs, Sylvester Broomfield, Maud Davis, Ed Murphy. Back: Wayne Murphy, Ab Murphy trustee, Frank Peach, George Coats trustee, Blondie Sutton, Isaac Gidcombs trustee, Ray Coats, Charlie Martin, Robert Dever, Willie Peach, Charles Dever, Ida Vance, Mag Cox, Mary Dever, Maggie Sutton, Addie Mae Fieldon, Georgie Mitchel.*

*Upper Point School 1924. (Listed right to left.) 1: Wm. Irvin Brown, Matthew Tichenor, Robert Wilson Smith, Edwin Clark Brown, Archie Jones, Lois Tichenor, Luva Mae Condit, Marie Stewart, Geneva Carter, Ruth Hicks, Rollie Lee Smith. 2: Walter Fisk Condit, Shelby Bishop, Roy Ansel Smith, Louverine Igleheart Bishop, Rachel Corinne Massey, Mary Simpson, Lorene Bennett, Esther Bell Johnson, Anna Bell Martin, Grace Jones, Mary Gail Condit, Oscar Carter, Johnnie Simpson, Leaburn. 3: Sudie Mae Bennett, Lillian Jackson, Elizabeth Montgomery, Ruva Belle Condit, Gerrald Massey, David Johnson, Nathel Stewart, Harry Taylor, Ray Jones, Viola Hoskins, Helen Catherine Brown, Alma Kathryn Taylor, Grace Marie Massey, Violet Howell, Ivo Hick. 4: 3 unk., Cebern Tichenor, Mac Bullock, Reathel Hoskins, Versie Minton, Anna Carter, Nettie B. Jones, Geneva Tichenor, Ada Ree Bennett, Bessie Hoskins, Nora Carter, Robert Hoskins, Myrl Massey, Edwin Martin. Back Norine Maddox, Eva Bell Smith, Florine Whittaker teacher.*

*Deanefield, 1934-1935. 1: Carl Whitehouse, Floyd Fitsgerald, Buster Hardin, Charles Rhoads, Gilbert Finley, Vernon Fuqua, Louis Bellamy. 2: Gertrude Hardin, Emma Jean Babbit, Alton Wilson, Edwina Wade, Virginia Greenwell, J.R. Tierney, Vivian Powell, Mike Tierney, Kenneth Lowe, Anna Bell Greenville, Betty Greenville. 3: June Powell, Reba Phillips, Ogal Wade, J.R. Hardin, Juanita Griffith, Hoover J. Haynes, Reba Hardin, Drexel Phillips, Charolette Russell, Dorothy Greenville, Chester B. Norris. 4: Daily Ray Fuqua, Cecil Phillips, Ernest "Jake" Kaysinger, Lanelle Babbit, Lucille Bellamy, Effie "Bennie" Wade, Bertha Mae Hardin, Zoinia Whitehouse, Helen Whitely Phillips, Aline Tatum, Gladys Phillips teacher.*

*Hartford High School, 1920s.*

*Oaks Dell School, 1930, Leonard Nabors, teacher.*

*Banquet sponsored by Beaver Dam Deposit Bank for Ohio Co. teachers, 1967. Bryan Taylor, Charles Ranney, Alva Bennett, Mrs. Austin Miller, Audra Hoxworth, Dorothy McKee, Anna Stewart.*

*Beaver Dam Grade School, Grade 6, 1939-1940. Top: Oscar Coleman, Virginia B., Mallam May, Jean Blakenship, Arthur Ram, Eugene Sandefur, M. May. 3: Clara Bennett, Virginia Render, U. Wallace, Mary Simpson, Kathleen McKenney, Jean Knight. 2: J.L. Burgess, Jimmy Butler, Archie Nelson, J.W. Duvall, Morton Roy, J.R. Gilstrap, Harold Wells, Glenn Coleman. Front: Wilma McCormick, Edna Stewart, Malcolm Carden, Tillie Shields, Billy Ashby, Wendell Sandefur, Nancy Stevens, Mildred Hazelrigg. Ellis T. Sandefur teacher.*

*Hickory Ridge School, Miss Argent Barnes teacher, ca. 1914. Back, Heavrin Everly on right. Front, Bertie Everly second from right.*

*Central Park School, McHenry, 6th grade, 1923. Back: Johnnie Maddox, Joe Mitchell, 3 unk., Mary Brown, 2 unk., Clarence Givens, Edward Rock. 2: unk., Mary Stevens?, Clara Shropshire, Ora Dinno?, Mabel Pierce, Martine Taylor, Verna Ruth Hawes, unk, Marguerite Warner. 3: Mallam Lake, Paul Maddox, Martha Rock, unk., Ruby Rowe, Corine Stewart, unk., Thelma Hibbs, Ariel Porter, Virginia Hardin, unk. 1: unk., Noble Sandefur?, unk., James Smith, Charles Allen?, unk., Wando Miller?*

*Rockport High School, 1933. 1: Guy Shenk teacher, Martha Barnard, Sylvia Chancellor, Bill Tooley, Evelyn Burden, Jimmy Gray, Margaret Reid, Mae Ashby, Neil Bratcher, Gladys Welborn, Martha Reid, Loretta Schacklett, Olga Robertson, Cleo Burden. 2: Naomi Tilford, Edith Elmore, Ray Hines, Leslie Hopper, Hazel Elmore, Darrell Ashby, Marnell Grobarger, Christine Robertson, Willie Lee Swain, Wanda Rowe, Ivan Rogers. 3: Hershel Kimmel, Ethel Robinson, Hugh Ferris Mason, Linsey Williams, R.C. Hines, Melborn Everly, L.W. Harrell, Lenalda Swain, Winston Hicks, Thelma Tooley, Helen Hicks, Jane Woodburn. 4: Carlos Duncan, Ernest Hopper, Gus Dodge, Netter Hester, Margaret Sullivan, Pat Chancellor, Gilbert Lamb teacher and coach, Edmund Park, Carolyn Wilson, Jenny Burger, Maurine Everly, Lottie Hicks, Esther (Buggs) Barnard, Mae Woodburn.*

*Rayburn, Idola, and Greyford Render with teacher Analtha Ross.*

*Prof. E.E. Tartar, principal Beaver Dam School. 1940s.*

*Reathel Goff, superintendent of Ohio Co. Schools, sign contracts. Looking on is Bob Shown, acting chairman of the board.*

*Grade 2, 1950, Rockport. 1: Wanda Phelps, Charles Devine, Betty Scott, Daisy Brown, Janice Heltsley, Millie Fulkerson, Patty Smith, Brenda Thomas, Wilma Fulkerson, Mary Jane Brown. 2: Linda Stevens, Shirley Chinn, Peggy Saling, Jackie Scott, James Goff, Philip Devine, Lewis Chapman, George Blackburn, Hugh Cummins, Doris Cardwell. 3: Anna Decker, Randall Phelps, Dicky Johnson, Miss Novia Ross.*

*Rockport, 7-8 grades, 1949. 1: James Brown, Fay Fulkerson, R.L. Goff, Analee Fulkerson, Lillian Key, Anna Barnes, Myrtle Likens, Ralph Fuller, Lake Holland, Milton Brown. 2: Betty Maddox, Clemmer Curtis, Gleda Brown, Shirley Blair, Nola White, Evelyn Fulkerson, Marlene Hoskins, Peggy Render, Eunice McKee teacher. 3: James Geary, Bobby Singleton, Raymond Maddox, Marnell Evans, William Givens, Billy Sharp, James Fuller, Lake Saling, Charles O'Brien.*

*Sugar Grove, 1908, two teacher school. Verna Rae Magan, standing left; a Mr. Roach?, standing right.*

*Fordsville High School, torn down in 1935.*

*Central Park School, 1917.*

*Central Park School, after the fire, 1930.*

*Rockport School, graduating class of 1946. Front: Hazel Tooley, Lelda Doris Fulkerson, Ruth Herrald. Back, Sylvia Warfield teacher. Rurel Brown, D.B. Lutz principal, Duane (Buckie) Stewart, James Curtis.*

*Central Park School, new gym being built, 1927.*

*Ohio Co. Teachers Banquet, 1966. Anne B. Barnes, Marshall Barnes, Betty Baker Jackson, Janie Taylor Phelps.*

*High View School. Top: Eugene Ashby, Raymond Robertson teacher, Mitchell Maddox, Earnest Hopper. 2: Purcell Hopper, Esther Barnard Brown, Willard Maddox, Cathrine Hopper Blackburn, Melburn Elmore, Martha Barnard James, William Wilson, Coleman Maddox. 3: Harry Elmore, Lois Hopper, unk., Nellie Francis, Electa Barnard Chinn, Una Southard, Mary Wilson, Ruby Nell Cardon, Adah Barnard Raymond, Chester Francis. Bottom: Valdie Elmore, Forest Southard, Tommy Hopper, Woodrow Brown, Len Brown, Glen Brown, Joe Maddox, James Maddox, Chestyne Maddox.*

*Beaver Dam School 1970-1971. 2nd grade. Front: Lynette Brown, unk., Becky Stewart, Kathy Vaught, Angie Saint, unk., Karen McClain, Glenna Armstrong, Teresa Hulsey, Dana Long. 2: unk., Randy Dowell, 3 unk., Michael Dockery, Jerry Mayes, Marty Allen, Randy Cain, 2 unk., Lana Davenport, teacher. 3: Daniel Clouse, Janice Everly, Shane Ferguson, Terry Jones, Robbie Wydick, unk., Van Roberts, Gerald Hardison, Brent DeSoto, Ricky Brizentine. 4: unk., Camilla Rowe, Steve Daniels, Kristi Taylor, Kamille Johnson, Lisa Stewart, Richie ___, Betty Hunt, Glenda Dockery, Bonnie ___, unk.*

*Lower Point School, Matanzas.*

*Faculty at Rockport, 1950. Mrs. Aaron Chapman, Cliffie Austin, Dorothy Park, G.R. Reynolds, Woodrow Park, Juanita Park, Nova Ross.*

*Pearl Brown, teacher.*

*Report book, 1919.*

*Ricketts School.*

*An American Red Cross class in 1930 at old Beaver Dam High School. Top: Mrs. Ellis Sandefur, Edith Wison Reeves, ___ Elliott, Mrs. Morgan James Smith, Bess Chick, Bess Barrass, unk., Annie Addison. Bottom, Mrs. Lena Duvall, Mrs. G. Barnes, unk., Emma Fair Young, unk., Marguerite Main Taylor, Bess Wilson.*

*First grade, Centertown elementary, Mrs. Hines teacher, Spring 1975. Robert Dockery back, third from right.*

*Hartford, Grades 7-8, 1933-1934, Mrs. S.O Keown teacher. Autry Duncan, 2nd boy on first row.*

*Dundee, 1937-1938, grades 1-2.*

*Kindergarten class, Beaver Dam Elementary program 1992. Paul Dockery in black shirt.*

*Taylortown 1939-1940. Back: Rose C. Duke, teacher, Annie Peay, Rose Catherine James Duke, Jimmy Taylor, Gene McKee, Lofton Maddox, Bill McKee, Henry Aldridge, Maurice Maddox, Juanita Maddox, Oakley Peay, Lindie Maddox. Front, unk., Rufus Lee, Wanda Jeline McKinley, unk., Gene Slack, Joe Maddox, unk., Clarron Neal Berryman.*

*Vine Hill, 1930, L.L. Embry teacher. Back: Nokel Hoheimer, Joseph Wright, Wymon Tucker, Clifford Rains, James Long, Thomas Watson. 2: Junior Ashford, Lucille Long, Artie Wilson, Cora Mae Long, Ruby Young, Martha Long, Wilda Tucker, Jessie Young, James Hoheimer. Front: Sonnie Wilson, Lynis Kennedy, Thomas Long, Tommy Kennedy, Onis Rains, Charles Wilson, Clarence Wright.*

*Dundee High School, 1931.*

*Ohio County teachers' meeting, July 29-30, 1926.*

*Beaver Dam High School.*

*Joint meeting of Daviess Co. and Ohio Co. school boards and superintendents. Pleasant Ridge, April 10, 1929. Bottom: Prof. Oscar Shultz, Harrison Flener, W.R. Carson, Mr. Stevens, Horace B. Martin.*

*Grade 9, Cromwell School, 1948-1949. Mrs. John Martin teacher.*

*Midway School, 1923. Myrl Bishop Ward Ashby, Artie Tatum James, 2nd row from top, 2-3 respectively.*

*Central Grove Spring School, 1919.*

*White Oak School, 1924. Front: Earl Payton, Cecil Jamison. 2: Earl D. Mitchell, Nelson Jamison, Jesse N. Berkeley, Bulah Raley, Gertrude Dugan, Bessie Likens, Opal Dugan. Back: R. May Byers Moore teacher Halam M. Berkeley on horse.*

*Washington School, 1902. Top: Porter Bailey, Mattie Hicks, Ethel Allen, Katie Trogden, Myrtle Trogden, Lee Hicks, Frances Smith, Vena Crabtree, Lonzo Bailey, Nutie Travis. 2: Damon Tinsley, Cliffie Tinsley, Margaret Sapp, Myrtie Hicks, James Henry Sapp, Albert Bailey, Lula Bailey, Mary Etta Sapp, Elmer Allen, Ernest Felix. 3: Weaver Bennett, Lilburn Smith, Gene Allen, Iola Mercer, Monroe Smith, Dora Hicks, Otis Howard, Emma Smith, Theodore Bailey, Cora Trogden, Dora Travis. Front: Ulysis Trogden, Esker Mercer, Hobert Tinsley, Bay Crabtree, Almond Tinsley, Estil Smith, Charley Bennett, Ellis Allen, Elsie Bennett. Teacher, Wayne Stratton.*

*Jubilee School, 1934. Front: Arthur Miller, Azim Johnson, Billy Williams, Billy Engler, Sam Graves, Billy Johnson, R.J. Williams. 2: R.C. Stevens, Wesley (Buckie) Overton, Robert Peyton, Bobby Shull, Rurel Brown, Marilyn Miller, Guy Lee Kennedy, Ruby Johnson, Hazel Johnson, Veachel Shull, Marjorie Stevens, Perry (Pete) Graves. 3: Leon Winchester, Charlotte Brown, Jack Brown, Nellie Brown, Carol Engler, Lucille Peyton, Kenneth Engler, Helen Stevens, Marjorie Overton, Wilda Graves, Lillie Chinn teacher.*

*Mt. Moriah School, near Taffy, 1932. Yates Everly teacher, standing first in row 3. Myrtle Smith 4th row past middle by girl with bow on dress.*

*Beaver Dam High School 1948-1949, Sophomore class, Anna Francis Smith teacher. Front: Daisy Fergerson, Jeanie Kimbrel, Kay Chinn, Mary Evelyn Hines, Delois Kitchens, Hildred Hines, Imogene Hert, Wilma Havens, Virginia Shultz, Jean Johnson, Ruth Ann Taylor. 2: Berchel Bishop, Flo Cardwell, Thelma Peyton, Gaynell Heflin, Kathryn Belle Brown, Myrtle Lou Buck, Helen Lois Brown, Mary Black, Mary Catherine Mercer, Mary Sue Ragland, Betty Black, Peggy Schroader, Nancy Paxton, Nadine Westerfield, Patsy Stevens, Anna Francis Smith. 3: Henry Leach, Carol Iler, Billy Himes, Alva Bennett, Billy Johnson, Roy Mason, Frank Shultz, Jerry Taylor, Logan (Buddy) Shown, Fred Newhouse, Hubert (Sonny) Myers, Bobby Young, Lawrence Pearl, James Monroe.*

*Western Seminary College, used later for Beaver Dam Grade and High School.*

Union School Number 11, 1897. Front: Cecil Cooper, J.J. Blankenship, R.C. Hocker, Arthur Plummer, Roy Blankenship, Ercil Balnkenship, Bessie Smith, Noble Taylor, Effie Taylor, Ethel Plummer, Annie D. Reid, Audra Bennett. 2: Travis Davis, Mary E. Davis, Lillie Stevens, Mallie Johnson, Vernie Stevens, Lessie Taylor, Mertie Taylor, Lennie Williams, Minnie Wright, Anna Blankenship, Robert Hodges. 3: Elvis Mauzy, Sam Mauzy, Robert Matthews, Wade Hodges, Maggie Davidson, Arlis Plummer, Sid Davidson teacher, Mammie Plummer, Pete Hodges, Zilpah Smith, Malin Williams.

Central Park School, 4th grade, Claude Park teacher. Bottom, Janice Albin, Alma Ann Hoskins, Alma S. Schroader, Betty Schroader, Martha Gail Hillard, Sharon Lacefield, Linda Joan Rock, Dorothy Schroader, Linda Kitchens. Middle: Nancy Chapman, Patricia Matthews, Ernie Moore, Jack Park Warren, Ernie Brown, Charles Whitler, Carroll Moseley, Mary Ann McClure. Top: Mr. Park, Jimmy Warren, Alison C. Embry, Larry James, June Nell Likens, Ronald I. Hillard, Ray Dowell, Ronald Sandefur.

WPA sewing project, 1937-1938, Hartford. Miss Ann Pirtle, Instructor. 2nd. row, 2nd. seat Bell Duncan.

Mary Maggard Watts, McHenry, retired as teacher on Central Park.

Olaton, 1936-1937. Front: Kathern Miller, Derwood Ford, Imogene Ford, Douglas Ford, Alice Keith, Henry Felix, Mary England, Lynnal Puyton, Pryse Patterson. 2: Maxine Duggins, Bernard Ford, Marjorie Faught, Carmon Daniel, Karmon Keith, Buda Patterson, Carl Dugan, Barbara Oller. 3: Fred Crume teacher, Ruth Myers, Bernard Hurt, Hazel Cooksey, Charlie England, Mildred Felix, Maxie Lynch, Mamie Rea Myers.

Rockport, 1-2 grade, 1935-1936. Back: Geneva Clark, Audrey Maddox, Randolph Clark, Lindy Rowe, Dicky Smith, Albert Lee Maddox, Gene Bowers, Thomas Jesse Jr., George Herbert Akin. Middle: Alva Fogle Jr., John Graves Jr., Jimmie Barnard, George Lee Lewis, Harold Mabrey, Neal Maples, Jewel Fogle, Hilliard Geary, Clemmie Everley. Front, Glen Malloy, Perry O'Neal Williams, Kathleen Dunn, Margaret Brown Wilson, Elizabeth Ann Clark, Betty Tooley, ___ Mabrey, Martine Wilson, Nancy Turley, Coleen Hoskins.

Taylortown, 1940-1941, Mrs. Rose C. Duke teacher. Back: Joe Maddox, Gene McKee, Jaunita Maddox, Jimmy Taylor, Gene Slack, Rose Catherine James. Front: Lois McKinley, unk., Freddie Newhouse, Jeline McKinley, Clarron Neal Berryman, Rufus Lee, Margaret Slattery.

Front: Franklin Jackson, Winona Everly, Margaret Stenburg, Ruby Combs, Mary Durham, Alta Ross. 2: Cecil Faulkerson teacher, Virginia Thomblinson, Grace Jones, Carlos Stewart, Walton Bishop. 3: Crowe Pate, Wilma ___, Oscar Bond James, Helen Morton, Mary Beth Morton.

Horse Branch High, 1931.

Wm. Paul Richards coach, Helen Hunter, Robert Snodgrass, bus driver and owner, 1941

1: Bill Stanley, Martha Heflin, Sam Plummer, Linda Burden Perry Lewis. 2: Avery Hill, Shirley Geary, Monty Leach, Nelda Barnes. 3: Jean Green, Hewlett Pryor, Camellia Sorrels, Don Ferguson, Shirrel Frizzell, Jackie Spinks.

Late 1800s, rural school near Fordsville.

Williams Mines School, 1908.

Rockport High, 1914-1915, J.W. O'Dell principal

*McHenry, 4th grade, 1928. Top: Ernest Trogden, Myrl Howard, Orvil Austin, Irene Fuller teacher, Dorthy Cox, Martha Rock, Marjorie Jones, Flossie Butler, Mercedes Lewis. 2: Jesse Lee James, Carl Ray Harden, Catherine Fulkerson, Hanna Nelson, Opal Peach, Laudella Peach, Dorthy Warren, Bertha Pierce. 3: Osville Hawes, Ruth Fisher, Margaret Allen, Claudine Warren, Rosa K. James, Ruby Shoulders, Gladys Hocker, Lucile Shields. 4: Clifford Parritt, Leon Autry, Clarence Hopper, Reynold Craddock, Benny Nelson, Charles James, Henry Cooper, Howard Doirs.*

*Horton School, 1948-1949. Front: Edith Minton teacher, Virginia Smith, Mildred Burden, Helen Smith, Ruby Smith, Loretta Baize. 2: Billy Burden, Reathel Monroe, R.V. Dockery, A.C. Dockery, John Minton, Marie Baize. 3: Warren Minton, Paxton Monroe, Lewis Burden, Roy Dockery, Linda Monroe, Doanie Smith, Margaret Dockery, Alice Minton.*

*Sophomore Class 1949-1950. Principal, M.S. Greer. Front: Richard Newton, A. Denton Huff, J.J. Coffield, Billy Jo Dalphies, "Cricket" Smith, Franklin Curtis. 2: Charles Wade, Alonzo Bellamy, Frank Schrader, Harold Clark, Charles Sullivan, Jospehine Richards, Dorthy Bruce Berch, Evelyn Mullen, Rebecca Richards, Edna Earl Moxely, Betty Deloris Matthews, Mary Elizabeth Williams, Anna Rea Patton. 3: Lillian Tierney, Alice Pierce, Artie Sexton, Betty Jo Neighbors, Nancy Fuller, Jo Nell Rhodes, Charlotte Robey, Barbara Heddon, Betty Joyce Craig, Martha Ann Stewart, Maggie Walker, Shirley Whitt, Lucille Payne, Vivian Williams, Betty Jean Moffett, Janet Rusher.*

*Sulphur Springs School, 1906. Georgie Larkin teacher.*

*Bailey School. Ethel Duvall, 4th from top left. Floyd Duvall, 7th from top left. Sadie (Goff) Baise, 8th from top left.*

*Cool Springs School, ca. 1911.*

*Pleasant Ridge School, 1907*

*Tea Given for Beaver Dam School Teachers, ca. 1950.*

*Beaver Dam Grade School, 3rd grade. Ruth Stanley, teacher. Students include George Duvall, Diana Bevil.*

*Maypole Dance at Beaver Dam School, 1953-1954.*

*Belmont (Ralph) School, 1927. Lola Field, teacher. Floy Diane Russell in front of teacher. Evan Ray Russell, 3rd row end, standing.*

*Beaver Dam School, 1934. grades 1-2. Betty Renfrow, teacher.*

*South Beaver School, 1897. Mrs. Carl Taylor, teacher. Front left: Everett and Sylvester Kendall.*

*Flint Springs, 1934-1935. Mrs. Jesse Romans, teacher.*

*Students from South Beaver Dam. Bess Chick, teacher.*

Schroader School, 1895, Lee Sandefur, teacher. Front: Etta Schroader, Clem Schroader, Minnie Schroader, Lon Schroader, Mima, Schroader, Andy Schroader, Netter Ziggler, Dee Tucker, Bennie Boswell, Cora Tucker, Della Peach, Essie Peach, Effie York, Archie Ziggler, Sibert, Ida Wright, Annie Gray, Annie York, Bessie Wright, Mary Minton, Leslie B. Wright, Henry Minton, Prudy Miller, Verdie Minton, Marvin, Eve Wright, Ivy Potts, Harlan Potts, Dora Schroader, Pearlie Warner, Marvin Warner. 2: Hiram Schroader, Dillard Schroader, George Schroader, Henry Wright, Mrs. George Schroader, Mrs. Tucker, Aaron Royals, Loersia Wright, Noah Schroader, Mag. Wright, George Tucker, Linda Gray, Isaac Schroader, Mary Belle Wright, Mrs. Jim Wright, Kate Wimsatt, Jim Wright, Mahalla Ann Wright, Maude Action, Nanney Duggins, Gassie York, Lula Crowder, Annie Crowder, Janie Ziggler. Back: Anyer Warner, Joseph Schroader, John Filbeck, Mede Schroader, George Schroader, Tommy Schroader, Hallie Bruton, Eldred Bruton, William Henry Potts, Richard Wright, Jack Barnett, Melvin Kessinger, Shelby Wright, Frank Wright. In window, Fannie Burton. Sitting, Alice Fielding.

Pleasant Walk School, 1934, Crossroads. Front: Ida Elizabeth Johnson, Kelly Johnson, Nellie Johnson, Edna Earle Decker, Doreen Slack, Bessie Whitten, Bethel Harder, Opal Mae Grant. 2: C.J. White, J.C. White, James Harder, Marie Robinson, Dinton Harder, Lee Roy Crow, Ivan White. Maxine Grant. Back, Welby Wilson, Elizabeth Slack, Crit Decker, Mary Grant, Monnie Harder, Everett Raidon.

Fordsville High School, trip to Mammoth Cave, April 26, 1941. Front: unk., Margaret Richards, Geneva McCardy, "Buddy" Hart, ___ Greer, 2 unk., Anna Mary Leach. 2: Eugene Bellamy, 2 unk., Canmom Carden, Mr. Westerfield, Clay Junior. Back: Mr. Bason, Mr. Lewis principal.

Fordsville, May 19, 1939, Grace Martin, teacher. Front: unk., Douglas Cheek, Mildred Stites, Sally Newton, unk., Buda Davison, Nina Mae Grant, 2 unk., "Buddy" Hart. 2: unk., Jackie Loyd, Eugene Bellamy, Marie Marsh, Genevieve Daulpher, unk., Anna Mary Leach, Drexel Phillips, Florence Fuqua, unk., Mildred Spencer, unk.

A.P. St. Clair, Logston, Juanita Baize, Onis Morris, Geoffrey Allan, Pirtle Sandefur, Ervin Minton, Gladys Park, Paul Wilson, Virginia Wilson, Harold Arnold.

LEFT: Beaver Dam Junior Rhythm Band, 1934.

*McHenry Senior Class, 1934-1935. Front: Margie Jones, Ronnie Givens, Katie Eden, Everette Hess, Lucille Phelps. 2: Margaret Allen, Iva James, Harold Kitchem, Catherine Culberts, ___ Moseley. Back: Lena Scott, Mrs. Burris (Fisher), ___ Sandefur, Prof. O.L. Shultz.*

*School Fair, Fall 1950, Horton Elementary School float.*

*Cromwell School, grade 7. Arthur Minton teacher. G.W. White principal.*

*Cool Springs 1939-1940. Miss Cliffie Austin teacher.*

*Simmons, 1928, Miss Austin.*

*Shirrel Frizzell, Nelda Barnes, Jean Green, June McKinley, Linda Burden, 1954, in front of old Beaver Dam School.*

RIGHT: Glendon Brown, 1946-1947.

MIDDLE: Six students from South Beaver Dam School.

FAR RIGHT: Mrs. Mary Lou Gossum, Stanley Phillips, Centertown teachers.

*Old Hartford College, 1880-1912.*

*West Kentucky College and Teacher Training School, 1898. Front: James Austin, Prof. Ray, Birch Hodges. Back, Beulah Coots, Maggie Smith, R.L. Barnes.*

*Green Brier School, Nov. 1909, G.W. White teacher. Top: Evie Wilson, Ernest Wilson, Edith Wilson, Lee Wilson, Emma Wilson, Hershel Ross, Opal Wilson, Alvin Chinn, Thomas Neal, Lizzie Wilson, Clayton Ross. 2: Blanch Chinn, David Wilson, Eugene Neal, Willie Chinn, Nellie Wilson, Corene Shultz, Daisy Chinn, unk., Pat Wilson, Taylor, John Bennett, John Roach. 3: Elijah Wilson, Pansy Wilson, Mable Neal, Cora Belle Wilson, Lizzie Wilson, Audry Brown, Sesnie Shultz, Haverin Brown, Susie Wilson, Tom Wilson, Lillie Chinn, Willard Douglas, Taylor. 4: 3 unk., Erdine Knight, Sally Mary Shultz, Beulah Wilson, Vergie Wilson, Jones, Daphne Knight, Maggie Wilson. 5: Beckham Wilson, Goebel Shultz, Randall Brown, Carroll Chinn, R.P. Brown, Raymond Brown, Karl Brown.*

*Shreve, 1909, Irene Whittinghill teacher.*

*Sunny Dale School, 1909.*

*Hartford College, 1908.*

*Ohio Co. Teachers Institute, 1909.*

# GRADUATIONS

Beaver Dam High, Class of 1930.

Beaver Dam High, Class of 1926. Front: Ben H. Rumage, Bennett Cohran, Sterling Maddox, Estill A. Hazelrigg. 2: Vivian Robertson, Hubert Greer, William Raley, E. Rhea Render, Malcolm L. Barnes, Karl T. Brown. 3: Virgil Lee Couch, Hayward Stevens, Audra Martin, Mildred Greer, Verna Lucille Baker, Beulah Kane, Lucille Couch.

Hartford High School, 1947 graduates. Back: Prof. L.G. Shultz, Annie Davidson, Jean Gray Magan, Virginia Carson-Statam, Bennie Smith Horn, Sara Berry-Smith, Remus Hudson, Mrs. Ray Barnhill. 2: Eddie Wood, Antha Bell Shown Ralph, Katheryn Phipps Maddox, Cecil Bristow Jr., H. Dean Moore Wilson, Margaret Holland, Delores James Vanfleet. Front: Teddy Ward, Bobby Westerfield, Cora Glen Trogden Vincent, Ernie Goodman Baird, Anna Rae Westerfield Gray, Jean Nell Acton Goff, Minnie, unk., James Duff Miller.

1945. 1: Donnie Carnes, Donnie Wakeland, Emogene Miller. 2: Noah Phelps Jr., Olivia Craddock, Lyndon Raymond, Irene Hunter teacher.

### Hartford College, 1916 graduating class.
#### Class Roll

Geneva Brown
Leon H. Bishop
Matthew H. Benton
Ellis D. Bell
Eva Garland Butler
Evelyn Clark
Sally H. Coleman
James V. Coleman
Nancy Eliz'th Davidson
Edward Duke
Marvin Hoover
Hula Allen King
Oliver Gilmore Keown
Willie B. Lindley
Beulah May Moore
Halley Gray Maddox
Arthur Minton
J. Worden Newbolt
Mary Laura Pendleton
J. Russell Pirtle
Pearl Lee Sandefur
Charles M. Ward

Class Color:
White and Green

Class Flower:
White Rose and Fern

Class Motto:
Nunc deducemus ubi stabimus

Faculty
H. E. Brown, Superintendent
Henry Leach, Principal
Lelia Glenn

1950. 1: Virginia Schroader, Elizabeth Warren, Margaret Owens, Catherine Embry, Ruby Minton, Norma Owens. 2: Charles S. Allen, Bruce Stewart, Jerry Nemo, Billy Goodall, Bobby Goodall. 3: Floyd Schroader, Clarence William Austin, Ralph Warren, Charles Ralph, Welzie Dockery.

1942. 1: Billy Render Chinn, W. Tinsley, K. Miller, Jr. White, Noble Baize. 2: Chester Warner, A. Arbuckle, Wilodean Givens, Ruby Nell Hudson, Versie Mosley, Fred Nelson. 3: R.P. Brown teacher, Leon Barnes, C.W. Ford, Earl Bishop Jr., O.L. Shultz principal.

1944. 1: Doris Jean Phelps, Harlan B. Ford, Virginia McConnell, Victor Baize, Margaret Maddox, Roby Daugherty Jr. 2: O.L. Shultz principal, Goble McConnell, John Givens Jr., Alma Chumley, Orville Warren Jr., Robert Nelson, Zora Embry teacher.

1941 graduates, Rockport. Dorothy Burger, Virginia Wilcox, Jean Reid, Virginia Ross, June Kimmel, Dorothy Brown, Dorothy Bell Brown, John O'Brien, Bobby Tilford, Bill Bennett, Paul Bowers, Valdie Elmore, Charles Grant, D.B. Lutz teacher, Edward Crunk.

Centertown High School, Class of 1965. Back: Wayne Bullock, Gary Jackson, Ronald Smiley, unk., Doug Porter, Jerry Coppage, Shelby Burden, Frank Durham, Larry Ross, Gary Porter, Randy Swan teacher. Middle: Janetta Wilson, Gean Frances, Glendale Snodgrass, Jackie Sheffield, Ronnie Southard, Montie Graham, Phillip Bradley, Connie Burden, Barry Barnes, Roland Geary Jr., Dannie Decker, Billy Kirk. Front: Linda Givens, Ann Coffman, Donnita Gillim, Wanda Everly, Linda Owens, Martha Adams, Doris Flener, Peggy Davis, Deloris Martin, Claudia Shrull.

*1981 Kindergarten graduation, Beaver Dam Elementary. Center, Daniel Dockery.*

*1990 Headstart graduation, Beaver Dam Elementary. Center, Kristi Dockery.*

*1991 Headstart graduation, Beaver Dam Elementary. Paul Dockery.*

*Eula Rhea Wilson Barrett, May 1930, in graduation dress, Beaver Dam School.*

*Cromwell High School Seniors.*

*Dundee Senior class, 1935. 1: Mildred Roach Miles, Lily Huff?, Helen Hardesty, Ruby Quisenberry. 2: Margaret Duke Walden, Edna Neighbors Bozarth, Abby Whittingly, Dora Frances Parker, Elma Miller Harrison Wright.*

*Centertown 8th grade graduation, 1966. Wanda Daugherty, Janice Porter, Sally Allen, Ruby Barrett, Brenda (Daugherty) Dockery, Faye English, Judy Barrett.*

# CHURCHES

*Fordsville Christian Church, Sept. 1955.*

*Union Sunday School Class, Cromwell.*

*Children's Dept. Beaver Dam ME Church, 1932. Teachers: Mrs. Birkhead (Francis) Barnes, Grace Margaret Williams, Mrs. Wilsie (Blanche) Taylor, Andra Martin.*

*Christian Church and Masonic Hall, Beaver Dam.*

*Independence Baptist Church, near McHenry. Believed to be homecoming June 24, 1923. Pastor at the time, Rev. I.B. Stewart.*

*Baptist Church, Hartford.*

*Centertown Baptist Church, 1930.*

*West Providence Missionary Baptist Church.*

*Tent Revival in Williams Mines, McHenry, early 1900s.*

*Hartford Methodist Church.*

*Beaver Dam Baptist Church, Vacation Bible School, ca. 1940.*

1948. Front: Zilbia Trogden, Tommie Tinsley, Earl Ray Trogden, Joyce Tinsley, Chas. York, Curtiss Trogden, James Trogden. 2: Lynn Rowe, Damon Trogden, Ethel Trogden, Zula Trogden, Mamie Trogden holding Hettie Glenn Trogden, Cora Tinsley, Katie Clark, Leah Trogden, Josie Rowe, Gala York, Nellie Trogden, Alpha Trogden holding Willis Trogden. 3: Chesley Trogden, Cora Glenn Trogden, Ulysses Trogden, Alice Edna Trogden, Mae Condit, Ernestine Clark, Elseworth Trogden, Mabel Hoover, Sylvester Clark, Madelyn Tinsley, Royse Tinsley, Violet Harris, Lelah Ruth York, Gary Bennett, Betty York, Fielder York, Edward Trogden.

McHenry Baptist BYPU Seniors, 1928. 1: Zora Romas, Myrl Bishop, Artelia Tichenor, Versie Baize, Grace Reynolds. 2: Anna Myrl Fisher, Ainsworth Allen, Velma Langley, M.R. (Jelly) Hatley, Lucille Miller, Roy James. 3: Louise Reynolds, B.F. Hudson, Bertha Toll.

Christian Church, Hartford.

Adult class of Bible School, Beaver Dam Church of Christ, Aug. 1952. Bro Kenneth Fielder, teacher. Bertha Westerfield, unk., Ruth Burris, Dorothy Johnson, Misa, Glenna Berryman, Kenneth Fielder, Christine Fielder and son, Lena Gray Johnson, Imogene Letty, Sarah Haven.

Ricketts Church congregation, 1942,

Longview General Baptist Church, 1991.

Women of Beaver Dam Baptist Church, 1898. Sunday School class.

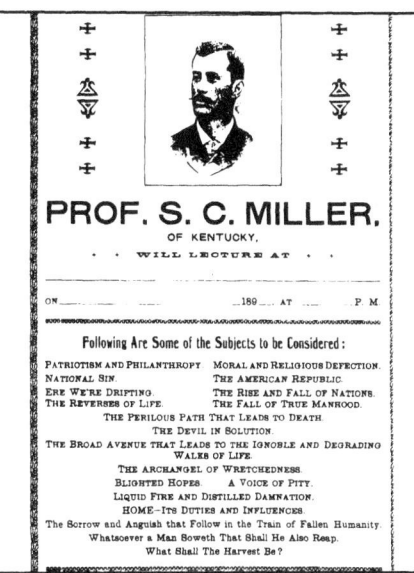
*Prof. Samuel Columbus Miller, ordained July 22, 1911, Newton Springs Baptist Church.*

*Cool Springs Baptist Church, ca. 1958.*

*Clear Run Church, 1973.*

*Ohio Co. WPA Nursery program, 1936. Bob Himes is in group.*

*Deacon Johnson in his 90s, Fordsville, 1920s.*

*Zion Baptist Church, Reynolds Station, mission group leaving to aid tornado victims in Petersburg, IN, 1990. Front: Robert Ralph, Andrew Ralph, Julie Rust, Julie Ralph, Sarah Saltsman, Jennifer Rusher, Liana Estes. Middle: Debbie Rust, Allison Rearden, Nancy Readen, Judith Ralph, Jennifer Rearden. Back: Todd Rust, Emogene Moseley.*

*"The Goat Church," Methodist Church, Dundee. Wood goat on steeple.*

*McHenry Baptist Church Christmas carolers, Dec. 1955.*

*R.L. (Les) and Susan Taylor, song leader and deacon of Bells Run Baptist Church.*

*Thanksgiving 1914 at Central Grove Church.*

*Rev. B.F. Burden, 1966.*

*Singing class, Liberty Methodist Church, 1925. Front: Mattie Taylor, Horace Taylor, Lois Black. Middle: John A. Barrett, Mabel Black, Lydia Williams, Una Stevens Leach, Cora Black, unk., Otha Birch Taylor, Ethel Royal, Ruby Royal. Back: Emma Taylor, Claude Taylor, Lee Royal?, unk., Eunice Cook, Ellis Cook, F.M. (Kip) Williams, Susie Stevens, Matt Stewart, Iva Lee, Chester Royal, Charlie Lee.*

*Friendly Boys Sunday School Class, Beaver Dam Methodist, Aug. 23, 1936. Front: Leonard Hocker, Vernie Nimmo, Charlie Stevens, W.R. Newcom, Darrell Ashby, Arvin Leisure, R.T Shields, Henry Nall Schultz, Leo Wilson, Percy Tilford. 2: Fred Hocker, Vernie Dabney, Bunyon Harreld, Mutt Crowder, Frank Barnes, Ernie Martin, Jess Blankenship, J.W. Tratt, Jess W. Smith, Harvey Sampley. 3: J.L. Carson, J.D. Renfrow, Biscoe Shown, Everett Mercer, Barney Baugh, Bart McPeak, Kyjoe McKenney, Courtland Taylor, James Hodge, Bill Ashby, Edward Taylor, Cecil Leisure, unk., Henry Haven. Back: Boyd Baugh, Ernie Baldwin, Jim Martin, Oscar Kelly, Birkhead Barnes, Granville Ingram, ___ Hoops.*

*Front: Martyne Lucas, Barbara Hodge, Anna Laura Duncan, Hazel Embry, Ruby Gaines. 2: Shirley Westerfield, Glen Vincent, Susan Brooks, Arline Leach, Emma Lou Ratcliff, Margaret Westerfield, Rae Parks, Jewell Renfrow. Back: Judy Miller, Barbara McQueen, Joan Johnson, Mitzi Chinn, Velma Lake, Madeline Tichenor, Bessie Lynn Hunley, Doris Bennett.*

*Marvins Chapel Methodist Church, early 1930s, Sunday School Class. C. Gray, Mertie Dotson, Mag Ferguson, Lillian Baker, Eva Miller, Fannie Duke, Louise Stone, unk., Louise Feemster, unk., Lucille Brown.*

*Sunday School class BDME church ca. 1950. Top: Mame D., Rhoda Havens, Carrie Greer, Mable Havens, Mattie Phelps, Sallie Renfrow, Alice Martin, Dona Martin, Effie Crowder, Bessie Hert, C. Black. Bottom: Laura K., Effie Taylor, Elizabeth Elliott, Viola Likes, Ada Vinson, Mattie Tichenor, Bertha Sandefur, Mallie Johnson.*

*Men's Bible Class, Beaver Dam Methodist Church, May 6, 1917. 1: Sam Stevens, Dick Stevens, Ernest Mathis, Byron Barnes, George Kane, Dee Barnes. 2: George R. Barnes Sr., Ben Thomas, Ed Kelley, Henry Stevens, Sam Taylor, Lee Barnes, Rev. Frank, John Pate, Dock Beard. 3: Joe Hocker, William Cooper, Ben Rummage, Sam Taylor, Rob Taylor, George Burton, Wilbur Mitchel, unk., Luther Chinn, Charlie Taylor. 4: Harvey Tichenor, unk., R.C. Hocker, John K. Barnes, Cal Neighbors, Ellis Sandefur, Sant Rogers, Elvis Smith.*

*Carol Keene, Elzie Butt, J.M. Butt, Rob Brown, John Brown. Beaver Dam Baptist Church, 1930*

*Mt. Pleasant Baptist Church, 1800s. Today, Fordsville Baptist Church.*

*Small Hous Missionary Baptist Church, Small Hous, joined Daviess Co. Association 1898.*

*Goshen Church, 1894.*

*Rockport Baptist ladies group. Front: Martine Everly and daughter, Margaret Curtis, Bonnie Blair, Pearl Rains, Gladys Reid. Others include Mable Carter, Mrs. Fulkerson, Charlene Hill, Mrs. Dozier, Addie Singleton, Evelyn Heltsley, Katherine Blackburn, Evie Rone, Carrie Devine.*

*Old Rockport Presbyterian church, burned.*

*Statty Creek Church, ca. 1922. George McMellon, Cesney Taylor McMellon, Lee Taylor Baker, Slade Taylor, Ella Stevens, Birch Shields, Talmadge Rogers. Rev. Joe B. Rogers, Emmerson Rogers, Milly Taylor Rogers, Martha Joanne Blankenship, Jimmy Lloyd Rogers, J.B. Rogers, Bernice Rogers.*

*Ethel, Rich, Richie and Damon Trogden in front of Washington Church, Hartford.*

*Hopewell Church, near Echols. Torn down, congregation out of existence.*

*Sunday School Class of Myrtle Hoskins behind old Baptist church, Rockport. Back: Jean Welborn, Sam Maple, Gloria Heltsley, Dorothy Carter. Front: Boyd Carter, unk., Coleen Hoskins. Out front: Barbara Maples.*

*Senior citizens of Pleasant Ridge Church. Sitting: Thelma Morris, Mamie Massie, Charlene Whitt. Standing, unk., Mary Ambrose, unk., Elizabeth Ford, Clora Ray Davis, Galene Jewell.*

*Taylor Mines Baptist Church that burned Oct. 1993. James and Robert Ralph.*

*Old Bethel Church, Belltown Road, Jan. 1992.*

*Goshen Church after storm in 1929. Steeple stuck into ground.*

*Fordsville Methodist Church, 1930s.*

*Barbara Daugherty, Easter 1977, Centertown Holiness Church.*

*Horse Branch Union Church, Dec. 1967.*

*Liberty United Methodist Church, est. 1850.*

*RIGHT: Ignatius Barrett, one of the founders of Liberty Methodist Church. March 30, 1802- June 23, 1884.*

*Rosine Methodist Church dates back to 1886 with first minister, R.D. Bennett.Log Cabin Preacher*

## LOG CABIN PREACHER
*By Danny Downs*

The year is 1860. The place is Ohio County, Kentucky. On a farm just north of Hartford stands a little log cabin. Inside an elderly man sits motionless in a rocker. He is William Downs, one of the first Baptist preachers and school teachers in western Kentucky. Broke and overcome with the infirmities of old age, he lives with his son's family, reflecting back on days gone by.

William was born during 1782 in a fort at Hartford. Traveling from Pennsylvania, his parents were among the first settlers in Kentucky. In 1784 the family moved to Fort Vienna (Calhoun). They lived here until 1790, when tragedy struck, William's father, Thomas Downs Sr., was killed by Indians while looking for cows that had wandered off in the wilderness. He was found in the bushes, scalped and savagely mutilated. Soon after, Mrs. Downs died.

William's seventeen-year-old brother, Thomas, Jr., was old enough to make his own way. Eight-year-old William was sent to Nelson County. Here, not far from the mouth of Knob Creek, he was placed under the care of Evan Williams. William received a fair education, professed religion, and joined the Rolling Fork Church. In 1799 he married Rachael Ashby in Muhlenburg County. She was 13 years older than he.

It was probably in the Rolling Fork Church that William was inspired to become a minister. Joshua Carman, the pastor, was an enthusiastic Emancipationist. Soon after he was baptized, William began preaching in public. He was one of the most fascinating and brilliant orators in the Kentucky pulpit in his day. Many times during his ministry, William engaged in debates. He was fond of controversy. His exceeding familiarity with the scriptures, his ready wit, keen sarcasm, and brilliant oratory attracted thousands.

William possessed such extraordinary

gifts that the church too hastily had him ordained. He had preached but a short time when he was summoned before the church. The charge was intoxication. He soon sought membership in a Separate Baptist Church to avoid the trial and was received. In 1805 Rolling Fork Church publicly excluded him and requested Salem Association to advertise him.

In 1809, William Downs formed a large church near Hodgenville called Little Mount. Among the members were Thomas and Nancy Lincoln, and their son Abraham. William would become the first to have a direct antislavery influence on Abraham. By 1810, William was composing hymns and poems for the members to sing. In 1816 he published an entire hymn book for Kentucky Christians of all denominations. Also in 1816, Abraham's teacher, Caleb Hazel, and Mary Stevens were married by William. Before the Lincolns moved to Indiana, William baptized Thomas in Knob Creek.

William dressed very shabbily. He wore a pair of course, short tow-lined pantaloons, and course cow skin shoes, without socks. He also wore an old wool hat with a piece of leather sewed in the crown.

While William lived in Hardin County, he traveled back and forth to Centertown to teach school. He instructed the students in reading, English grammar, common arithmetic, algebra, and the theory of surveying.

About the year 1828, William moved back to Ohio County and held debates with preachers of other religions, always coming away the victor. From 1829 to 1835 he pastored in Bethabara at Habit. He preached at Bell's Run from 1833 to 1839. In 1838 William built Shiloh and in 1839, Sardis. Both of these churches were built near Pleasant Ridge, Ky. In 1843 he joined the Panther Creek Association and began retirement.

William Downs died in poverty and obscurity in 1860. In remembrance to his years of service, the Kentucky Historical Society honored him with a highway marker on September 15, 1988. The marker stands at the entrance to the Ohio County Museum.

*Relocated Shiloh Baptist Church, Pleasant Ridge, 1968.*

*Laura Duncan inside relocated Shiloh Church*

*Church of God of Prophecy, McHenry, 1950.*

*Sulphur Springs Sunday School, Aug. 31, 1913*

*Oct. 19, 1902. Bertha Basham Miller Baptism, in front of Bill Tierney's house.*

# BEAVER DAM BAPTIST CHURCH

Beaver Dam Baptist Church dates her pioneer organization to March 5, 1798. Five Baptists, James Keel, Aaron Atherton, his wife Christina, John Atherton, his wife Sallie, covenanted together to labor as a church for the Master's cause. James Keel became their first Undershepherd and Aaron Atherton, the first clerk. This mother church in the Green River area was named for the nearby Beaver Dam Fork of Muddy Creek, in an area of vast wilderness. Members met in homes or barns until its first structure was built in 1807, a crude log cabin with dirt floors, heated by a fire in the center. The land where this meeting house stood was deeded to this collective body of believers on January 13, 1811, by Philip Fulkerson for the amount of fifty cents. When fire broke out in the surrounding woods, this building was destroyed in 1839.

The second building was also made of logs and stood from 1839 to 1850. It was sold and replaced with a frame structure in 1850. This third building was accidentally burned down in 1869.

James S. Coleman, Undershepherd, led its members to construct the fourth building, a frame structure in 1869. Later a bell tower was added to this structure in 1901. The first sound of organ music was heard in this structure in 1887. The first Sunday School was organized in 1872 with 20 members as services were held one Sunday a month to its membership totaling 160. Members gathered for worship as some walked, rode horseback, or came in buggies and wagons pulled by horses.

The Beaver Dam Baptist Church joined with other churches and formed the Ohio County Baptist Association in 1901, and is still a member of this association- Land lying to the north of the church was used as a public park and many social functions were held by the church and community at this site. By 1912, the membership numbered 402 and a mission was established at Taylor Mines. This mission later became the Ridgecrest Baptist Church.

The first full-time preacher was Brother C. C. Daves employed in 1920. Under his leadership the fifth house of worship was constructed of brick. The church continued a dedication to mission that was a part of its heritage. All the Baptist churches in a 50 mile radius from Beaver Darn were established by its outreaching members.

By March 7, 1948, the church membership numbered 777 as the Beaver Dam Baptist Church reached 150 years since its inception. Additional structures were added to house educational and worship space, including a sanctuary dedicated in 1973. A church building designed to strengthen Christian fellowship and physical activity was completed in 1993.

The last 31 years, Beaver Dam Baptist Church has been blessed with the consistent leadership of Dr. Glenn Armstrong. He is supported by John Cashion, Minister of Music, Doug King, Minister of Youth and Lena Romans, Minister of Education as they minister to this family numbering 901, still called His children - God's Church.

*1998, 200 years old.*

*LEFT and ABOVE: Previous versions of the Beaver Dam Baptist Church, "the Church that started Beaver Dam," according to David C. Taylor.*

*Youth choir, 1983.*

*Pastor, Glenn Armstrong.*

# BEAVER DAM UNITED METHODIST CHURCH

*The original church structure (left) was located at the corner of West Second Street and North Madison Street. It was completed in 1901. The Sunday School addition was constructed between 1915 and 1917. The original church building was in use until the current facility (right) was completed in 1952. There have been no additions to the 1952 building. However, in 1997, the congregation purchased the former West family home, located at the corner of West Third and Mulberry Streets, and are currently using the structure as a community meeting center.*

The Beaver Dam United Methodist Church began as members of nearby Methodist circuit churches felt a need to establish a church home in Beaver Dam. Early meetings were held in the homes of members. As numbers increased, preaching services were held in the large frame school building which was located where Mid-Town Plaza stands today. A Union Sunday School was also held in the same building for a time. Rev. Enoch M. Crowe and Rev. Eldred E. Pate were pastors during these years.

On March 8, 1900, a lot was purchased at the corner of Second and Broad Streets for construction of a permanent church facility. Rev. James C. Petrie was pastor when the congregation moved into the new church in 1901. A Sunday School annex was added during the 1915-1917 pastorate of Rev. W.C. Frank.

The current brick parsonage, located at 312 N. Lafayette Street, was constructed in 1948 while Rev. Marvin B. Whitmer was pastor.

In 1950-1951, during the pastorate of Rev. Fred R. Pfisterer, the congregation built a new brick structure at the corner of West Third and North Lafayette Streets. The original property was sold and the church was torn down.

In 1997, during the pastorate of Rev. Gary W. Graves, the 275 member congregation purchased the West home located behind the church at the corner of Third & Mulberry Streets. The building is currently used as a community wellness and meeting center.

### Pastors of Beaver Dam United Methodist Church
*1901 -Present*

| | | | |
|---|---|---|---|
| 1899-03: | James C. Petrie | 1943-46: | Ira R. Crenshaw |
| 1903-05: | W.T. Miller | 1946-48: | Marvin B. Whitmer |
| 1905-07: | James Lewis/Frank Baker | 1948-54: | Fred R. Pfisterer |
| 1907-09: | Virgil Elgin | 1954-55: | H.B. Hilburn |
| 1909-13: | A.L. Mell | 1955-56: | A.C. Johnson |
| 1913-15: | L.M. Russell | 1956-58: | J.T. Walker |
| 1915-17: | W.C. Frank | 1958-63: | G. Edward Henry |
| 1917-20: | E.S. Moore | 1963-67: | Owen Hoskinson |
| 1920-23: | W.S. Buckner | 1967-71: | Gene Lovell |
| 1923-24: | F. E. Lewis | 1971-76: | James Lyle |
| 1924-26: | F.D. Ryan | 1976-80: | Roy E. Clark |
| 1926-29: | M.D. Allen | 1980-85: | William Price |
| 1929-33: | F.A. Sanders | 1985-89: | Keith F. Switzer |
| 1933-36: | D.L. Vance | 1989-90: | Michael Marx |
| 1936-38: | T.J. Wade | 1990-93: | Ken Spurrier |
| 1938-39: | W.D. Milliken | 1993-97: | Carlton Puryear |
| 1939-41: | W.N. Taylor | 1997- : | Gary W. Graves |
| 1941-43: | J.R. McAfee | | |

*Ground was broken for the current parsonage in 1948 by Rev. Marvin Whitmer and Mr. Biscoe Shown (left) while members of the congregation (right) gathered for a service of celebration.*

*Rev. Fred Pfisterer, Biscoe Shown, Ross Duvall, & Ted Monte at the Cornerstone Laying Service in 1950.*

*Members of the Beaver Dam Methodist Episcopal Church Sunday School were photographed on May 6, 1917.*

# CLUBS

*Ladies Rural Club, of Washington community, Ohio County, KY, taken in 1916. Top row (left to right) Lidie Gott Casteel, Merl Lake, Cora Trogden Tinsley, Eva Renfrow Shown, Manda Smith Travis, & Willie Lake Lowe. Bottom row: Mrs. Shelby Wallace (leader of group), Katie Belle Trogden Travis, Daisy Newcom Travis, Sode Travis Casteel, Amy Lake Funk, & Mrs. Bessie Lake (mother of Amy & Willie). Sode Casteel daughter of Henry Travis & Margaret Long; Manda Travis, Katie Bell Travis & Daisy Travis, wives of Frank, Nutie & John Travis, sons of Henry Travis & Margaret Long. Taken at home of Mrs. Bessie Ashley Lake on Owensboro-Hartford Road.*

Leadership Ohio Co, Class of 1996.

Red Ribbon Lodge.

Literary Club, early 1900s.

*McHenry Homemakers Club, Christmas Party, Dec. 1955.*

*Beaver Dam Woman's Club, May 1938.*

*Rockport Glee Club, 1937. Kneeling: Adah Barnard, Francis Boswell, Mildred Elmore, Martine Stewart, Mildred Crunk, Juanita Stewart. Seated: Nadine Wood, Joan Malloy, Ruth Hicks, Jewell Bowen, Mary Wilson, Ruby Carden, Gertrude Barnard, Dorothy Park, Mary Brown. Standing: Hazel Harrel, Virginia Mabrey, Katherine Hopper, Dora Mae Fulton, Louise Maddox, Electa Barnard, Doris Tilford, Bertie Wilson.*

*Masonic meeting, Oldham Park, Beaver Dam. Gordon Chinn, Dr. W.H. Washburn, Henry Burgess, H. Dell Stevens, Buddy Bradley, Boyd Baugh, Jessie Carl Hill, Roy Baugh, Hoyt Wilson.*

*Hartford Lodge # 675.*

*Beaver Dam Woman's Club. Front: Betty Jackson, Ventia Abner, Elizabeth Keown, Mattie Young, Audra Hoxworth, Thelma Stewart, Imogene Ferguson. Back, Norma Barrett, Lena Romans, Tonja Johnson, Leola Johnson, Edna Goff, Tammy Goff, Beulah Bray, Jean Chavis, Ima Danks, Katrina Bullington.*

*Grace Chapter #37, Order of the Eastern Star, org. 1905. Present membership 126. Officers front: Janice Cook, Christine Allen, Carla Williams, Martha Patterson, C.J. Ford, Anna Bratcher. Back: Colleen Cox, Jannet Kidd, Lurlene Ford, Rodney Chinn, Ruth James, Thomas Jackson, Frances Burgess, Nancy Embry, Cynthia Woodrum.*

*McHenry Boy Scout Troop, 1949. Glen Berryman, Neil T. Ashby, Sherrill G. Ashby, Roger Gray, Danny Raymond, Owen Dale Gray, Roger Given, Hershel White.*

*Masonic Lodge walking for Will Iler's funeral.*

*Lions Club. Bottom: Maurice Martin, Marshall Barnes, Elmer Embry, Paxton Casebier, Eugene Jackson, Frank K. Casebier. Top: Dr. W.H. Washburn, Mallam Lake, Bill Spinks, unk., Porter Barnes.*

# Sports

Native of Ohio Co., William Tichenor, s/o Jack and Ruth Tichenor of Beaver Dam, was a jockey. He rode in 7,000 races, winning 812 from 1969-1975.

Central Park Basketball team, 1947-1948. Bud Allen, mgr., Back: Carroll Gray, Ralph Warren, Charles Ralph, Bobby Mann, Layman Hoskins. Front: Clemen Nance, Gene Warren, Bobby Espey, Richard Hillard, Keith Martin, Bill Leach coach.

Old team from Echols Mine.

Rockport, 2nd team, 1950. Back L.H. Harper, R.L. Goff, Don White, James Geary, Lake Saling, Wm., C.D. Givens, Woodrow Park coach. Front: Fay Fulkerson, Shirley Danks, Shirley Blair, Joyce McCoy, Clemmer Curtis, Harold Welborn.

*WKS Women's Basketball team, 1912.*

*Front: Willie Maddox, David Smith, Ray Hocker. Middle: unk., Arthur Maddox, John Austin, Ozna Shultz, unk., Noah Phelps Sr. Back: 3 unk., Monk Trail, Willie Davis, Paul Espey, Frankie Wilson, unk., ca. 1907.*

*Central Park Basketball Team. Front: Billy Watts, Chas. McDaniels, Chas. Faught, Jr. Maddox, Jack Fisher. 2: Jouette Crowe, James Wallace, Chas. Fisher, Rodney Robinson, James Albin, Ralph Chinn, Claudius Blanchard, Mutt Burden. 3: Conrad Phelps, James Blackburn, J.C. Hoskins, James Embry mgr., Wm. Reynolds, Miles Jones, O.L. Shultz. Back: Coach J.B. Garner, Pirtle Ashby, Paul Smith asst. coach, Jack Lewis, Bud Hawes, Edwin Mosley, Russell Crowe.*

*Rob Roy Basketball Team. Joseph M. Bartlett, Fielden M. Williams, Martin Porter, Alfred Westerfield or Roy Rains, Bert Davis, Jim Sandefur, Clay Leach or Roy Rains, Rob and Roy Williams, 1920-1930.*

*Hartford High School Girls Basketball Team, 1925-1926. Record 21-1. Zula Burklow, Inez Burklow, Vancyneta Travis, Alice (Henry) Triplett, Gala (Henry) Funk.*

*1965 Beaver Dam Basketball Team. Coach Jim Guess, Jim Reid, Jim Burden, John Curtis, Don Williams, Jerry Bradley, Pete Gilstrap, Johnny White, Mike Givens, Lowell Tarrant. Asst. Coach Gerald Roscoe. Bottom: Mgr. David Greene, Mike Montgomery, John Burden, Kenneth Embry, Steve Alexander, Mgr. Bruce Curtis.*

*Bruce Basketball Team, 1934 State Champs. Front: Everett Berry, Kenneth Edison, Billy Render, Nolan Finn, Nathanel Thomas, Walter Mason, Milton Taylor. Standing: Coach Jackson, Harlan Monroe, Sylvester Render, Robert Finn, Elmer Rogers, Nan Owens, C.V. Haynes.*

*HHS 1927. Donald Mitchell coach, Gala Henry, Helen Pirtle, Lena Rae Sooh, Anna Pirtle, Artie Mae Snell, Lucile Schroeter, Coxie Birkhead, Charlotte Pirtle, Betsy Duff, Cova Wilson, Mary Lou Smith, Vancyneta Travis.*

*Centertown School Freshman Team. Top: Don Brown, Charles McCulla. Middle: Kendall Render, Jerry Faith, Donny Brock, Billy Joe Boyd. J.C. Carter, coach Raymond Robinson. Cheerleaders: Adeline Render Bohler, Lou Everly, Patsy Lewis, Wanda Little Snodgrass.*

*HHS 1927. Donald Mitchell coach, Robert Barnett, Harold Haynes, Allison Beard, Bratcher Bilbro, Tipin Alford, J.C. Casebier, Edwin Davidson, Jimmie Ward, Louis Ward, Nolan Ranney.*

*Everett Nelson and Ruel Cairnes, Central Park School.*

*Grace Reynolds and Anna M. Fisher, MHS 1926.*

*Damon Trogden.*

*Dundee High School Basketball Team, 1937-1938.*

*Central Park Cheerleaders, 1948-1949. Margaret Earl Owens, Shirley Watson, Mary Lou Miller, Opal Lou Austin.*

*Orange Crush Aces: Russel Ward, Porter Hundley, Carlos Duncan, Bill Hultz, Lynn Barrett, Edward Oldham, Flop Fulkerson.*

*1937 Basketball Team. 1: Conrad Phelps, Godfrey Robinson, James Albin, Claudis Blanchard, James (Mutt) Burden. 2: O.L. Shultz principal, Bill Watts, L.R. Craddock, J.O. Wallace, Rodney Robinson, Charles R. Fisher, Buford Garner coach. Front: Reathel Wallace.*

*Beaver Dam Boys Basketball Team 1952-1953. Front: Bill Stanley, Sandy Pearl, Curtis Dement, Jack Gaither, Phillip Stewart, Doug Ashby, John A. Westerfield, Edwin Render, Bill Robinson, Bill Weedman, Jimmy Trail, Jackie Spinks. Back: Prof. Forsythe principal, Monty Leach, Bob Shown, Charles McCormick, Homer Geary, Sam Plummer, Avery Hill, Jessee Carl Hill, John Haven, Jimmy Casey, Joe Romans, Conett Bruce Austin.*

LEFT: *1924-1925 Beaver Dam Girl's Basketball Team. Back: Augusta Shaver, Coach Frances Hart Render, Thelma Arbuckle. Middle: Ruth Renfrow, Geneva Flener, Frances Stevens, Hazel Bennett. Front: Rachel Hayes McKinney, Allene Southard, Virginia McKinney Birkhead.*

*Centertown Basketball Team, 1924. Wm. Coffman, Noble Early, Alton Gillespie, Aaron Chapman.*

*Centertown Demons 6-7 Grade Team. Front: Tim Shultz, Bob Williams, Billy Garner. Back: Coach Danny Southard, Randy Park, Richard Johnston, Kenny Whitten, Bobby Scott, Joey Brown, Jeff Johnston, Chris Gaither.*

*Centertown Demons 8th Grade Team, 1974-1975. Front: Ray Daugherty, Jeff Wilkerson. Middle: Tim Daugherty, Barry Tichenor, Timmy Faith, Tommy Singleton, Benny Fray. Back: Coach Danny Southard, Chris Patton, Rodney Daugherty, David Campbell, David Geary, Danny Fleming, Joe Bishop.*

*Jimmy Tichenor, Chuck Embry, Lori Mayes, Karen Wiggins, A.V. Conway III. 2: Chris Ellen Johnson, Kerry Driskill, Sammy Knight, Mindy Martin, Chris Higdon. 3: Tony Parks, Susan Burgess, unk., Dalton Maples. Top: Teresa Myers, unk., Susie Elliott, Marty Martin, Jerry Mayes.*

*Bill Leach Baseball Field.*

*BELOW: McHenry Team, 1926.*

*Beaver Dam Basketball Team, 1945-1946. Top: Gary Coffee, Billy Martin, W.C. Peeks, Charles Reed, Earl Reed, Marvin Phelps, Clyde Danks. Middle: Maxey Martin, William Crow, Earl Davis, Eugene Leach, Ted Reed Kelley, Bobby Iler, Bobby Taylor. Bottom: Warren Hines, George Duvall, Gail Givens, Tommy Baines, Wayne Crow.*

*Ray Chapman, baseball player, killed while playing a game. Born in McHenry.*

*Centertown, 1928. Douglas Morton, Gilbert Balls, Fred Stenberg, Elvis Brown, R.C. Ashby, Eugene Morton, Fred Heflin, Walton Morton, Wid Ross, Marvin Ross.*

*Ohio County Champions. Top: Ed Whitehead, Tony Whitehead, Jimmy Tichenor, Wendell Tichenor, Carl Boyd, John Jackson, Edsell Whitton, Ralph Boyd, Frank McLain. Bottom: Ray Lyn McLain, Philip and Hoyt Kimmel, Charles Loyd, Paul Kerson, David Leach, Don Bartlett.*

*Carolyn Reneer Hopper, Wanda Little Snodgrass, Betty Roeder Maddox, Jo Carolyn Render Patton, Adeline Render Bohler.*

*Hartford, 1929. H.A. Ward, Norman Bilbro, Warden Owen, Birkhead Carter, Jakie Keith, Emmett Murphy, Amel Taul, Imon Lee Baughn, unk., Irvin White, Clifton Roe, Byron Mitchell, Chapman, Ellis Maddox Foster, William Spinks, Homer Smith.*

*Centertown. Glen Fraim, Ernest Brown, Bernard Tichenor, Lane Brown, Sonny Stewart, Kenneth Duncan, Bobby Brock, Hershel White, Ad Marlowe, Arnold Fieldon, Tony Rowe, Phillip Kimmel. Coach Bill Leach.*

*Rockport High Team, 1939-1940. Back: Charles Crane, George Boyd, Autry Duncan, Curtis Maddox, Truman Everley. Front: H.J. Kennedy, Billy Bennett, Edward Crunk, Bobby Tilford, Junior Devine.*

*Beaver Dam Cheerleaders, 1954-1955. 1: Nancy Lampson, Martha Heflin, Ora Lee Wydick. 2: Sue Young, Linda Burden, Mike Stenburg.*

1944 3rd Region Champions, Central Park School. James R. Daugherty Jr., John Givens Jr., W.O. Warren Jr., Bobby Borah, Lyndon J. Raymond, Coach Raymond Robertson.

Beaver Dam High Team, ca. 1920.

Horse Branch School Basketball team.

Rockport High Cheerleaders, 1946-1947. Coleen Hoskins, Gladys Robinson, Bette Tooley, Bobby Fulkerson, Peggy Fulkerson.

*Beaver Dam 7-8 Grade Cheerleaders. Linda Burden, Carolyn Ashby, Sue Young, Martha Heflin.*

*Fordsville High School Varsity, 1965-66. Front: Coach Carroll Harrison, Jerry Coppage, Cletas Greer, Steve Phillips, Phillip Johnson, Donnie Davis, Coach Dan Chapman. Back: Sherwood Kirk, James McGrew, Bill Freer, Joe Johnson, Alan Tucker, Doug Rearden, Eddy Young.*

Ohio County High School Basketball Team.

# Map of Downtown Beaver Dam

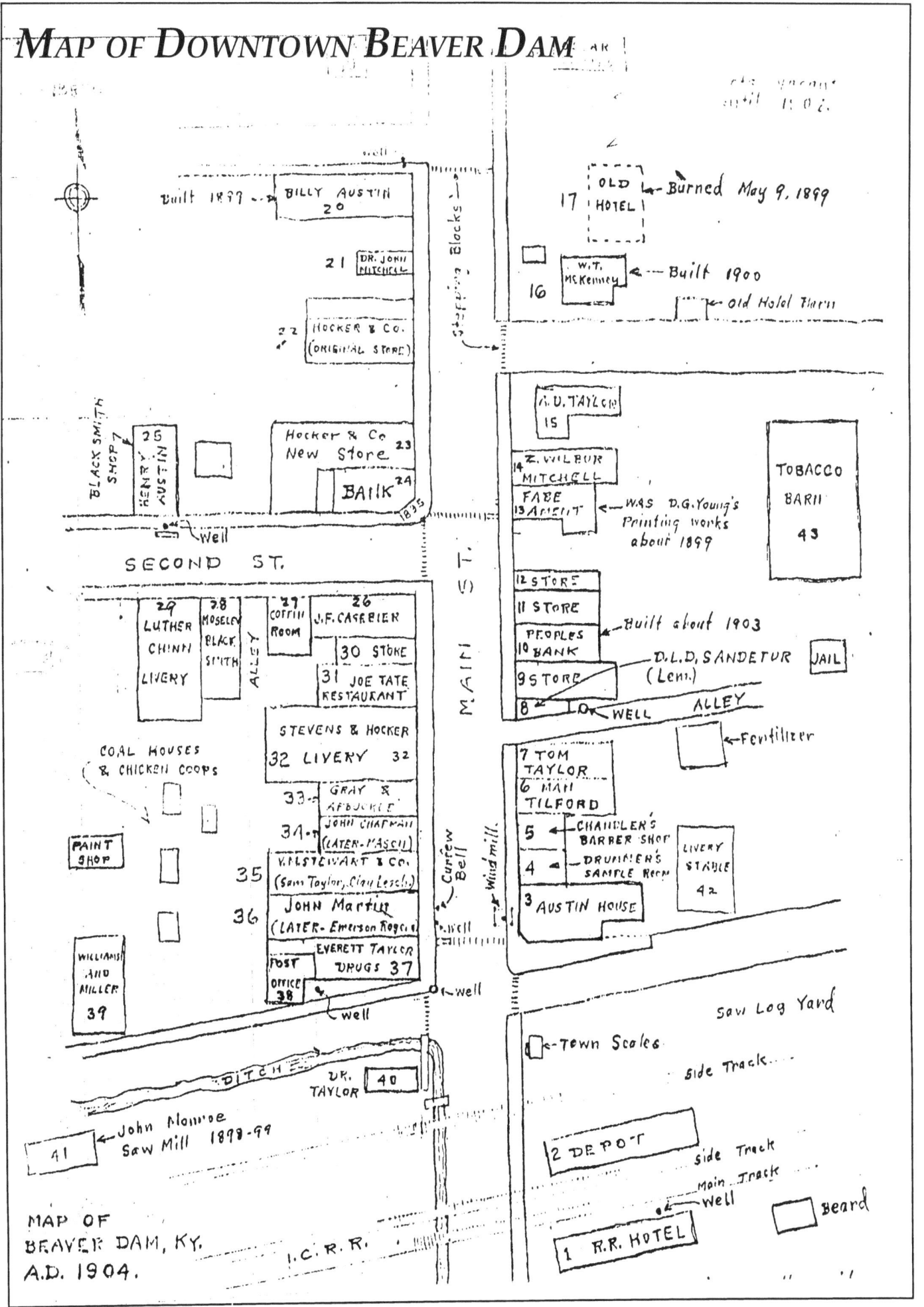

# Post Offices

*Percipial Aurthine Swain married Willie Angle, first postmaster of Prentiss.*

*Beaver Dam Post Office employees, June 1952. Glena Cooper, Kelly Kane, Verna Patton, Geneva Williams, Postmaster Ernest M. Martin.*

*Echols Post Office.*

*Vada L. Stagner, Rosine Postmaster to 1996.*

*Green River Post Office, 1912, Chiggerville, KY.*

*Fordsville Post Office, ca. 1900, between Main St. and Harl Funeral Home.*

*McHenry Post Office and McHenry Coal Co. Store, 1890.*

*Beaver Dam Post Office Employees in remodeled building. Verna Patton, Geneva Williams, Postmaster Ernest M. Martin, Glena Cooper, Kelly Kane.*

*Beaver Dam Post Office employees, June 1952. Geneva Williams, Postmaster Ernest M. Martin, Glena Cooper, Verna Patton.*

*Mail boat "Leona," next to last one.*

*Richard Harlan Taylor and M. Effie Swain. First rural mail carrier, 1905, Beaver Dam, and first agent for Standard Oil in county.*

# HISTORY OF ROSINE POST OFFICE
*by: Wendell Allen*

*Rosine Post Office and Barber Shop.*

In two short years after the arrival of the Elizabethtown and Paducah railroad in 1870, a post office was established as Pigeon Roost that would become known as Rosine. The name Pigeon Roost came about, story has it, because of large flocks of Pigeons roosting in the cedar trees that grew up the new railroad line toward the tunnel and east end of Front Street that would become the business section of the new settlement carved from a vast timberland soon to emerge as a railroad "boom town" and mercantile center. As the settlement grew into a bonafide city, Col. Henry D. McHenry, businessman and legislator, saw the need for plans to develop the town and he set out to map boundaries, lots, streets and a new name.

The post office was established on January 16, 1872, would be renamed "Rosine" on June 10, 1873. There are any number of stories for whom, by whom, and why, the name "Rosine" was chosen but most agree the new name was chosen for the town founder's wife, Jenny Taylor or McHenry, a native of Hardinsburg, Breckenridge County, who was the author of many articles and poetry, writing under the pen name of "Rosine" and published in the Louisville paper, predecessor, the Courier-Journal. A book of her poems titled, "Forget Me Not", can be found in the Waterson Collection in the Louisville Library at 4th and York Streets.

The first postmaster for Rosine (Pigeon Roost) was G. B. Van Nort, January 16, 1872. Mr. Van Nort also operated the Van Nort Hotel that stood next to the railway station later becoming the Summit Hotel. The first post office building historians believe was located on Front Street, the business sector. On August 1, 1900, fire swept through the entire block of the businesses along Front Street from McHenry to McLeod destroying all but the Post Office. Water from the public well on Front Street was used to fight the fire, saving the post office. Thomas Allen was postmaster (1897-1910). Through the years since 1872, it is known that the post office operated in six sites other than Front Street location. In 1910 Logan Crowder was Rosine postmaster and the office site was located on McLeod Street near the present home of Oval and Irene Swift. Walter Earp, cousin of the infamous lawman, Wyatt Earp, was named postmaster in 1914-1918, and the post office was at the corner of Front and McLeod streets across from Andy Alford's store, said Dorothy Crowder Gary. In 1918, Nora Kessenger became postmaster serving until 1926 and the office was operated from the Kessenger home near the corner of I st and McHenry streets next to the present Rosine Community Park according to Golda Johnson Ruby. In 1926, Logan P. Crowder's daughter, Mayme Crowder Embry became postmaster at the building on McLeod Street next to Frank Lindsey's mill. One side was the barber shop where Willis Peach was barber and the other side, the post office. They were across the street from Dr. Theodore Dunes office. The post office was still there in 1935 said Loretta Leach Allen. Later located to the corner of Front and McHenry in the grocery store operated by Mrs. Embry and husband, L. L. Embry. Mrs. Embry served 24 years as postmaster, longest of any officer, next was Boyce Taylor, 23 years (1950-1973) who succeeded Mrs. Embry. Mail first reached Rosine by horse and rider and by stage coach. The stage coach line preceeded the railroad. Coming of the railroad meant mail would arrive by train. Twice a day, morning and afternoon, mail arrived to the depot and from there transported to the post office that was within a block of the station, most likely, carried by the postmaster. In 1932, Loney Crowder was the Illinois Central Railway depot agent when the station closed, and until 1936 when he went to work at the IC LaSalle Street Station in Chicago, he carried the mail to, and from, the post office. He, at the south end of the passenger platform, would place the mail bag on a big metal arm, for a mechanical device from the train's mail car to grab in passing as a person in the mail car tossed a mail bag off. This method continued until 1958 when all rail passenger service of the Illinois Central Railroad was discontinued. Three other men carried mail from the depot to the post office from 1936 to 1958. Orville Embry, who also did clock and watch repair, Rollo Stewart and last Jimmy Collard. In 1950 when Boyce Taylor was appointed postmaster, the office was located in the former Rosine Cream Station located in front of the Rosine Barn Jamboree building. Later, to a building which still stands between the Jamboree and former Woosley's Grocery, before moving it to its present site on Highway #62.

During the past one hundred and twenty-five years (1872 - 1997) of service, seventeen postmasters and three officer-in-charge have served. According to the U. S. Postal Service, the name Rosine is the only post office in America. The Rosine post mark has reached all corners of the globe with request of the cancellation mark numbering in the hundreds,, as Rosine being home to the Father of Bluegrass Music, Bill Monroe and the "Home of Bluegrass Music".

Note: Information for this story came from Rosine residents and U.S. Postal Service, Washington, D.C.

*The Ohio County Postal Customer council. organized in 1996, is made up of the Postmaster and one representative from each of the 12 areas in the county. Pictured are: bottom row: Esther Paxton, Suzie Renfrow, Wilda Hardesty, Wanda Watson, Paula Taylor, Pat Burch, June Greenwell. Top row: Marlene Morris, Kenny Crowe, Delbert Rice, Glen Sears, Bob Ballard, Bob Clark, Rose Wieder.*

## BEAVER DAM POST OFFICE

| NAME | TITLE | DATE APPOINTED |
|---|---|---|
| James S. Coleman | Postmaster | 04/10/1852 |
| Henry W. Harris | Postmaster | 01/20/1853 |
| Elijah G. Williams | Postmaster | 04/28/1853 |
| Parmenus Hocker | Postmaster | 01/22/1861 |
| Elisha H. Coleman | Postmaster | 02/10/1863 |
| Owen M. Barber | Postmaster | 01/08/1875 |
| William H. Murrell | Postmaster | 03/14/1876 |
| Weaver H. Barnes | Postmaster | 09/25/1876 |
| Ignatius P. Barnard | Postmaster | 05/09/1878 |
| George W. Cooper | Postmaster | 04/08/1879 |
| John B. Bir | Postmaster | O6/15/1883 |
| Thomas J. Stevens | Postmaster | 05/05/1885 |
| John H. Nave | Postmaster | 11/02/188G |
| William T. Austin | Postmaster | 10/13/1887 |
| William H. Blankenship | Postmaster | 04/24/1889 |
| Emma Barnes | Postmaster | 06/03/1893 |
| Henry C. Leach | Postmaster | 05/14/1897 |
| Richard C. Jarnagin | Postmaster | 04/25/1901 |
| Jacob D. Williams | Postmaster | 01/12/1903 |
| Everett P. Taylor | Postmaster | 03/24/1908 |
| Otho Dexter | Postmaster | 07/14/1916 |
| Edith Porter | Acting Postmaster | 01/01/1918 |
| Edith Porter | Postmaster | 10/03/1918 |
| James A. Leach | Postmaster | 02/05/1923 |
| Ernest Martin | Acting Postmaster | 11/16/1933 |
| Thomas E. Cooper | Postmaster | 05/12/1934 |
| Miss Verna L. Patton | Acting Postmaster | 06/30/1949 |
| Ernest M. Martin | Postmaster | 05/15/1950 |
| Mrs. Bertha Schroader | Acting Postmaster | 10/31/1956 |
| Kermit W. Cook | Postmaster | 07/03/1958 |
| Jesse C. Neal | Officer-In-Charge | 02/26/1983 |
| Michael J. Pyfferson | Officer-In-Charge | 05/28/1983 |
| Patricia F. Paxton | Postmaster | 06/25/1983 |
| Paul Embry | Officer-In-Charge | 08/26/1993 |
| Lee Taylor | Officer-In-Charge | 10/25/1993 |
| Robert W. Clark | Postmaster | 02/19/1994 |

*Kermit W. Cook, served as postmaster for more than 25 years.*

*Kermit Cook and Charles Black.*

*Hartford Post Office.*

*Last Echols Post Office.*

*Present Rosine Post Office.*

*New Centertown Post Office, 1988.*

*Old Centertown Post Office, before 1965, white building.*

BELOW: Ben Woods and Ras Smith on mail boat "The Daisy" after 1917.

*Present Horse Branch Post Office.*

## HORSE BRANCH

Horse Branch Unique in the fact it is the only town with a post office by that name. The exact date that horse branch was first called by that name is not know. Hallie Duncan said it was called by this name in 1868 when her father, Elmer Miller, was born. However, there are several theories of how horse branch got its name: some say a horse fell in a branch, or a horse drowned in quicksand while crossing a branch, or a doctor who was going on a house call had a horse fall into a branch and drown. From the records of the Illinois Central railroad office in Chicago, Illinois comes the most logical and believable theory. Their files state that years ago there was a stage-coach that went from Owensboro to Bowling Green which made a stop in horse branch to get fresh horses. The passengers on the stage coach occasionally stayed overnight here. The horses which were used to run the stage were kept in a corral by the branchthus the name Horse Branch.

The first house built in Horse Branch, located in the southwest corner of Horse Branch. This house was built by Makel Miller who lived there until the railroad was built. He moved to another house on the old cane run road to avoid the noise of the trains. This house was also the first post office of Horse Branch, which was started in 1871, and Makel Miller was the first postmaster.

*Copied in book by David Russell Sandefur entitled Footsteps to Follow*

# CARLOS B. EMBRY

**THE CHUCK EMBRY FAMILY**
Shown from left to right: C. B. "Brock" Embry IV, C. B. "Chuck" Embry III, Darlena Embry and Meredith Embry. The Embry's live in Beaver Dam.

**THE ROY WEST FAMILY**
Laura Ann (Embry) West, Roy West and twins April and Dale West. The West family live near Centertown.

John and Barbara Ann (Embry) Jordan. The Jordans live in Carrollton, Kentucky.

Shown above in this 1940's photo are Jane and Morgan Dougherty (on left) and Rev. Marion A. & Lola Embry. The Dougherty's were the foster parents of Zora Romans Embry, living first in Flint Springs, and later in Cromwell. The Embry's were the parents of Carlos B. Embry, Sr. Rev. M. A. Embry was the teacher at Baizetown School and the pastor at the New Zion Missionary Baptist Church (Baizetown) for many years and was a member of the Ohio County Fiscal Court when the present Ohio County Courthouse was built in 1941.

Shown above are Thilbert Finn (left) and C. B. Embry, Jr., at the Embry home in Beaver Dam in 1944. 45 years later Embry was serving as Ohio County Judge/Executive and Finn was his Deputy Judge/Executive.

**MRS. WANDA LOU (RALPH) EMBRY**

Mrs. Embry was born Nov. 15, 1942 in East Chicago, Indiana, the daughter of the late Cecil Bert Ralph and Lucille Trail Ralph. She graduated from Beaver Dam High School in 1960 and attended Bowling Green Business College. On August 25, 1962 she married C. B. Embry, Jr. and is the mother of Mrs. Laura Ann West, Mrs. Barbara Ann Jordan and C. B. "Chuck" Embry, III. She is the past president of the Sunshine Homemakers, past vice president of the Beaver Dam PTA, served two terms as state secretary of the Kentucky Young Republican Federation and was a member of the Beaver Dam Parks & Recreation Commission. In 1973 she was named the "Outstanding Young Republican Woman in Kentucky." She is presently vice president of the the Bowling Green East Camp Auxiliary of Gideons International. She serves as Policy and Procedure Officer for the multi-state law firm of Hughes & Coleman.

**CARLOS B. EMBRY, SR. 1906-1974**

Carlos B. Embry, Sr. was the son of the late Rev. Marion A. and Lola Albin Embry, of the Baizetown community. After graduation from Western Kentucky University at age 19, he served as Principal of a junior high in Bulloch County, Georgia, and of Lynnville High School, in White Mills, Kentucky. The founded the Ohio County Messenger in Beaver Dam in 1930 at the age of 24. At one time his Embry Newspapers, Inc. included seven weekly publications in western Kentucky. Embry served as State Senator for the 10th District 1946-49. While in the senate he led the effort to establish a school of medicine and surgery at the University of Kentucky. Speaking from the floor of the senate he pointed out that the new medical school would be the best way to produce more doctors for the rural areas of Kentucky. He became interested in real estate and developed Ohio County's first shopping in 1955, Embry's Valley Shopping Center in north Beaver Dam. His deep interest in the American Indian led to his book "American Concentration Camps - The Facts About Our Indian Reservations Today", published by McKay of New York in 1956. Embry married the late Zora Romans Embry in 1940. His son, C. B. Embry, Jr., served as Beaver Dam's Mayor and as Ohio County Judge/Executive. His daughter, Mrs. Jane Carroll Hardwick, of Louisville, is a retired teacher.

**ZORA ROMANS EMBRY 1907-1997**

Zora R. Embry was the daughter of the late Richard D. and Ora Haven Romans, of the Flint Springs community. She was reared by foster parents, the late Morgan and Jane Doughterty, of the same community. Mrs. Embry served as vice president and director of The Embry Newspapers, Inc. (Ohio County Messenger) for over 40 years, starting in 1944. She was a teacher at Central Park High School 1932-44 and was Principal of Pleasant Ridge Elementary School 1959- Mrs. Embry was a past president of the Beaver Dam Women's Club and the 20th Century Club, and served as First District Governor of the Kentucky Federation of Women's Clubs in 1954-55. She was past president of the Beaver Dam PTA and was second vice president of the Kentucky PTA. Mrs. Embry also served as treasurer of the Kentucky Federation of Republican Women's Clubs. She married Carlos B. Embry, Sr. in 1940 and lived in Beaver Dam, all but one year, until her death. Her son, C. B. Embry, Jr., served as Mayor of Beaver Dam and three terms as Ohio County Judge/Executive.

**MARY BELLE SMITH 1905-1990**

Miss Mary Belle Smith was the daughter of the late Dr. George H. Angie Plummer Smith. Dr. Smith was a well-known British cancer doctor. Miss Smith served as assistant business manager for the Ohio County Messenger for over 50 years. She was employed by the Messenger in 1933, after seven years as a teacher in the Ohio County School System. She was instrumental in getting street markers for the City of Beaver Dam. A long-time member of the Beaver Dam High Alumni Association, she served as their secretary twice.

**C. B. EMBRY, JR.**

C. B. Embry, Jr. was born in Louisville, Kentucky July 29, 1941 the son of the late Carlos B. Embry, Sr. and Zora Romans Embry. After graduation from Western Kentucky University in 1963 he became editor of the Ohio County Messenger, a post he held for 25 years. Embry served as Mayor of the City of Beaver Dam 1970-73, Ohio County Judge 1974-77 and Ohio County Judge/Executive 1982-89. He is the youngest person ever elected as Beaver Dam's Mayor and as Ohio County Judge. Embry is past president of the Beaver Dam High Alumni Association, Beaver Dam Jaycees, Lions Club, PTA and Little League. He was three times named Beaver Dam's Outstanding Young Man by the local Jaycees. Embry served two terms each as State Treasurer of the Republican Party, Chairman of the Kentucky Young Republican Federation and as Chairman of the Green River Area Development District. In 1975 he was named "The Outstanding Young Republican in the Nation" at a national convention in Atlanta, Georgia, the award being presented by the Honorable George Bush. He presently serves as General Manager of the regional law firm of Hughes & Coleman. Embry married Wanda Lou Ralph in 1962 and they presently live in Bowling Green, Kentucky. Their three children are Mrs. Laura Ann West, Mrs. Barbara Ann Jordon and C. B. "Chuck" Embry, III.

# IN MEMORY OF STOY LEE GEARY

That name might not mean much to some of you, but to his family and friends, he was our strength.

He was the kind of person who gave without question and asked for nothing in return. Stoy was born, February 28,1934 in Horton, Kentucky. He lived most of his life in Rosine, Kentucky. His parents were Vernie and Lizzie Geary-, but was raised by Granny (Arlona Geary.) He was the youngest of four children, brother and sisters are Roy Geary, (des.), Jewell (Geary) Crumes, (des.) and Leaner (Geary) Wallace.

Joyce E. (Mitchell) Geary was his beloved wife for 44 years. They were married January 16,1953. Stoy and Joyce had four children: Ronald Herbert, Steven Wayne, Drucilla Ann and Cynthia Lee. They have ten grandchildren and one great grandchild.

Stoy received his license to preach, April 20,1961 and ordained deacon, May 28, 1964. After ten years of active service, he retired, but was always willing to volunteer his help if a church needed a pastor for a short time. He also performed numerous marriage ceremonies including his children and nieces, nephews and started on his grandchildren. He was also deputy sheriff and county detective in the 70's and 80's. Stoy made Kentucky Colonel, July 25,1990 presented by Kirk Brandenberger.

He was a very big Bluegrass Music fan and promoter. Bill Monroe and Stoy were very close friends. He hosted several Bluegrass Festivals in Rosine and Hartford as fund raisers for the fire dept. Stoy was a member of the Rosine Original Bluegrass Music Association and the International Bluegrass Music Association. He was also involved in the festivals at the Ohio County Park and Owensboro. Being a retired Methodist Minister, he loved gospel music. We can still hear him singing "Amazing Grace" while he walked down the hall or working in the garden.

Stoy -was founder and chief of Rosine Volunteer Fire Department for more than 15 years. He loved the Fire Dept. and the work that went with it. He was always willing to help anyone he could, in fact he died in the line of duty at a house fire January 14,1997 a very cold and icy morning, due to a massive heart attack. He passed on doing what he loved -to do best, helping others.

*Sept. 12, 1996, Stoy L. Geary inside the Rosine Fire Department.*

*Stoy's father, Vernon Geary.*

*Stoy's mother, Lizzie Geary.*

*Granny Geary.*

*Bill Monroe and Stoy.*

*Stoy, Jewell Geary Crumes, Leaner Geary Wallace, Roy Geary.*

*Stoy and Joyce's children. Ronnie, Steve, Drucilla, Cindy*

*1991, Kirk Brandenburg, Stoy, Don Hayes, Rosine Bluegrass Festival*

*Rosine fire truck, 1997.*

*Stoy in fire truck.*

*Stoy's grandson Jimmy Blacklock with watermelons, summer 1993.*

*Stoy, De McCurry and son Ronnie at Bill Monroe Funeral, Sept. 12, 1996.*

*Stoy, Ricky, and Sharon Skaggs at Bill Monroe's funeral.*

*Leon Burns, Stoy, Bertha (Bill Monroe's sister), Norman Howard at Rosine Bluegrass Festival.*

*Monument for Stoy L. Geary.*

# In Memory of
# C.W. (Lum) and Dessie Spinks Gray (Grey)

who were married in Ohio County on
November 5, 1903

Their deceased children are:
Hattie—1908-1909
Violet—1921-1935
Otha—1910-1949
Georgia—1907-1985
Claudie—1913-1994

Their remaining children:
Delbert
Hazel

*Lum and Dessie*

*Lum and Dessie, wed 64 years.*

*Violet*

Prepared and submitted by
Carrol & Oreva Grey

# In Memory of
## Dessie (Spinks), Lum, Essie (Haven), Otha, Oreva Billie (Evans), Mam & Dad, Carrol, Cheri and Barry E. Grey

Four Generations
Contributed by Oreva Grey

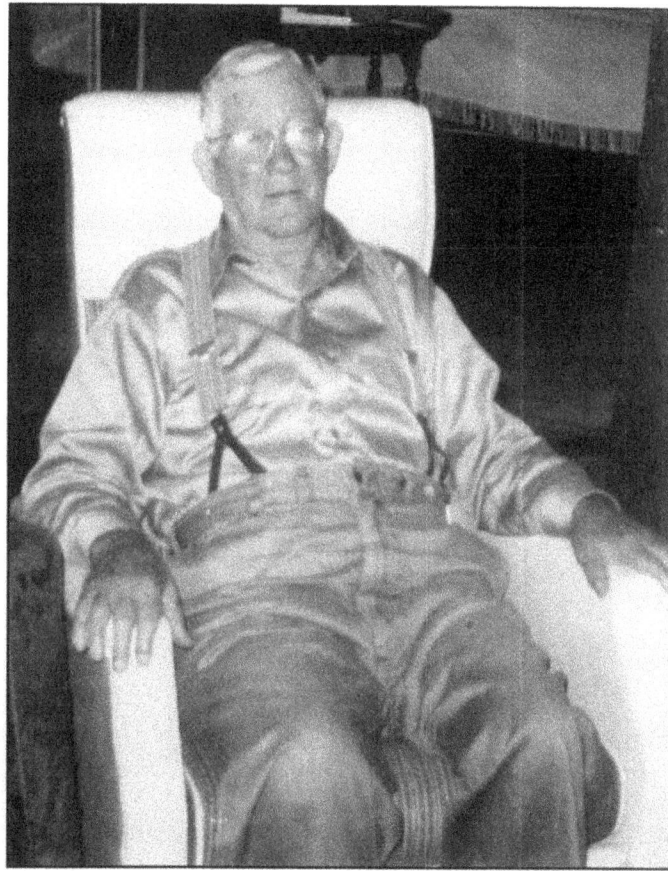

# JACKSON FAMILY

Mary Jane Jackson.

Sara Jackson-Maine.

Elizabeth Anne Jackson Burgess.

Mr. and Mrs. Thomas L. Jackson.

Mary Lane Jackson.

Thomas L. Jackson.

Dr. Elizabeth J. Burgess, Mark and Jordan.

Sara Jackson Maine, Miss Ohio Co., 1981.

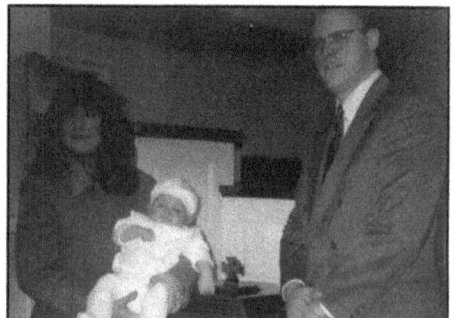
Sara J. and Wesley Maine and Asa Wesley.

# Tribute to
## Dona Rock Martin 1887-1968
## Thomas Crittenden Martin 1889-1935

Parents of
Mrs. Grethel Martin Stanley 1909-1989
and Mrs. Audra Martin Sprigg 1907-.

I am thankful for Christian parents, will cherish their teaching always, miss them more than words can say.

Daughter

*Audra Martin Sprigg, March 19, 1997. 90th birthday celebrated with Mr. and Mrs. Bill Stanley, Mr. and Mrs. Brad Stanley, Tyler Stanley, Mr. and Mrs. Charles G. Harrison, Mrs. Earl Reid, Mrs. Cleo Burden, Mary Taylor, and Mr. and Mrs. Ray Potter.*

# The Old Mobberly House

One of the oldest homes in Ohio County is the home of Mary Elizabeth Williams Young on Easton Road north of Fordsville. She and her sister, Margaret, were born in the house and she is the sixth generation to live here since the house was built around 1818.

John G. Mobberly bought the land in 1817 and built the house with help of slaves. There were two sides of the house - Mobberly side and slaves side with an adjoining hallway where wood was stored. A fireplace on each side of the house would hold 3'x18" logs. Under the exterior are large logs - some 53" long. One must go into the attic on both sides of the house to view the logs. Now bricked in with an insert for burning coal. The house has been upgraded to gas heat.

John G. Mobberly and his wife, Martha (Patsey) Hardin Mobberly were the parents of seven children - four of whom were born here. Patsey died in 1829 and is buried in the Wells Cemetery along with their son, Remus, who died in 1847.

In 1832, John G. Mobberly married Nancy Haynes who helped raise the children who were then ages 5-21. John G. and Nancy sold and/or quit claimed all their land and the home to their daughter, Delila, and her husband, Bradford Whitler in 1853 and moved to Daviess County, Ky.

Delila and Bradford Whitler had nine children. During the Civil war, soldiers would ride through their land on the way from Paducah to Mammoth Caves where gun powder was stored. If the soldiers had a lame horse they would leave it and take one of the Whitler horses. The soldiers would pay Mrs. Whitler in gold coins for the meals she prepared for them.

A railroad crossed the land and one time a "shister" was caught trying to blow up bridges. He was hung on a railroad trestle near their home.

Bradford Whitler died at the age 76 on July 9, 1887. Delila H. Whitler died November 2, 1887, at the age of 62, both are buried in the Whitler Cemetery on the property, along with others in the family.

On October 6, 1887, the Whitler children and their Mother, Delila, gave some of the land to their sister and daughter, Mary E. Lanum. Also on this date, part of the land was purchased by heirs. Mary and her husband, Quinton, had 4 children. Quinton died September 28, 1905. In 1909 Mary sold the property to E.S. Dunn with the agreement that she "holds possession of one room of the dwelling house, the North room of the main building, now known as the family room." Mr. and Mrs. Dunn would furnish "board at his table of wholesome diet." Mary Lanum was to "live as one of the family as they have been living for the past 18 months." Mary Lanum died December 12, 1912.

Ed Dunn and Delila Lanum were the fourth generation of the farm. Delila Dunn died in 1941. Ed Dunn continued to live on the farm where he died 1956. In 1929, Terell and his wife Pearl, who was the daughter of Annie Lanum, who came to live on the farm with Ed Dunn. The Williams were the fifth generation. They had two daughters, Mary Elizabeth Williams Young and Margaret Ann Williams Coffield. Margaret Ann died in 1983. Mary Elizabeth, who is the surviving Williams, moved to the farm in 1991, and is the sixth generation and is living there at present. Pearl Williams died in 1984 and Terrell Williams died in 1992 at age 91.

*The Mobberly house generations ago.*

*The Mobberly house, 1992.*

*John C. and Patsey Mobberly.*

*Ollie Cobb and Arch Lain driving hearse in 1800s.*

*Mary Young and Terrell Williams.*

*Delila M. Lanum Dunn, Ed Dunn, and Pearl Lain Williams.*

# Newcom Family

The family of Robert Renfrow and Becky Shown. The children are Belva, Ellis, and Lyman. Robert died in 1918 with influenza. Bessie married Clarence Patton in 1920 and they had one son, Sterlin, who is the only survivor and lives in Owensboro.

Aubrey Newcom and Belva Renfrow were married Nov. 6, 1920 (above) and were parents of 11 children. One son died in infancy. Seven sons and three daughters grew to adulthood (below).

The William F. Newcom family of the Washington Community. Front: Ruby, William, Tracy, Mary, Martha (Mattie), and Ruth. Back: Georgia, Ercel, Virgie, and Aubrey. Photo prior to 1917. Robbie was born in 1917, and is the only one surviving. She lives in Troy, MI.

Seated, Harold, Mary, Ray, and Everett. Standing, Virginia, Lawrence, Pearl, Ken, Shirley, and Max. The oldest son, Harold, died in 1994. Mary, Ray, Ken, Paul, and Lawrence now reside in Ohio County.

# Tribute to Greg Phelps

50th wedding anniversary, Oct. 1970, Noah and Lillian Phelps. Front: Lucille P. Kelly, Noah Sr., Lillian B. Phelps, Doris J. Haynes. Back: Conrad M. Phelps, Natomi Raywood, Noah Jr. The Phelps operated Phelps Grocery in McHenry 1941-1967.

Phelps Family Reunion, 1978, at central Park School, McHenry

Dec. 12, 1954, marriage of Noah Phelps Jr., and Anna Jane Taylor.

Debbie Monroe Phelps and Paul K. Phelps, June 10, 1978.

Gregory Dale Phelps, b. April 13, 1959, son of Mr. and Mrs. Noah Phelps, graduate of Ohio Co. High School, Western Kentucky University, and Cincinnati Conservatory of Music. He was a professional entertainer, a member of Actors Equity and Screen Actors Guild. He Died on December 12, 1989.

Conrad M. Phelps, McHenry, 1943-1946 USA. Deceased in 1995.

Retirement party Dec. 27, 1992 for Noah Phelps Jr. after 45 years in banking. Top: Debbie, Jordan, Paul, Branscott, and Renee Phelps. Bottom: Nicolas, Tyler, Janie, Noah Jr., and Nathan Phelps.

Lillian Beck Phelps, age 95, 1992.

# H.B. Stanley, Incorporated

Founded H.B. Stanley in 1941

*In Memory of Grethel Martin Stanley, 1909-1989.*

*In Memory of Martha Harrison Crawford, 1955-1995*

*In Memory of Henry Bradley Stanley, 1908-1991.*

*Bill, Brad and Tyler Stanley.*

*Martha Harrison Crawford, Mary Jo Stanley Harrison, Bill Stanley*

*Lisa, Tyler, Brad, Bill, Pat, Mary Jo, Charles, Martha, and Bobby.*

# MEMORIAL
# ALVIN L. TATE
*Aug. 7, 1924-Oct. 17, 1989*
*By Wanda (Rowe) Tate*

*Beaver Dam Police Dept., Oct. 1978. Alvin Tate, Bill Phelps, Off. Burr.*

*Chief Alvin L. Tate, 1973.*

*Chief Tate, Jan. 11, 1982, wedding anniversary, holding hat wife Wanda had bronzed for him*

(Captions left to right, by row.)

*Mr. and Mrs. Alvin Tate, 1982.*

*Wanda Rowe Tate at Ohio Co. Sheriff's Office, 1973, as dispatcher.*

*Lt. Alvin Tate, Chief Bill Phelps.*

*Wanda Rowe Tate and Bill Monroe, July 1975.*

*Back Helen (Rowe) Newton, Juanita Wright. Front: Patsy Newton, Linda Rowe, Wanda Rowe, Dorothy Rowe.*

*Vitula Ann Blanchard, Retha Blanchard, 1916.*

*Wanda Rowe Tate and father, Holley Floyd Rowe.*

*Cecil Byron Martin WWII veteran.*

He was originally, from Cloverport, resided in Ohio County from 1966-1989. He served as, a, police officer in Louisville until 1948. He served in the Air Force, where he retired in March 16, 1966. While he was in the military, he fought in World War II and Vietnam, he served about 23 years in the Military. He worked with Sheriff Lawrence Westerfield as a Chief Deputy, Ohio County Jail 1986-1987, he was Chief of Police at Beaver Dam from 1981-1985. He married Wanda Rowe on January 11, 1973.

He was a member of the Centertown Baptist Church.

# Myrl Taylor, Jr.

Myrl Taylor, Jr. was killed in WWII on Leyte island. 1920-1944.

Warren Taylor, a farmer from Cromwell, 1848-1938, father of Myrl Taylor Sr.

Myrl Taylor Sr., Cromwell, with his small children on a sled and his team of horses, 1940.

Myrl Taylor Sr., 1899-1980. Virginia Sandefur Taylor, 1903-1991. Feb. 1970, 50th Wedding Anniversary.

# WALLACE-WITHROW FAMILY

*Hugh and Elizabeth (Wallace) Withrow celebrated their 50th wedding anniversary January 28, 1994 with a dinner-dance in Lufkin, TX with more than 100 friends and relatives in attendance, hosted by their three children, Shelby, Ray, beth, and grandaughter Shannon Withrow. The Withrows are formally from Centertown, KY.*

*Back: Victoria Barnard, Mayworth Barnard, Charlotte Wallace Barnard, 3 unk., Mabel Ward, Mary Catherine Wallace Ward, Dillis Ward, Monty Barnard, Ina Wallace Barnard. Middle: Hannah Wallace, Beatrice Wallace, William Cleo Wallace, Omar Thomas Wallace, Elton Williams Wallace, Nellie Lee Wallace, Deliah Wallace Pirtle, John Franklin Wallace, Clara Wallace, Lillie Ann Royal Wallace, Shelby Franklin Wallace holding John Wesley Wallace. Front: Clarice Ward, Clarence or Charles Barnard, Violet Barnard, Charles or Clarence Barnard, John Ward, Bertha Ward, Etta Wallace, Willie Pirtle, Clyde H. Wallace, Ivy Wallace, Irene Ward. On Floor: Jimmy Pirtle, Ernie Wallace, Henry Curry Wallace, Mary Pirtle (Deliah).*

*Lonnie Morton Hatcher family. Baby in picture is Ann Wallace Mason, daughter of Mr. and Mrs. Clyde Wallace on Nannie Hatcher's 21st birthday, Mar 27, 1921.*

*Wedding pictures and vase. Left: Clyde H. Wallace and Nannie Elizabeth Hatcher, m. May 26, 1919. Right: Lonnie Morton Hatcher and Martha Elizabeth Williams, m. 1886. Vase was a wedding gift to Lonnie and Mattie Hatcher from S.W. Anderwon who owned a store at Cervalvo, and later in Owensboro.*

*Nell Wallace Burgess and Ruth Wallace Whitely, double cousins, 1997, after Nell's 95th birthday.*

# In Memory of
# The Warrens

*Everett E. Warren*

*Dona Morris Warren*

EVERETT E. WARREN
DONA MORRIS WARREN
JAMES LOGAN WARREN
WILLIAM O. WARREN,
EVERETT A. "RED" WARREN

*Living Children of Dona and Everett*
M. EVELYN WARREN RAGLAND
M. ELIZABETH WARREN MOSELEY

*James Logan Warren*

*William O. Warren*

*Everett A. "Red" Warren*

*M. Evelyn Warren Ragland and M. Elizabeth Warren Moseley*

**JAMES LOGAN WARREN**, b. July 5, 1917. Graduated McHenry High School and attended Bowling Green Teachers College for one year. 1936 m. Opal Butler; five children—Sue C. James E., Edward E., Patricia L., and John L. He was well known as a song leader in churches of Christ in Ohio and Butler counties. He died Dec. 15, 1960.

**WILLIAM ODDEST WARREN**, b. February 6, 1920, near Warren's Mill. Graduated from McHenry High School and served in US Army in Europe during WWII. He married Julia Buza in New York City, September 29, 1944; two daughters Cynthia Jo and Dona Debra. He received his Bachelors and Masters degrees from Western Kentucky State Collete and was an educator in Ohio County. He was serving as principal at Horse Brance High School when he was killed in a tractor-automobile accident july 4, 1956.

**EVERETT "RED" WARREN**, b. in Ohio Co. in 1926. Graduated from McHenry High School. served in Germany after WWII. He received an undergraduate degree from Western Kentucky State College, a masters degree in mathematics from Iowa State college, and did graduate work at Purdue University, the University of Minnesota and george Peabody University. He married Shelda Jacobson in 1960; one daughter, Dona. He taught at Moorhead State University, Moorhead, MN from 1960 until his death in 1973.

*Elizabeth Moseley, Jimmie Warren, and Evelyn Ragland*

## In Memory of
# THE WARRENS

*Bill Warren.*

*Pansy Warren*

**WILLIAM ORVILLE WARREN**
**LULA MORRIS WARREN**
**PANSY MAURENE WARREN**
**WILLIAM ORVILLE "BILL" WARREN**

*Living*
**GENEVA ROSS**
**GENE WARREN**
**RALPH MORRIS WARREN**

*Gene, Bill, and Ralph Warren.*

**BILL WARREN**, b. Aug. 14, 1926, McHenry; d. 1996. Education: Central Park High School 1944; Western Kentucky University, AB-MA-Rank 1, 1950-1970. Occupation: Teacher and coach for 30 year at Cromwell, Calhoun, Butler Co., Ft. Knox.

**PANSY WARREN**, b. Nov. 2, 1915; d. April 30, 1995. Education: Central Park High School; Western Kentucky University, AB-MA-Rank 1. Occupation: Teacher at Horse Branch, Rockport, Valley High school.

*Ralph, Gene, Claudean, and Teresa Wright, Bill and Pansy Warren.*

# Tribute to
# C. T. (Benny) Young

C. T. Young became a part of the history of Beaver Dam, when he was born there on November 30, 1909, to his parents, D.G and Eva Young. He attended Beaver Dam School and during high school, he played the character of "Benny" in a play. This became his nickname for the remainder of his life. He was President of the Beaver Dam High School Class 1927. He continued his education at Western University of Kentucky and Bowling Green Business College.

Young Hardware Co., located on North Main Street in Beaver Dam, became his first business venture in 1930. It continues to be an active downtown business, selling hardware and household furnishings. His basement workshop at his home on 522 South Main Street in Beaver Dam, was where he developed his unique porch swing design. Continuing his wood products interest he founded Young Manufacturing Co. on South Main Street in Beaver Dam in 1946. He manufactured oak sills, thresholds and risers and was President of this Corporation. Its continued growth and expansion has become an important source of revenue and employment to Beaver Dam residents. An addition to his success as an entrepeneur in the wood industry, was his creation and ownership of Young Sawmill in South Beaver Dam.

C.T. Young married Mattie Oglesby in 1936, and they had three children, Sue Hitchell, Connie Hoskins, and Robert Young. He was a member of the Beaver Dam Methodist Church and devoted Father. His love of the outdoor life led to many hunting and boating trips. He was a charter member of the Beaver Dam Lions Club and was actively involved in civic and professional organizations in his community and state.

His last challenge in the wood industry was the acquisition of a 126 acre farm in 1990. His goal was to develop a show place that demonstrated multiple resource conservation at the Young Tree Farm. His outstanding stewardship and forest management earned him the 1992 Master Conservationist Award by the Ohio County Conservation District and the 1993 Kentucky Tree Farmer of the Year.

With his trademark Colonel Sanders tie, C.T. Young remained a vital resident of Beaver Dam until his death on July 24, 1995.

*Submitted by:*
*Connie Hoskins - daughter*

*C.T. (Benny) Young.*

*Sign for Young's Sawmill, Hwy 231S, Beaver Dam.*

*The Young Family. Back: Sue Hitchell, Connie Hoskins, Robert Henry Young, C.T. (Benny) Young. Front: Mattie Elizabeth Oglesby Young.*

*Young, 1993 KY tree farmer of the year.*

*Mattie (Oglesby) Young trophy for Strawberry festival 1933, and picture 1934 Miss Ohio Co. pageant.*

*Reading blueprints with son, Robert.*

*With Robert at new structure.*

*Plaque in memory of Young on his tree farm, Beaver Dam.*

# Render

Lou and Raymond Render, Centertown, owned and operated Blue Bus Cafe and Barber Shop, 1942. They specialized in hamburgers and lemonade. During WWII everyone had ration stamps for sugar, gas, and a number of things. Lou used all her sugar stamps for lemonade, and some of her mother's stamps, too.

They moved to Louisville so Raymond could work in the ship yard. Robert Lee and Sylvia Durham took the cafe and then in a few years it closed and was used to strip tobacco.

JoCarolyn Patton and Greta Whitehead. The Render sisters began singing at ages 7 and 8 with their dad, Raymond Render on guitar. They would also sing at Walton's Creek Baptist Church with Elizabeth Hoover at the piano. They were on WOMI radio in Owensboro with preacher Maurice Davies. When WWII was over they sang at the court house in Hartford. Songs included "When Johnny Comes Marching Home," "White Cliffs of Dover," and "There's a Star Spangled Banner Waving Somewhere." They would go to Mose Ragers' barber shop in Drakesboro and sing shile Mose and their father played guitar. One of their favorite songs was "Keep Your Chin Up" written by their mother, Louverine. JoCarolyn and Greta have been singing together for 58 years and have sung at nearly 200 funeral services, still harmonizing together with their soprano and alto voices. Bottom: Raymond Render and Lote Tichenor.

Lou and Raymond Render.

Ed Whitehead, Otha Dodson, Clarence Morris, Jasper Whitehead, Cleve Heflin in tobacco warehouse, 1964, formerly the Blue Bus Cafe and Barber Shop.

Nancy Elizabeth (Cook) Taylor, Anna Mariah (Williams) Taylor, Myron Hoy Taylor, Horace Leslie Taylor, Lilburn Blackstone Taylor holding Lilburn Blackstone Jr., Claude Liles Taylor holding Louise Williams Taylor, Emma Elizabeth (Liles) Taylor, Robert Lee Taylor.

# BANK OF OHIO COUNTY

The Bank of Dundee was organized in 1922 by a group of citizens for the purpose of serving the financial needs of the community. It was one of only a few banks in the state which continued to pay dividends during the depression. The main office of the bank has occupied three structures in Dundee. With an expanded customer base and more mobile society, the bank name was changed in 1990 to the Bank of Ohio County. A branch was located in Beaver Dam in 1991 and facilities were expanded in 1993 to include a busy supermarket location in Houchen's Grocery. Three ATM machines have also increased the availability and convenience of banking services. The Bank of Ohio County has it's roots in Ohio County and retains it's Independent Community Bank status reinvesting Ohio Countian's funds in the the economy of local citizens.

### PRESIDENTS OF THE BANK OF OHIO COUNTY
*FORMERLY BANK OF DUNDEE*

R.P. McDowell
S.P. McDowell
Dr. J.A. Duff
C.C. King
J.J. Turner
Percy Landrum
Jon A. Lawson

# THE HISTORY OF BEAVER DAM

*By C. B. Embry, Jr.*

Over 200 years ago early settlers, Daniel Boone among them, passed through or near the present site of the City of Beaver Dam. It was Martin Kohlmann (German spelling version which later ancestors changed to the English spelling of Coleman) who first built a home for his family and located them on a farm near Beaver Dam Creek.

Kohlmann found a rich fertile valley. At the foot of the Southern slope and through the lowland was a creek inhabited by many beavers. Several dams had been constructed by the industrious little animals. Kohlmann named the creek "Beaver Dam Creek" and located his home and farm nearby in 1795.

In 1798 a church was built at the top of the slope by Elder James Kiel, John Atherton and his wife, Sally, and Aaron Atherton and his wife, Christina. The church was named the Beaver Dam Baptist Church.

Kentucky became a state in 1792 and Ohio County only had a population of 1,223 in 1800. The Beaver Dam Community continued to grow slowly but got a boost following the earthquakes of 1811-12.

In 1852 a post office was established and Elisha Coleman (English spelling) was named postmaster. The population of the Beaver Dam area was 55 in 1855.

It was the coming of the railroad that changed the Beaver Dam community from one of the small communities in Ohio County into a town. A town that would later become the largest city in Ohio County.

In 1871 Beaver Dam had its first doctors. They were John J. Mitchell, his brother, Dr. George F. Mitchell and Dr. William J. Berry.

A city government was formed in 1873 and Beaver Dam became officially a sixth class city. Under that form of city government, the town was governed by a Board of Trustees. The first members of the Town Board were J. Austin, A. L. Chick, Owen Barber and William Austin.

There were 55 houses in Beaver Dam in 1895, as the town continued its growth. In 1900, south Beaver Dam was annexed to the City, adding 125 people to the population. Beaver Dam's population now approached 1,000.

In 1926, Beaver Dam was named a Fifth Class City. J. T. Casebier was elected the cities' first Mayor. In 1930 Latna Oldham became the cities' third Mayor and held that position for 28 years to become the longest serving Mayor in the history of this city.

In 1932, the Strawberry Festival was founded in Beaver Dam. It was recognized as one of the largest events in the county at that time. They held parades, gave away prizes, held games as well as many other activities. It was noted that over 500 acres of strawberries was being grown and they expected the crop to bring in close to $100,000.00. This was a tremendous amount of money at that time, especially during the depression.

In 1940 Beaver Dam's population was 1,161. In 1955, street and mail delivery was started.

The current Officers are: **Mayor** - David C. Taylor, **Commissioners** - Robert Cox, Dwight Westerfield, Charles Patton, and Gerry (Rip) Wright. **City Clerk** - Brenda Dockery and **City Treasurer** - Lois Geary, **City Superintendent** - Larry Carter and **Water/Wastewater Superintendent** - Kevin Bradley.

While Royal Crown Bottling Company, Cowden Manufacturing and Thomas Industries, as well as others has played a major part in the past industrial history of Beaver Dam, many companies continue to make Beaver Dam a strong industrial center. Today, such companies as American Fabri-Tec, Inc., BF1 Medical Waste Systems, Nationwide Lure Manufacturing Company, Neo Industries, Nestaway, Young Manufacturing Company and Young Sawmill continue to present a strong work force in the city.

There are four major shopping areas in the city. Besides the down-town area, the Mid-Town Plaza developed by Hayward Spinks and is located on the former property of the Beaver Dam High School; the former Embry Valley Shopping Center developed by the late Carlos B. Embry, Sr. and the Walmart Shopping Center located on the extreme north corner of the city.

## SCENES FROM THE BEAVER DAM BICENTENNIAL 1998

*Miss Strawberry Queens—Mattie Oglesby Young, 1933, and Sarah Neal, 1998. Their trophies in inset.*

# CITY OF BEAVER DAM

Beaver Dam City Hall, Police Department, and Fire Station, 309 West Second Street.

The Welcome to Beaver Dam Sign, Hwy. 231 North and South.

City Commission, 1998. Dwight Westerfield, Robert Cox, Mayor David C. Taylor, Charles Patton, Gerry "Rip" Wright.

City Government Week, Beaver Dam, 1998. Commissioners Cox, Westerfield, and Wright instruct children from Beaver Dam Elementary about City Government in City Hall.

Beaver Dam City Police Force: Chief Gene Gaither, past officers Deannie Minton and R.L. Goff, present officers James Burke, Lt. Don Beemer, Kenny Wright. Not pictured Leroy Embry, Chris Shephard.

Beaver Dam Volunteer Fire Dept. Front: Chief Jerry Shephard, Courtney Reisz, John Gaither, Jeremy Nance, Paul Shephard. Back: Dwight Westerfield, Nancy Miller, Jimmy Duke, Chris Shephard, Ralph Miller, Roger Burgess.

City employees hard at work. Larry Carter, Dudley Casteel, Ben Bard.

Ms. Lois Geary, treasurer.

Rodger Burgess and Joe Bennett, city employees.

Clerk Brenda Dockery.

Ms. Amy Puckett.

# Beaver Dam Deposit Bank

## A Kentucky Tradition

*Downtown—274-9654*
*Owensboro—684-0044*
*Northside—274-6150*

In 1890 a group came together and chartered Beaver Dam Deposit Bank. In the heart of the Western Kentucky coalfields, the bank grew by providing quick, friendly service, meeting the financial needs of families throughout the community.

A lot of things have changed since we first opened our doors. Coal is no longer king as different employers are now calling this region home. From poultry to manufacturing, this diversity constantly adds strength and stability to our economic climate. Banking has changed, too. Merger and acquisition have transferred much decision making authority to corporate headquarters in other cities and states.

Some things, however, have remained constant, solid and strong. As we progress into our second century, Beaver Dam Deposit Bank is still an independent, community bank. Decisions regarding our growing customer base are made right here, quickly, with a special touch the corporations caught up in being bigger and bigger just can't deliver.

With our loan center in Bowling Green and full service offices in Owensboro and Ohio County, folks are continuously discovering just how good a banking relationship can still be. Meanwhile, in Ohio County we're serving fifth and sixth generations who simply expect and receive the best banking service available anywhere.

Down through the years, we have adopted the motto, "None will serve you better, few as well." It's very true. Independence, strength and the best service available - this and more awaits you at Beaver Dam Deposit Bank. We're ready to work for you. After all, it's tradition.

# BFI MEDICAL SERVICES

BFI Kentucky Medical Services is one of the most technologically advanced medical waste treatment facilities in the eastern United States. It is owned by BFI Waste Systems of North America, Incorporated of Houston, Texas. The facility sets on seven enclosed acres in the rolling hills of Ohio County in western Kentucky and has been providing safe and reliable medical waste treatment and disposal services to our customers since 1991.

The 25,000 square foot autoclave facility is capable of treating and disposing of your medical waste, safely and effectively, both now and far into the future. Our facility operates three steam injected autoclaves, secondary back-up systems for steam generation, automated process controllers, and a state-of-the-art material handling system, allowing the processing capability of over 70 tons per day with minimal downtime. We have incorporated these secondary systems to assure your medical waste is treated and disposed of in a timely manner with the utmost respect for safety and efficiency.

Waste is received seven days per week with facility operations to process the waste continuing 24 hours per day. We have thousands of customers from a fourteen state area that utilize our services. From major metropolitan hospitals to suburban clinics to rural physicians, BFI Beaver Dam is committed to "cradle to grave" regulatory compliance for every customer we serve.

We have installed security measures such as warning fences, natural barriers, and secured entrances to our facility to prevent access of any unauthorized personnel. Radiation defectors have been installed at the processing area to monitor every container received for treatment.

Every employee at BFI - Beaver Dam goes through an extensive health assessment program, both before and during their employment with BFI. All employees are thoroughly trained in health and safety programs to ensure their on-the-job safety.

BFI - Beaver Dam has the capability of handling many different types of medical waste containers. Three box sizes, reusable waste tubs, and 150 gallon wheeled carts are just a sample of the various containers offered by your local BFI collection company.

BFI operates the nation's largest network of medical waste treatment facilities and offers broad based support in hygiene, safety, engineering transformation, regulatory activities and environmental affairs. Look to the leader for all your medical waste needs. We welcome you to visit our facility to see for yourself how we work to protect you.

## BFI MEDICAL SERVICES
### ONE TECHNOLOGY PLACE
### BEAVER DAM, KENTUCKY 42320

# COMMONWEALTH COMMUNITY BANK

Commonwealth Community Bank Inc. was chartered on July 2, 1928. The original name was Hartford Deposit Bank. The bank later changed its name to The Hartford Bank and Trust Company, and continued to operate under that name until May, 1994. At that time, the name was changed to Commonwealth Community Bank Inc. to better reflect our entire countywide presence.

In June, 1967 the bank acquired Farmers Bank in Centertown. It continues to operate as a branch today. In August, 1994 Commonwealth Community Bank acquired The Bank of Fordsville. We serve that area as a full service branch. Bob's IGA Supermarket Branch was opened in November, 1996. That branch provides extended hours to better serve our customers.

This bank is proud to be locally owned and operated. Our Board of Directors consists of: Gary W. Miller, President and CEO; Victoria Anderson, Chairman of the Board; James H. Higginbotham, Vice-Chairman; Billy W. Luttrell, Executive Vice-President; Roily Tichenor; Hugh Smaltz; Robert Higdon; and Andy Alan Anderson. Some of the past presidents are: Andy Anderson, Doyle Crenshaw, and James H. Higginbotham.

We are especially proud that our institution was rated one of the best in the nation by Sheshunoff Information Services, a highly respected bank rating service. This was for the period ending December 31, 1997. We will be included in the publication of SHESHUNOFF HIGHEST RATED BANKS AND S&LS IN AMERICA.

Commonwealth Community Bank appreciates the support our customers have given us through the years. We are committed to providing the best customer service available.

# WILLIAM L. DANKS FUNERAL HOME

An article written by Dorothy Gentry in September 18,1986, stated that the Home was once owned by Thomas H. Faught in 1895-1899, and considered to be the oldest home in Beaver Dam. Mrs. D. Lee Barnes wrote once about the Funeral Home and stated that two of the rooms that were in the original house are still there. According to Mrs. H. Kenneth Birkhead, it had been modernized, had electricity and furnace and once was one of the few houses in town with water and bath. The place had a well and its own electric system. The property again changed ownership when Hubert and Thelma Myers became owners on March 8,1948. They kept it only until April 1, 1951 when Erwin Casebier and his wife, Annabelle, purchased it and converted it into a funeral home. William L. Danks served as funeral director and embalmer with Erwin Casebier Funeral Home for seven years and purchased it on April 1,1966. The name was then changed to William L. Danks Funeral Home. The home was extensively remodeled in 1972 and a chapel with a church-like atmosphere was added. Jeffrey Danks joined his parents in 1979 and is now in charge of caring for and preparing the deceased. He is secretary of the corporation. Also employed by the funeral home is Pat Gilstrap, Jerry Crowe and Chris Burns. William L. Danks is a past president of the Funeral Directors Association of Kentucky and presently is a director of the Kentucky Funeral Directors.

# DUKE-BEVIL BROS. FUNERAL HOMES, INC.

## CENTERTOWN-HARTFORD
## KENTUCKY

Duke-Bevil Bros. Funeral Homes, Inc. originally was the Birkhead Funeral Home in Hartford. It was started around 1914 by Ernest Birkhead. After his death Kenneth & Virginia Birkhead (Ernest's son & daughter-in-law) took over the operation. Birkhead Funeral Home sold to Haley-McGinnis Funeral Home in Owensboro in 1961.

The funeral home then was sold to Duke Funeral Homes, Inc. in 1966. This firm consisted of Hugh E. Duke, Sr., Hugh E. Duke, Jr., an I. B. Duke. The Duke Funeral Home was started in 1915 by Edgar F. Duke in Dundee. When Edgar Duke died in 1956 Hugh E. Duke, Sr. Took over the business. Along with his sons (Hugh E. Duke, jr. & Thomas B. Duke) Mr. Duke opened a funeral home in Centertown in 1962. In 1966 they purchased the Birkhead Funeral Home from Haley-Mcginnis Funeral Home in Hartford. The Duke family kept the three funeral homes until 1980, at which time they closed the Dundee Funeral Home & in 1986 they sold the funeral homes in Centertown & Hartford to Larry & Kathy, Jerry & Judy, David & Cydnee Bevil. The name then became Duke-Bevil bros. Funeral Homes, Inc. In 1989 the Bevil bros. added a monument business to their funeral home. This was & is the only locally owned & operated monument business in Ohio County.

# MILLER-SCHAPMIRE FUNERAL HOME

The Miller-Schapmire Funeral Home, located on Walnut Street in Hartford, KY, was founded in 1966 by D.M. Miller, Jr. and Daniel M. Schapmire, along with their wives, Elizabeth Ann Miller and Suzanne E. Schapmire. The property was formerly known as the Benton-Felix home and is believed to have been constructed in 1849.

Although major additions and improvements have been completed, there have been no structural changes of the original homestead since it was converted to a funeral home. The home, with its original flooring and I 0-foot ceilings, is also enhanced by an antique staircase with a hand carved railing as well as a large wood sliding door that separates the front hall from the parlor.

Another unique feature of the home is a prismatic superstructure which extends above the roofline on the east side. The cupola, which was perhaps once used as a vault, has three circular windows and exposes the original handmade scalloped gingerbread shingles.

Since acquiring the historic home in 1966, a large chapel, private office, entryway and lounge have been added which were all designed with the comfort of the families we serve in mind.

Having served Ohio County for over 32 years, the owners and funeral directors at Miller-Schapmire Funeral Home believe their success is based on their reputation for integrity and for their personal care during a family's time of need.

*Prior to 1966.*

*1966.*

*Present.*

# OHIO COUNTY CHAMBER OF COMMERCE

Hwy 69 & Clay Street
HARTFORD, KY 42347
(502) 298-3551

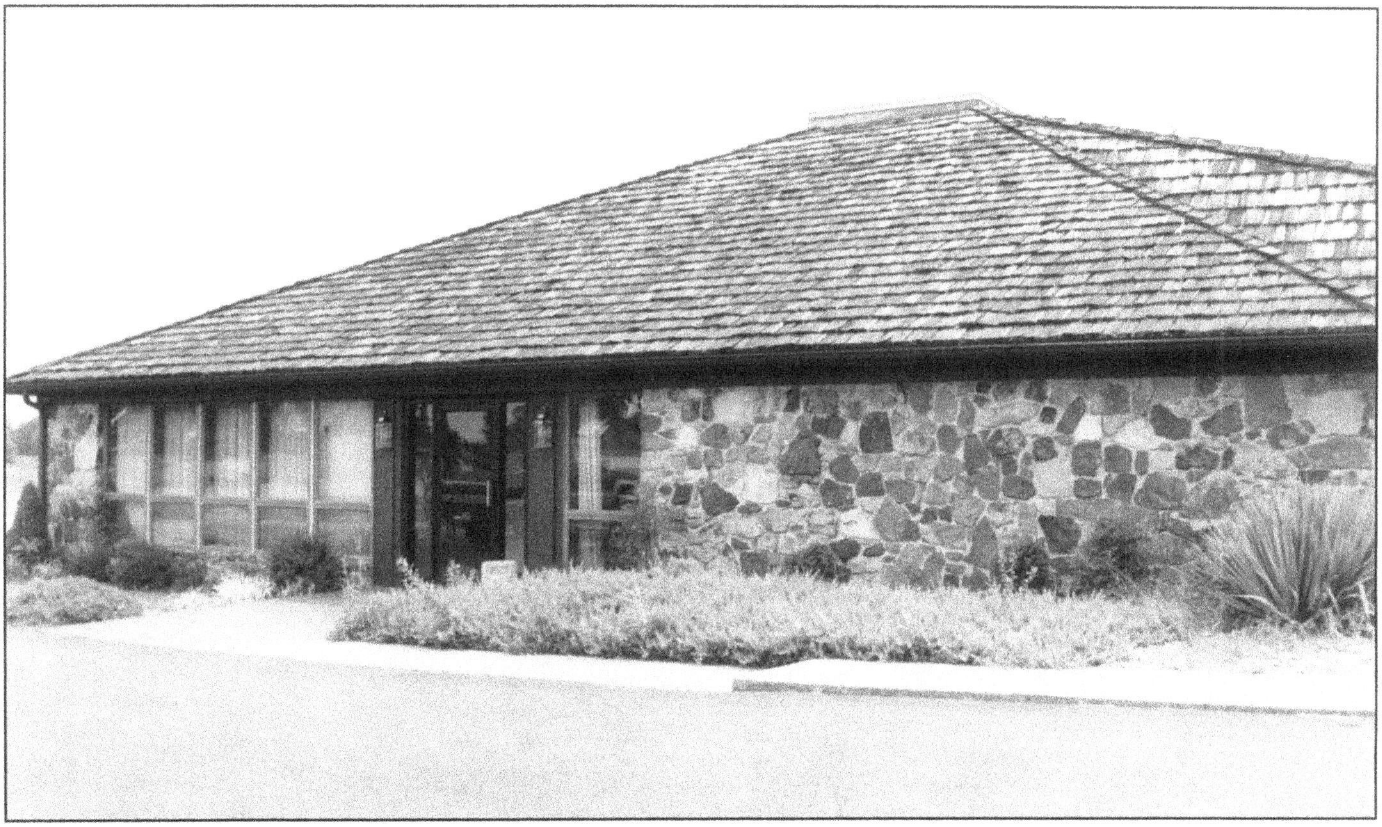

The mission of the Ohio County Chamber of Commerce is to lead in the enhancement and maintenance of a favorable business climate, and serve as an advocate to promote economic well being, quality of life, growth, and community development for Ohio County and the region.

# OHIO COUNTY COURTHOUSE

Ohio County's third courthouse, erected 1865-1867 on the square, on the site of the one burned in Dec. 1864 by Gen. H.B. Lyon "as a military necessity."

Sheriff's Dept. 1906-1910. Front: S.A. Bratcher sheriff 1916, Harriett Flener, Ransom B. Martin sheriff. Back: Wade Martin, W.C. Ashley, Grant Pollard.

## COUNTY OFFICIALS—1998

COUNTY JUDGE/EXECUTIVE
Dudley Cooper

COUNTY ATTORNEY
E. Glenn Miller

SHERIFF
Elvis Doolin

COUNTY CLERK
Lessie R. Johnson

PROPERTY VALUATION
Emma Geary

CIRCUIT CLERK
Gaynell Allen

COMMONWEALTH *ATTORNEY*
Greg Seelig

OHIO COUNTY JAILER
Darrell "Shotty" Curtis

OHIO COUNTY CORONER
Larry Bevil

MAGISTRATE DISTRICT #1
Dwight Smith

MAGISTRATE DISTRICT #2
Dorothy P. Bennett

MAGISTRATE DISTRICT #3
David Jones

MAGISTRATE DISTRICT #4
Larry Keown

MAGISTRATE DISTRICT #5
Billy R. Burden

## ABOUT OHIO COUNTY

Ohio County, formed in 1798 as the 35th county in Kentucky was carved from an outlying section of Hardin. When formed, it extended all the way to the Ohio River, from where its name was derived. It has been able to retain a sizeable portion (596 square miles) of its territory to rank 5th in size among Kentucky's 120 counties. Bordering counties include Daviess, Hancock, Breckinridge, Grayson, Butler, Muhlenberg and McLean.

*Old Fort Hartford*, located on Rough River, was established in 1782. The name *Hartford*, was said to have come from the Rough River ford (hard ford), used by deer and other animals. Hartford is the county seat. The courthouse at Hartford is Ohio County's fourth. The first one constructed in 1799, was made of log. It was the Jail and Hall of Justice. According to the marker in the courtyard, it collapsed in 1813, and its logs used to build a bon-fire in celebration of Perry's victory on Lake Erie. A brick courthouse built in 1813, was one of seven in the area burned by Confederates. General Hylan G. Lyon yielded to the request by Dr. Samuel O. Peyton to save the records of the courthouse before burning it.

Landmarks around Hartford include old Hartford Academy plus the home of the pioneer carpenter and contractor, Charles Wallace, who built Ohio County's first two courthouses.

### The First County Court

The first county court was organized on the second of July, 1799, by the following gentlemen who were commissioned by Governor James Garrard. They were sworn and took their seats as justice of the peace: Jesse Cravens, Stephen Cleaver, Harrison Taylor, David Glenn, Robert Barnett, and Christopher Jackson; and the court was fully organized by the appointment of William Rowan, clerk and Stephen Statler, Sheriff.

*Present Day Courthouse.*

*Fiscal Court 1939. Bottom: Clifton Black court clerk, Otto Martin county attorney, Lon Ralph county judge, J.J. Blankenship, Jess Johnson. Top: John Chapman, Jess Smith, Herman Render, Orville Craig, M.A. Embry, Ches Tichenor.*

*Ohio County Courthouse in the 1920s.*

# OHIO COUNTY HOSPITAL

1956

1981

## A HISTORY OF CARING

The dream of a medical facility for Ohio County became a reality in 1936. A 12 patient clinic was built by Dr. Marion O. Crowder on the corner of Center Street and Apple Alley in Hartford. In 1953, a bond issue to finance a hospital was approved by voters, construction began in 1955. Ohio County Hospital opened its 30 bed-facility in September, 1956 on land donated by Hartford businessman Leslie B. Carden. Since that time, the hospital has undergone several major construction and renovation projects to keep pace with the changing needs of area residents.

Today, Ohio County Hospital is a progressive 68 bed, acute care facility. A broad range of medical, surgical and ancillary services are available with the latest in medical technology and expertise. Our history is providing the care you need, close to home.

1211 Main Street
Hartford, Kentucky 42347
(502) 298-7411

*caring for your health*

# OHIO COUNTY PUBLIC LIBRARY

## HISTORY OF THE OHIO COUNTY PUBLIC LIBRARY
*"Building Knowledge for the 21st Century"*

The Ohio County Public Library was created in 1937. Each town in the county was asked to send a Works Project Administration worker into Hartford to work on a rural library project. The library that was established in Hartford was first housed in Hartford High School, services included pick up and delivery of materials that were collected by the W.P.A. workers. In the future, the library was to be housed in several buildings, including a tool shed.

In 1942, the W.P.A. asked the Hartford Women's Club to take over the administration of the tool shed library. The group agreed and began raising money for the library through rummage sales and contributions. The city of Hartford donated $13.00 per month for library operations. Materials were obtained through a traveling library provided by the Library Extension of the Kentucky State Department of Libraries.

The library received its first bookmobile in 1954, as a memorial from a patron, the Ohio County School Board agreed to appropriate funds to operate the Bookmobile. The Bookmobile route was developed by the county health nurse.

In 1962, plans were presented to the Hartford City Council, the Ohio County Board of Education, and the Ohio County Fiscal Court to establish a regional library. Ohio County would be the headquarters for six other counties The library would be funded through taxes.

In 1965, the library applied for funds under the Library Services and Construction Act to build a new library. The library received $82,511 in federal matching funds. The total cost of construction was $104,720. The new Ohio County Public Library was dedicated on October 15, 1965.

Thirty years later, Library Trustees launched a fundraising campaign for an addition to the building. In March, 1996, the Ohio County Public Library was awarded a $300,000 construction grant from the Kentucky Department for Libraries and Archives. In October, 1996, the library began construction on a two-story addition to the existing facility. In the summer of 1997, the addition was complete, however, the old side had to be remodeled in order to tie the two sides together. In October, 1997, ribbon cutting ceremonies dedicated the entire new building to library services for the citizens of Ohio County.

*Ohio County Public Library Groundbreaking Ceremony 1997. Judge Dudley Cooper, David Bevil, Melissa Acquaviva, Betty Jackson.*

# WILLIAMS HARDWARE

The business, started by J.D. Williams in 1891, began as a blacksmith and machinery shop on the corner of First and Main Streets with a post office in the back of the building. His sons, J.R. and J.M., joined him and after their f fathers' death in 1918 added hardware. They built the present building beside Beaver Dam Bank in 1927. In 1939, J.M. bought into the B.D. Planing Mill Go. JR Williams, sole owner then, renamed the store JR Williams Hardware. After failing health, JR sold his business to his brothers-in-law, Carl & Henry McKenney, Glendon Stevens, and Everett Hill. In later years, Everett Hill became sole owner. Virginia Hill, granddaughter of J.D. Williams, and her husband, Everett Hill continued the hardware business with the help of their son, Joe Mac Hill. In 1993, Jeff W. Black became partners with Joe Hill expanding the appliances and electronics areas. The two now own and operate JR Williams T.V. and Appliances.

Jeff Black and Joe Hill are proud to have such a historic establishment and look forward to continuing their service for years to come!

*North Main Street, Beaver Dam, current location of Williams Hardware.*

*Top: J.R. Williams 1912-1946, J.D. Williams 1891-1914, J.M. Williams 1912-1927. 2: H.H. McKenney 1946-1971, Carl McKenney 1946-1953, Glendon Stevens 1946-1976. 3: Joe Hill 1973-present owner, Everett Hill 1946-1993, Jeff Black 1993-present owner employed 1975-1993.*

*J.D. Williams house, 1980.*

*Joe Mac Hill, first street in Beaver Dam.*

*Businesses in Beaver Dam.*

*Williams on Main Street, Beaver Dam.*

*Everett Hill, Williams & Miller Blacksmith shop, 1915. Tornado hit plow.*

# W.S. TAYLOR & SONS

## FORTY YEARS OF DEPENDABLE SERVICE
# 1927-1967

## From business founded by W.S. Taylor & Sons

Opened for business December 7, 1927 as agency for Willy-Overland
Selected as Ohio County dealer for Chrysler in 1932

W.S. Taylor remained active in the business until his retirement in 1946
The business was operated by Roy and Joe S. Taylor as partners until 1952 when Joe S. Taylor became sole owner.

*(Recreation of 1967 advertisement.)*

*Present business in Beaver Dam. The Bannister House and Tea Room, 1998, 217 n. Main.*

# NEO Industries

NEO Industries Ltd., the parent company of NEO's worldwide operations, was established in 1952 with the head office located in Burlington, Ontario, Canada, The head office was moved from Canada to Portage, Indiana in 1995.

In 1964, NEO Industries plated trial work rolls for the Steel Company of Canada. The results were excellent in both cold and temper mills. This success prompted the development of specialized plating plants worldwide.

The company specializes in wear resistant surface treatment for industrial applications. NEO pioneered the first hard chrome plating of work rolls for flat rolled products which is now the company's core business. Today NEO services more than 125 flat rolled operations throughout the world for their texturing and chrome plating needs. Chrome plating has continued to provide a value added service to customers that have sought to minimize roll maintenance processing cost while maximizing mill operational performance,

Each NEO plant uses world standards as a benchmark and through our technologically advanced computerized plating process we are able to achieve a superior product. We are committed to establishing safe and environmentally sound facilities. In addition, NEO is ISO 9000 certified which enables us to provide top quality products.

NEO Industries currently has plants located in France, Slovakia, Australia, and in the United States in Indiana, West Virginia, Tennessee, and Kentucky. Currently NEO Industries is expanding in Alabama as well. Each plant was built and designed to meet various customer needs and their continually increasing quality requirements. Customers send work from as far as 500 miles for NEO Chrome. Continuous improvement and solidly based customer working relationships have resulted in consistent and repeatable sheet surface improvements and customer satisfaction. NEO continues to lead all competitors with the latest technology and equipment research, flexibility and capability.

NEO Industries Kentucky location started staffing the facility in late 1992. The manufacturing facility is located in Beaver Dam at 10 Technology Place off of U S Highway 231, in Industrial Park Fast.

NEO's presence has been a positive one for Ohio County and the Commonwealth. In addition to creating jobs for this area, purchases from Kentucky vendors play a part in protecting our economic future, and local school and state tax represent a contribution as well.

# DESCENDANTS OF ROBERT LEE TAYLOR

1 Robert Lee Taylor Born: May 08, 1870 Died: September 0 1, 1937
.. + Emma Elizabeth Liles Born: April 22, 1879 Died: November 30, 1969 Married: January 06, 1897
... 2 Lilburn Blackstone Taylor Born: November 7, 1898 Died: March 20, 1980
...... +Nancy Elizabeth Cook Born: December 18, 1901 Married: March 11, 1923
...... 3 Emma Elizabeth Taylor Born: March 04. 1924 Died: March 18, 1924
...... 3 Lilbern Blackstone Taylor, Jr Born: June 12, 1925
.......... +Nellie Jeanette Burden Born: October 2 5, 192 8 M arried: J u ne 0 1, 194 7
.......... 4 Dana Jean Taylor Born: July 18, 1954
.............. +David Neal McGregor Born: October 27, 1952 Married: Septembcr 30, 1972
..............   5 Bryan Davis McGregor Born: January 3 1, 198 1
........... 4 Alan Lee Taylor Born: January 12, 1963
...............  +Marian Christine Smith Born: June 15, 1965 Married: July 26, 1986
................ 5 Austin Lucas Taylor Born: October 05, 1994
...... 3 Robert Conrad Taylor Born: August 08, 1928
.......... +Betty Ann Turner Born: January 28, 1928 Married: July 02, 1950
.......... 4 Paula Ann Taylor Born: August 20, 1955
............  +Webster Vernon Rogers III Born: July 03, 1962 Married: 1993
............ 5 Webster Vernon Rogers IV Born: September 03, 1993
............ 5 Robert Lee Rogers Born: September 03, 1994
...........4 Marla Ann Taylor Born: August 20, 1955
.. ............+David Phillip McChesney Born: December 06, 1950 Married: December 15, 1973
................5 Shannon Lee McChesney Born: February 19, 1976
...................+Chris Spann Born: January 01, 1974 Married: August 19, 1991
................... 6 Holly Leann Spann Born: Febr uary 20, 1992
................... 6 Amber Ashley Spann Born: May 19, 1994
................ 5 David Phillip McChesney, Jr Born: June 04, 1978
................ 5 Clinton Conrad McChesney Born: February 22, 1980
.......3 Defrosia Ann Taylor Born: April 20, 1930
...........+Charles Marshall Richard Born: November 13, 1923 Married: June 0 1, 1946
...........4 Charles Marshall Richard, Jr Born: August 07, 1949
..............  +Sharr'an Marie Rojas Born: July 27, 1952 Married: January 20, 1973
...............  5 Cassie Marie Richard Born: June 28, 1978
...............  5 Charles Marshall Richard III Born: August 18, 1981
...............  5 Chelsee Marie Richard Born: May 12, 1986
...........4 James Taylor Richard Born: April 27, 1951 Died: December 07, 1951
...........4 Cynthia Ann Richard Born: March 29, 1953
..............  +Randall Kent Terman Born: December 15, 1947 Married: February 16, 1974
...............  5 Amanda Jane Terman Born: October 23. 1975
....................  +Douglas Lawrence Hawkins Born: September 09, 1973 Married: October 07, 1995
....................  6 Holden Gage Hawkins Born: June 01, 1996
...............  5 Ashley Delynn Terman Born: November 15, 1980
.......... 4 Connie Lynette Richard Born: December 09, 1954
................+Horst Dieter Matthes Born: April 09, 1949 Married: April 19, 1975
................5 Crista Ann Matthes Born: August 25, 1980
................5 Kent Richard Matthes Born: January 08, 1987
...........4 Chad Taylor Richard Born: March 02, 1970
...... 3 Jerry Russell Taylor Born: June 02, 1932
...........+Betty Lou Coleman Born: February 03, 1936 Married: April 07, 1955
...........4 Jerry Russell Taylor, Jr Born: March 03, 1956
................+Cynthia Darlene Simms Born: November 2 1, 1958 Married: October 03, 1987
................5 Jennifer Kathryn Taylor Born: June 06, 1989
................5 Allison Nicole Taylor Born: October 15, 1993
...........4   Ronald Steven Taylor Born: August 25, 1959
...........4   Robin Lynn Taylor Born: August 03, 1971 Died: August 03, 197 1
.......3 David Cook Taylor Born: May 14, 1934
...........+Peggy Ann Bozarth Born: April 15, 1937 Married: June 16, 1955
...........4 Abby Lynn Taylor Born: September 26, 1959
...............+Ricky Filback Married: May 16, 1977
...............5 Jarrod Wayne Filback Born: December 12, 1977
...........*2nd Husband of Abby Lynn Taylor:
................+Mike Collard Married: March 19, 1983
................ 5 Alison Taylor Collard Born: August 14. 1985
...........4 Kristi Gay Taylor Born: March 16, 1963
................+Bruce R Hall Born: September 09, 1959 Married: June 17, 1994
......... ....5 Trent Taylor Hall Born: October 16, 1995
.......3 Peggy Lucille Taylor Born: August 26, 1936 Died: July 13, 1939
.......3 James Ray Taylor Born: March 10, 1939 Died: July 27, 1939
.......3 Donald Edward Taylor Born: January 17, 1940
...........+Betty Lou Pierce Born: July 30. 1939 Married: July 05, 1959

..........4 Donald Edward Taylor, Jr Born: July 28, 1962
...............+Karolyn Lynn Foster Born: February 19. 1964 Married: July 14, 1990
...............5 Jacqueline Paige Taylor Born: December 30, 1995
..........4   Patricia Ann Taylor Born: September 09, 1963
..........4   Emma Mae Taylor Born: March 20, 1971
...............Michael Scott Richards Born- October 23, 1962 Married: July 24, 1993
...............5 Taylor Scott Richards Born- February 03, 1997
....2  Infant Daughter Born: February 24, 1900 Died- March 23, 1900
....2 Claude Liles Taylor Born: June 24, 1901 Died: April 09, 1956
..........+Anna Mariah Williams Born: April 23, 1900 Died: September 19, 1932 Married- December 0 1. 1920
..........3 Louise Williams Taylor Born: November 16, 1924
...............+Joseph Thurmond Maupin Born: December 1 1, 1924 Married- November 11, 1945
...............4 Suzanne Maupin Born: June 28, 1946
....................+Lee Robert Nelsen Born: November 21, 1946 Married: August 06, 1966
....................5 Christopher John Nelsen Born: March 11, 1967
....................5 Eric Taft Nelsen Born: October 29. 1969
....................5 Amanda Louise Nelsen Born: April 20, 1976
.................4 Harold Joseph Maupin Born: January 0 1. 1950
....................+Patty Carmody Born: March 09, 1953 Married: June 16, 1979
.................4 Stephen Earl Maupin Born: March 18, 1951
....................+Nancy Moran Born: January 13, 1951 Married: August 23, 1980
....................5 Jennifer Maupin Born: January 0 1, 1992
.................4 Kenneth Taylor Maupin Born: September 22. 1960
..........3 Lois Christine Taylor Born: September 19, 1932 Died: September 19, 1932
........*2nd Wife of Claude LilesTaylor:
..........Annabel Johnson Born: July 04, 1911 Married: December 04, 1937
..........3 Claude Lewis  Taylor Born: February 14, 1942
...............+Janice Sue Spinks Born: October 13, 1943 Married: December 26, 1963
...............4 Shannon Lea Taylor Born: April 17, 1967
....................+Kevin Lee Brotherton Born: May 18, 1970 Married: September 2 1, 199 1
........................5 Hannah Elizabeth Brotherton Born: April 18, 1996
............. 4 Eric Jon Taylor Born: May 22. 1971
..........3 Shelby Lee Taylor Born: February 05, 1945
...............+Judy Rae Compton Born: April 25, 1946 Married: September 10, 1966
...............4 Courtney Lynn Taylor Born: February 23, 1975
...............4 Susan Lee Taylor Born: December 29, 1977
.......2 Myron Hoy Taylor Born: September 02, 1903 Died: July 18, 1962
..........+Dora Belle Boswell Born: June 0 1, 1912 Married: March 11, 1933
..........3 Willie Lee Taylor Born: February 16, 1940 Died: February 16, 1940
..........3 Brenda Sue Taylor Born: March 09, 1949
...............+Ivan Jeffrey Warren Born: July 30, 1947 Married: June 30, 1973
...............4 Jeremy Taylor Warren Born: August 13, 1981
...............4 Jonathan Park Warren Born: November 19, 1985

# Index

## A

Abbott 5
Abner 102, 147
Acker 91
Acquaviva 194
Adams 6, 99, 130
Adcock 19, 108
Addington 102
Addison 8, 118
Adkins 6
Akin 121
Akins 48
Albin 10, 51, 121, 149, 151
Albright 46
Aldridge 118
Alexander 149
Alford 70, 107, 150
Allan 125
Allen 25, 29, 40, 47, 69, 99, 100, 106, 107, 108, 115, 117, 120, 123, 126, 130, 131, 134, 147, 148, 160, 192
Ambrose 22, 26, 139
Anderson 11, 56, 81, 187
Andes 12
Angle 158
Arbuckle 10, 130, 151
Armstrong 117, 143
Arnold 125
Ashby 11, 102, 107, 109, 113, 115, 117, 119, 137, 147, 149, 151, 154, 156
Ashford 118
Ashley 7, 192
Ashton 111
Atherton 143, 182
Austin 13, 106, 117, 123, 126, 127, 130, 149, 151, 182
Autry 28, 32, 107, 123

## B

Babbit 114
Babbitt 102
Baggarly 108
Bailey 48, 120
Baines 152
Baird 129
Baise 123
Baize 13, 23, 25, 107, 112, 123, 125, 130, 134
Baker 8, 10, 12, 15, 54, 129, 137, 138
Baldwin 137
Ball 113
Ballard 114, 160
Balls 154
Barber 182
Bard 184
Barnard 8, 14, 24, 48, 86, 113, 115, 117, 121, 146, 176
Barnes 8, 23, 44, 107, 111, 112, 113, 115, 116, 118, 122, 126, 127, 129, 130, 132, 137, 147
Barnett 93, 125, 150, 192
Barnhill 129
Barrass 80, 118
Barrett 14, 26, 28, 43, 69, 81, 85, 86, 104, 111, 131, 136, 140, 147, 151
Bartlett 111, 149
Basham 6, 26
Bason 125
Baugh 11, 17, 137
Baughn 154
Bean 16
Beard 137, 150
Beck 33, 49, 51
Beemer 184
Bell 46, 48, 52
Bellamy 114, 123, 125
Benadinto 10
Bennett 7, 13, 14, 15, 19, 32, 49, 69, 113, 114, 115, 120, 127, 130, 134, 137, 140, 151, 154, 184, 192
Bennington 67
Berch 123
Berkeley 24, 120
Berkley 108, 110
Berry 150, 182
Berryman 13, 22, 25, 107, 118, 122, 134, 147
Bevil 64, 124, 189, 192, 194
Bibb 107
Bilbro 102, 150, 154
Birchwell 91
Birkhead 150, 151, 188, 189
Bishop 9, 29, 32, 68, 103, 106, 107, 108, 110, 113, 114, 120, 122, 130, 134, 152
Bivins 15, 49, 57, 83, 112
Black 30, 45, 50, 51, 81, 84, 120, 136, 161, 192, 195
Blackburn 26, 27, 103, 104, 107, 116, 117, 138, 149
Blacklock 22, 73, 82, 165
Blackstone 12, 180
Blades 49, 89
Blair 24, 47, 107, 116, 138, 148
Blakenship 115
Blanchard 113, 149, 151, 174
Blankenship 10, 121, 137, 138, 192
Blanton 11
Bohler 150
Bondurant 99
Boone 182
Borah 107, 110, 155
Boswell 6, 16, 48, 81, 108, 113, 125, 146, 199
Bowen 109, 146
Bowers 121, 130
Boyd 20, 56, 108, 112, 113, 150, 154
Bozarth 25, 33, 34, 42, 131, 198
Bradley 130, 149, 182
Bradshaw 113
Brandenburg 164
Brannon 102
Bratcher 61, 108, 112, 113, 115, 147, 192
Bray 147
Bristow 129
Brizendine 110
Brizentine 117
Brock 150, 154
Brooks 54, 137
Broomfield 114
Brown 8, 12, 13, 14, 18, 19, 21, 24, 25, 27, 30, 42, 48, 54, 65, 66, 78, 82, 84, 89, 102, 106, 107, 108, 109, 112, 114, 115, 116, 117, 120, 121, 126, 127, 129, 130, 137, 138, 146, 150, 152, 154
Bruton 125
Buck 26, 111, 120
Buckner 99
Buell 103
Bullington 147
Bullock 113, 114, 130
Burbridge 99
Burch 160
Burchett 12
Burde 24
Burden 25, 33, 73, 82, 83, 84, 85, 108, 110, 112, 115, 123, 126, 130, 136, 149, 151, 154, 156, 169, 192, 198
Burger 115, 130
Burgess 12, 24, 112, 113, 115, 147, 152, 168, 176, 184
Burke 8, 184
Burklow 149
Burns 165, 188
Burris 47, 126, 134
Burriss 47
Burton 67, 112, 125, 137
Butler 11, 50, 107, 115, 123, 177
Butt 138
Buza 177
Byers 111
Byrd 106

## C

Cain 117
Cairnes 106, 150
Caldwell 47
Calloway 110
Campbell 152
Campfield 48
Carden 115, 125, 146
Cardon 117
Cardwell 58, 103, 116, 120
Carmody 199
Carnes 107, 110, 129
Carson 50, 119, 137
Carter 18, 112, 113, 114, 138, 139, 150, 154, 182, 184
Casebier 14, 57, 73, 147, 150, 182, 188
Casey 55
Cashion 143
Casteel 106, 145, 184
Cates 110
Cavender 10, 102
Cawthorn 48, 49
Chancellor 115
Chandler 91
Chapman 20, 24, 106, 107, 110, 111, 112, 113, 116, 117, 121, 152, 154, 156, 192
Chavis 147
Cheek 6, 125
Chenowith 98
Chick 8, 12, 17, 118, 124, 182
Chinn 12, 19, 24, 25, 26, 29, 43, 46, 48, 49, 52, 108, 109, 110, 111, 112, 116, 117, 120, 127, 130, 137, 147, 149
Chumley 107, 130
Chungler 110
Clark 9, 109, 121, 123, 134
Cleaver 192
Clouse 117
Clovis 12
Coats 13, 114
Cochran 13
Coffee 152
Coffield 123, 170
Coffman 130, 152
Cohran 129
Cohron 8
Coleman 33, 71, 102, 109, 112, 115, 143, 182, 198
Collard 198
Combs 122
Compton 199
Condit 114, 134
Conway 152
Cook 10, 13, 15, 18, 30, 33, 67, 81, 108, 136, 147, 161, 180, 198
Cooke 11
Cooksey 108, 110, 121
Cooper 57, 92, 102, 109, 111, 121, 123, 137, 158, 159, 192, 194
Coots 127
Coppage 130, 156
Couch 8, 129
Cowell 30
Cox 10, 100, 107, 114, 123, 147, 182, 184
Coy 106
Crabtree 112, 120
Craddock 7, 107, 123, 129, 151
Craig 123, 192
Crane 154
Cravens 192
Crawford 44, 173
Crenshaw 187
Crow 11, 125, 152
Crowder 24, 49, 60, 109, 125, 137, 160, 193
Crowe 107, 144, 149, 160, 188
Crume 121
Crumes 54, 164
Crunk 30, 48, 49, 130, 146, 154
Culberts 126
Culbertson 49, 107
Cummins 102, 109, 116
Cunningham 99
Cup 31
Curtis 40, 52, 63, 89, 106, 107, 108, 112, 116, 123, 138, 148, 149, 192

## D

Dabney 137
Dale 70
Dalphies 123
Daniel 107, 110, 121
Daniels 113, 117
Danks 147, 148, 152, 188
Daugherty 15, 19, 72, 130, 131, 152, 155
Daughterty 13
Daughtery 54, 140
Daulpher 125
Davenport 61, 108, 117
Daves 143
David 106, 110
Davidson 121, 129, 150
Davis 20, 54, 70, 106, 107, 108, 114, 121, 130, 139, 149, 152, 156
Davison 125
Day 8, 91
Decker 52, 106, 108, 110, 116, 125, 130
Deeter 108
Dehart 20, 32
Dement 151
Dennis 71
DeSoto 117
Dever 114
Devine 106, 111, 116, 138, 154
Deweese 93
Dexter 113
Dickerson 99
Dinno 115
Dockery 5, 24, 72, 117, 118, 123, 130, 131, 182, 184
Dodge 48, 115
Dodson 180
Doirs 123
Doolin 192
Dortch 108
Dotson 137
Dougherty 28, 163
Douglas 107, 127
Dowell 107, 117, 121
Downey 108
Downs 140
Dozier 106, 138
Drake 30
Driskill 152
Duff 55, 150, 181
Dugan 120, 121
Duggins 121, 125
Duke 27, 30, 118, 122, 137, 184, 189
Duncan 11, 28, 86, 115, 118, 121, 137, 141, 151, 154, 162
Dunes 160
Dunn 108, 121, 170
Durall 32
Durbin 59
Durham 49, 89, 111, 122, 130, 180
Duvall 22, 61, 62, 115, 118, 123, 124, 144, 152

## E

Early 152
Earp 160
Easterday 21, 30
Eden 126
Edison 150
Elder 107
Elliott 118, 137, 152
Elmore 49, 112, 115, 117, 130, 146
Embry 13, 15, 52, 69, 104, 110, 118, 121, 130, 137, 147, 149, 152, 160, 163, 182, 184
England 25, 102, 108, 121
Engler 109, 120
English 71, 131
Eskridge 23, 31, 46, 70
Espey 70, 107, 148, 149
Estes 135
Evans 10, 13, 48, 61, 116
Everley 121, 154
Everly 19, 48, 56, 115, 117, 120, 122, 130, 138, 150
Ezell 108, 113

## F

Faith 150, 152
Farmer 5
Farris 61, 106, 107, 108
Faught 108, 110, 121, 149, 188
Faulkerson 122
Faulkner 98
Feemster 137
Felix 120, 121
Fergerson 120
Ferguson 29, 113, 117, 122, 137, 147
Ferris 13
Field 124
Fielder 134
Fielding 125
Fieldon 114, 154
Filbeck 125
Fink 12
Finley 114
Finn 150, 163
Fisher 8, 15, 17, 55, 56, 105, 107, 110, 123, 126, 134, 149, 150, 151
Fitsgerald 114
Fitzgerald 54
Fleming 152
Flener 32, 33, 34, 119, 130, 151, 192
Flickenger 56
Fogle 121
Ford 18, 106, 110, 112, 121, 130, 139, 147
Forrest 98
Forsythe 111, 151
Foster 25, 154, 199
Fraim 154
Frances 130
Francis 89, 113, 117
Fray 152
Freer 156
Frizzell 122, 126
Fulkerson 17, 28, 46, 106, 107, 109, 111, 112, 116, 123, 138, 143, 148, 151, 155
Fuller 106, 107, 112, 116, 123
Fulton 108, 109, 146
Funk 145, 149
Fuqua 58, 114, 125

## G

Gaines 137
Gaither 151, 152, 184
Galloway 6
Garner 149, 151, 152
Garrett 112
Gatten 91
Geary 20, 54, 92, 106, 108, 109, 111, 112, 113, 116, 121, 122, 130, 151, 152, 164, 165, 182, 184, 192

Geaves 32
Gentry 9, 13, 188
Gidcombs 114
Gillespie 152
Gillim 130
Gilstrap 64, 115, 149, 188
Gipson 91
Given 147
Givens 51, 70, 89, 104, 107, 110, 112, 115, 116, 126, 130, 148, 149, 152, 155
Glenn 192
Goff 112, 115, 116, 129, 147, 148, 184
Goodall 5, 32, 83, 84, 130
Goodman 30, 49
Gossum 126
Gracey 99
Graham 109, 130
Grant 49, 125, 130
Graves 120, 121, 144
Gray 111, 115, 125, 129, 147, 148, 166
Green 122, 126
Greene 149
Greenville 114
Greenwell 114, 160
Greer 8, 123, 125, 129, 137, 156
Gregory 13, 18
Grey 166, 167
Griffith 13, 49, 56, 114
Gripentrog 56
Grobarger 49, 115
Growbarger 33, 106
Guess 149

## H

Hacker 9, 13, 58
Hagan 99
Hale 27, 44
Hall 39
Hamilton 49
Hammon 108
Hammond 9, 106, 109
Hammons 14
Hanes 108
Harden 123
Harder 102, 125
Hardesty 131, 160
Hardie 99
Hardin 114, 115
Hardison 117
Hardwick 163
Harper 106, 148
Harrel 146
Harreld 46, 137
Harrell 115
Harris 23, 106, 112, 134
Harrison 156, 169, 173
Hart 125

Hatcher 176
Hatley 134
Haven 13, 16, 70, 111, 134, 137, 151
Havens 34, 49, 120, 137
Hawes 8, 52, 106, 107, 108, 115, 123, 149
Hawkins 44, 93, 99
Hayes 19, 27, 164
Haynes 114, 150, 172
Hazelrig 18
Hazelrigg 26, 112, 115, 129
Heddon 123
Heflin 30, 43, 48, 57, 111, 113, 120, 122, 154, 156, 180
Heltsley 48, 116, 138, 139
Hendricks 108
Henry 150
Herrald 116
Herrel 108
Hert 48, 107, 120, 137
Hess 27, 126
Hester 115
Hibbs 106, 108, 115
Hick 114
Hicks 31, 46, 49, 108, 112, 114, 115, 120, 146
Higdon 152, 187
Higginbotham 187
Hill 5, 46, 101, 108, 111, 122, 138, 151, 195
Hillard 121, 148
Himes 90, 120, 135
Hines 48, 49, 86, 110, 115, 118, 120, 152
Hinton 26
Hitchell 179
Hobbs 6
Hobdy 40
Hocker 46, 81, 90, 113, 121, 123, 137, 149
Hodge 137
Hodges 121, 127
Hoheimer 118
Holdman 19
Holland 106, 112, 116, 129
Holman 105
Hood 98, 99
Hoops 110, 137
Hoover 23, 93, 134
Hopper 102, 115, 117, 123, 146
Horn 129
Hoskins 7, 10, 14, 16, 89, 92, 106, 107, 112, 113, 114, 116, 121, 139, 148, 149, 155, 179
House 110
Howard 120, 123, 165
Howell 114
Hoxworth 44, 114, 147
Huckleberry 26
Hudson 110, 129, 130, 134
Huff 123, 131

Hughes 47
Hulse 108
Hulsey 117
Hultz 151
Hundley 151
Hunley 109, 137
Hunt 102, 117
Hunter 17, 33, 49, 54, 107, 109, 122, 129
Hurd 91
Hurst 56
Hurt 121

## I

Iler 65, 120, 147, 152
Ingram 106, 112, 137

## J

Jackson 5, 12, 13, 15, 24, 44, 46, 79, 99, 104, 114, 116, 122, 130, 147, 150, 168, 192, 194
Jacob 22
Jacobson 177
James 8, 10, 11, 20, 21, 22, 24, 25, 28, 29, 54, 66, 72, 102, 106, 107, 108, 117, 119, 121, 122, 123, 126, 134, 147
Jamison 120
Janes 92
Jennings 113
Jesse 121
Jewell 139
Jimbo 11
Johnson 5, 22, 26, 27, 30, 40, 44, 58, 64, 85, 86, 98, 103, 108, 109, 112, 114, 116, 117, 120, 121, 125, 134, 135, 137, 147, 152, 156, 192
Johnston 6, 47, 99, 152
Jones 61, 107, 108, 114, 117, 122, 123, 126, 127, 149, 192
Jordon 163
Junior 125

## K

Kalnai 12
Kane 129, 137, 158, 159
Kaysinger 114
Keel 143
Keene 138
Keith 108, 110, 121, 154
Kelley 107, 137, 152
Kelly 137, 172
Kendall 124
Kennedy 49, 106, 118, 120, 154
Keown 28, 63, 118, 147, 192
Kessinger 49, 105, 125
Key 107, 108, 112, 116

Kidd 147
Kiel 182
Kimbrel 120
Kimmel 107, 115, 130, 154
Kincade 108
Kincheloe 113
King 54, 89, 143, 181
Kirk 9, 93, 130, 156
Kirtley 109
Kitchem 126
Kitchens 120, 121
Knight 8, 70, 108, 115, 127, 152
Kohlmann 182
Kuykendall 67

## L

Lace 111
Lacefield 69, 107, 121
LaGrange 98, 99
Lake 115, 137, 145, 147
Lamb 114, 115
Lampson 154
Landrum 108, 181
Langford 110
Langley 106, 107, 108, 134
Lanum 170
Larkin 123
Lawrence 72
Lawson 181
Leach 6, 11, 23, 24, 26, 34, 54, 69, 71, 90, 104, 120, 122, 125, 136, 137, 148, 149, 151, 152, 154
LeBlanc 29
Lee 10, 12, 26, 118, 122, 136
LeGrand 102
Leisure 74, 106, 108, 137
Lender 8
Leonard 12
Letty 134
Lewis 107, 111, 121, 122, 123, 125, 149, 150
Likens 107, 113, 116, 120, 121
Likes 137
Liles 198
Lindsey 108, 110, 160
Linkletter 48
Litsey 73
Loney 18
Long 67, 117, 118, 145
Lowe 114, 145
Loyal 6
Loyd 125
Lucas 137
Luce 22
Luttrell 187
Lutz 107, 116, 130
Lynch 110, 121
Lyon 98, 99, 192

Lyons 75

## M

Mabrey 24, 48, 121, 146
Maddos 69
Maddox 8, 17, 21, 25, 33, 48, 72, 106, 107, 108, 112, 114, 115, 116, 117, 118, 121, 122, 129, 130, 146, 149, 154
Magan 116, 129
Magas 12
Maggart 14
Main 107
Maine 168
Malloy 121, 146
Manford 12
Mann 148
Maple 89, 108, 139
Maples 92, 121, 152
Marlow 89
Marlowe 154
Marsh 125
Martin 8, 13, 24, 26, 32, 33, 34, 51, 53, 55, 64, 84, 85, 88, 102, 108, 110, 114, 119, 125, 129, 130, 132, 137, 147, 148, 152, 158, 159, 169, 174, 192
Martine 50
Mason 115, 120, 150
Massey 114
Massie 111, 139
Mathis 106, 137
Matthes 198
Matthews 6, 107, 121, 123
Mattingly 52, 108
Maupin 199
Mauzy 111, 121
May 115
Mayer 6
Mayes 117, 152
McBride 10
McCardy 125
McChesney 198
McClain 44, 117
McClure 121
McConnell 69, 106, 109, 130
McCook 98, 99
McCormick 115, 151
McCoy 89, 106, 108, 110, 148
McCulla 150
McDaniel 107, 108
McDaniels 149
McDowell 181
McElroy 61
McGill 91
McGregor 198
McGrew 52, 156
McHenry 98, 99, 100, 160

203

McIntyre 107, 113
McKee 106, 108, 114, 116, 118, 122
McKenney 11, 34, 115, 137, 195
McKenny 46
McKeown 27
McKinley 26, 118, 122, 126
McKinney 151
McMellon 138
McPeak 137
McQueen 137
Menton 107
Mercer 26, 120, 137
Midkiff 17, 20, 101, 109, 111
Miles 107, 131
Miller 6, 24, 28, 47, 59, 106, 107, 108, 109, 111, 114, 115, 120, 121, 129, 130, 134, 135, 137, 142, 151, 162, 184, 187, 190, 192
Mills 91
Minton 8, 67, 93, 107, 108, 123, 125, 126, 130, 184
Mitchel 114, 137
Mitchell 48, 107, 108, 115, 120, 150, 154, 182
Mobberly 170
Moffett 123
Monroe 10, 47, 48, 49, 55, 120, 123, 150, 164, 165, 174
Monte 144
Montgomery 114, 149
Moore 44, 107, 120, 121
Moorman 111, 112
Morris 5, 7, 11, 28, 52, 57, 93, 114, 125, 139, 160, 180
Morton 122, 154
Moseley 6, 23, 28, 69, 104, 107, 110, 121, 126, 135, 177
Mosley 107, 130, 149
Moxely 123
Mulhall 13
Mullen 123
Murphy 10, 114, 154
Myers 107, 110, 120, 121, 152, 188
Myres 111

## N

Nabors 114
Nall 108
Nance 107, 148, 184
Natcher 52
Neal 22, 127, 182
Neighbors 123, 137
Neil 24
Nellson 123
Nelsen 199
Nelson 67, 72, 107, 115, 123, 130, 150
Nemo 130
Newcom 137, 171

Newhouse 120, 122
Newton 123, 125, 174
Nichols 12
Nimmo 50, 137
Norris 114

## O

O'Bannon 78
O'Brien 61, 106, 107, 116, 130
O'Dell 22, 122
Oglesby 179, 182
Oldham 9, 14, 16, 51, 86, 110, 151, 182
Oliver 113
Oller 71, 108, 110, 121
Osborne 102
Overhults 52
Overton 109, 120
Owen 154
Owens 30, 107, 130, 150, 151
Owsley 99

## P

Park 6, 11, 17, 107, 115, 117, 121, 125, 146, 148, 152
Parker 131
Parks 25, 46, 106, 137, 152
Parritt 123
Parrott 106
Pate 122, 137, 144
Patterson 108, 110, 121, 147
Patton 18, 48, 113, 123, 152, 158, 159, 182, 184
Paxton 23, 120
Paye 19
Payne 123
Payton 16, 99, 108, 109, 110, 120, 121
Peach 67, 106, 107, 114, 123, 125
Pean 15
Pearl 111, 120
Peay 118
Peeks 152
Pendleton 99
Pennebaker 99
Peterson 110
Petrie 144
Peyton 120, 192
Pfisterer 144
Phelps 5, 11, 22, 24, 31, 32, 33, 34, 45, 48, 102, 105, 107, 108, 110, 112, 116, 126, 129, 130, 137, 149, 151, 152, 172
Phillips 114, 125, 126, 156
Pierce 33, 55, 106, 108, 115, 123
Pirtle 121, 150, 176
Plumer 114
Plummer 121, 122, 151
Pollard 192

Porter 10, 19, 30, 89, 102, 106, 108, 112, 115, 130, 131, 149
Post 43
Potter 169
Potts 59, 60, 125
Powell 114
Price 107
Pryor 111, 122
Puckett 184

## Q

Quinn 109
Quisenberry 131

## R

Ragers 180
Ragland 86, 120, 177
Raidon 125
Raines 49, 112
Rains 49, 107, 118, 138, 149
Raley 8, 120, 129
Ralph 6, 17, 39, 104, 113, 129, 130, 135, 139, 148, 163, 192
Ram 115
Ramney 33
Ranney 110, 114, 150
Ratcliff 24, 50, 137
Ray 127
Raymer 106
Raymond 24, 107, 110, 117, 129, 147, 155
Raywood 172
Read 30
Rearden 135, 156
Reed 152
Reedy 11
Reeves 118
Refrow 29
Reid 5, 13, 18, 23, 46, 48, 49, 63, 108, 115, 121, 130, 138, 149, 169
Reisz 184
Render 7, 8, 11, 26, 48, 71, 72, 89, 110, 111, 112, 113, 115, 116, 129, 150, 151, 180, 192
Renfrow 22, 85, 124, 137, 151, 160, 171
Renner 22
Reynolds 19, 30, 31, 110, 117, 134, 149, 150
Rhoads 12, 13, 114
Rhodes 110, 113, 123
Rice 160
Richard 33, 198
Richards 6, 122, 123, 125, 199
Rippy 106
Roach 116, 127
Roberts 59, 91, 117
Robertson 8, 109, 115, 117, 129, 155

Robey 123
Robinson 20, 48, 59, 107, 108, 109, 111, 112, 115, 125, 149, 150, 151, 155
Rock 110, 115, 121, 123
Roe 102, 154
Rogers 10, 115, 137, 138, 150, 198
Romans 13, 106, 124, 143, 147, 151, 163
Romas 134
Rone 138
Roscoe 149
Rosencrans 6
Rosine 45
Ross 18, 22, 30, 48, 57, 98, 109, 110, 113, 115, 116, 117, 122, 127, 130, 154, 178
Rowan 76, 192
Rowe 26, 48, 113, 115, 117, 121, 134, 154, 174
Roy 13, 115
Royal 107, 136
Royals 125
Ruby 160
Rumage 129
Rummage 8, 137
Rusher 123, 135
Russell 107, 109, 114, 124
Rust 135

## S

Saint 117
Saling 89, 106, 107, 116, 148
Saltsman 135
Sandefur 34, 107, 108, 115, 118, 121, 125, 126, 137, 149, 162
Sapp 102, 108, 110, 120
Scalf 12
Schacklett 102, 115
Schapmire 190
Schrader 123
Schroader 8, 10, 67, 120, 121, 125, 130
Schroeter 150
Schultz 13, 137
Scott 17, 106, 107, 116, 126, 152
Sears 160
Seelig 192
Sexton 123
Seyffer 56
Shafer 109
Shannon 13
Sharp 26, 107, 116
Shaver 92, 151
Shaw 92, 106, 108
Sheffield 52, 107, 130
Shenk 115
Shepard 54
Shephard 184
Shields 115, 123, 137, 138
Shoulders 8, 9, 110, 123

Shown 11, 12, 68, 81, 93, 115, 120, 137, 144, 145, 151, 171
Shows 9
Shropshire 106, 108, 115
Shrull 7, 102, 130
Shull 109, 120
Shultz 72, 109, 111, 113, 119, 120, 126, 127, 129, 130, 149, 151, 152
Simpson 13, 91, 99, 100, 107, 114, 115
Singleton 89, 92, 107, 116, 138, 152
Skaggs 165
Slack 64, 108, 118, 122, 125
Slattery 122
Smaltz 187
Smiley 111, 130
Smith 5, 13, 34, 42, 48, 52, 61, 102, 106, 107, 108, 112, 113, 114, 115, 116, 118, 120, 121, 123, 127, 129, 137, 149, 150, 154, 162, 163, 192, 198
Sneeden 92
Snell 150
Snodgrass 13, 87, 88, 107, 122, 130, 150
Snowden 13
Snyder 104
Sondefur 106
Sooh 150
Sorrels 24, 122
Southard 12, 69, 109, 117, 130, 151, 152
Spann 198
Sparks 122
Spencer 110, 125
Spinks 147, 151, 154, 199
Sprigg 169
Spriggs 43
Stanley 64, 101, 122, 124, 151, 169, 173
Statam 129
Statler 192
Stenberg 154
Stenburg 122, 154
Stevens 8, 12, 26, 34, 60, 71, 83, 108, 112, 115, 116, 119, 120, 121, 129, 136, 137, 138, 151, 195
Stewart 7, 10, 20, 57, 81, 88, 106, 107, 109, 113, 114, 115, 116, 117, 122, 123, 130, 132, 136, 146, 147, 151, 154
Stites 125
Stom 109
Stone 28, 31, 137
Strandell 56
Stratton 120
Struder 61
Stum 88
Suegeon 110
Sullivan 115, 123
Sutton 101, 114
Swain 21, 31, 46, 115, 158
Swan 130
Swarm 13
Swift 54, 160

Sypert 99

## T

Tanner 107
Tarrance 106
Tarrant 149
Tartar 115
Tate 64, 174
Tatum 50, 106, 110, 114
Taul 154
Taylor 5, 12, 13, 17, 18, 19, 21, 26, 28, 33, 34, 46, 49, 50, 51, 53, 54, 57, 67, 69, 71, 81, 86, 106, 107, 108, 113, 114, 115, 117, 118, 120, 121, 122, 124, 127, 132, 136, 137, 138, 150, 152, 160, 169, 172, 175, 180, 182, 184, 192, 196, 198, 199
Terman 198
Thomas 11, 12, 24, 98, 106, 116, 137, 150
Thomasson 10, 113
Thomblinson 122
Thurman 6
Tichenor 11, 13, 58, 113, 114, 134, 137, 148, 152, 154, 180, 187, 192
Tierney 37, 114, 123, 142
Tilford 48, 115, 130, 137, 146, 154
Tinsley 9, 27, 53, 108, 112, 120, 130, 134, 145
Toll 134
Tomblin 109
Tomblinson 19
Tomes 61
Tooley 48, 107, 108, 115, 116, 121, 155
Townsley 25
Trail 106, 108, 149, 151
Tratt 137
Travis 120, 145, 149, 150
Triplett 149
Trogden 9, 16, 18, 21, 23, 84, 120, 123, 129, 134, 139, 150
Trought 57
Truman 102
Tucker 27, 85, 118, 125, 156
Turley 48, 121
Turner 33, 107, 109, 181, 198

## V

Valentine 110
Van Nort 160
VanBecelaere 19
Vance 10, 114
Vandiver 48, 55
Vanfleet 129
Vaught 117
Veller 70
Vernon 49, 108

205

Vincent 46, 105, 107, 129, 137
Vinson 71, 108, 112, 137

# W

Wade 106, 110, 111, 114, 123
Wakeland 11, 107, 108, 129
Walden 131
Walker 123
Wallace 10, 72, 93, 103, 107, 111, 115, 145, 149, 151, 164, 176, 192
Waller 99
Ward 113, 129, 150, 151, 154, 176
Warfield 116
Warner 106, 107, 108, 115, 125, 130
Warren 5, 12, 25, 106, 107, 110, 121, 123, 130, 148, 155, 177, 178, 199
Washburn 147
Watkin 98
Watkins 98
Watson 27, 106, 118, 151, 160
Watt 107
Watts 14, 55, 90, 121, 149, 151
Webb 39
Weedman 151
Welborn 48, 106, 107, 112, 115, 139, 148
Wells 111, 115
West 34, 144, 163
Westerfield 7, 25, 63, 99, 112, 120, 125, 129, 134, 137, 149, 151, 182, 184
Whillinghill 14
White 13, 25, 42, 75, 106, 109, 112, 113, 116, 125, 126, 127, 130, 147, 148, 149, 154
Whitehead 20, 43, 72, 87, 88, 180
Whitehouse 112, 114
Whitely 54, 176
Whitler 25, 121, 170
Whitley 110
Whitmer 144
Whitt 123, 139
Whittaker 102, 114
Whitten 125, 152
Whittinghill 127
Whittingly 131
Wieder 160
Wiggins 152
Wilcox 108, 112, 130
Wilkerson 106, 152
Williams 11, 13, 14, 25, 26, 46, 48, 85, 86, 102, 104, 105, 106, 107, 109, 111, 113, 115, 120, 121, 123, 132, 136, 147, 149, 152, 158, 159, 170, 176, 180, 195, 199
Willingham 91
Willis 13
Wilmoth 59
Wilson 16, 22, 32, 48, 49, 63, 69, 101, 114, 115, 117, 118, 121, 125, 127, 129, 130, 137, 146, 149, 150
Wimsatt 125
Winchester 120
Withrow 176
Wood 129, 146
Woodburn 92, 108, 112, 115
Woodcock 108
Woodrum 147
Woods 162
Woolsley 6
Wright 6, 13, 18, 24, 118, 121, 125, 131, 174, 178, 182, 184
Wydic 109
Wydick 117, 154

# Y

Yates 101
Yonts 113
York 9, 125, 134
Young 118, 120, 147, 154, 156, 170, 179, 182

# Z

Ziggler 125
Zirkel 59

*1972 Class of Beaver Dam Elementary Graduation. 1: unk., Craig Frizzell, Diane Heflin, Carol Maupin, Kevin Likens, Darrel Maupin. 2: Ruth Dockery, Sandy Cox, Jill Durham, unk., Dawn Barnes, Lori Mayes, Cindy Harris, unk., 3: Stan Roberts, Dane Ferguson, unk., unk., Will Hines, Andrea Hurst, Jenny Manasco, unk.*

207

INCORPORATED UNDER THE LAWS OF KENTUCKY

UNITED WE STAND, DIVIDED WE FALL

NUMBER 11

SHARES 25

DUMMY

# Cooperative Canning Association

BEAVER DAM, KY.

This Certifies that ________
is the owner of Twenty five Shares of the Capital Stock of
COOPERATIVE CANNING ASSOCIATION
transferable only on the books of the Corporation by the holder hereof in person or by Attorney upon surrender of this Certificate properly endorsed.

IN WITNESS WHEREOF, the said Corporation has caused this Certificate to be signed by its duly authorized officers and its Corporate Seal to be hereunto affixed this 1st day of Aug. A.D. 19__

Secretary-Treasurer

President

SHARES One EACH

Homecoming for veterans at Renfrow Church of Christ, WWII, Sept. 29, 1946. 1: Carlos Tarrence, Edward Allen, Pirtle Bates, Clarence Smith, Moncie Taylor, Kermit Cook, Randolph Murphy, Carlos Allen, Pershing Rogers, Tilmon Rogers, Bobby Daugherty. 2: Rolo Stewart, Lafe Neighbors, John T. Burdin, Yeullis Renfrow, Reathel Morris, Ellis Raley, Leslie Raley, Gus Willoughby, Guffie

Morris, Harold Arnold, Wilmer Weedman, Clelland Cook. 3: Mauriece Morris, Carlos Morris, Lavelle Coy, Daymond Daugherty, Preston Geary, Fairdean Embry, Dencil Daugherty, V.C. Drake, Waymon Worley, Rodney Worley, Vanos Allen.

www.ingramcontent.com/pod-product-compliance
Lightning Source LLC
Chambersburg PA
CBHW060921170426
43191CB00025B/2452